WA 1010257 4

THE POLYTECHNIC OF WALES LIBRARY

Llantwit Road, Treforest, Pontypridd.
Telephone: Pontypridd 480480

Books are to be returned on or before
the last date below

– 4 MAY 1990	1 2 DEC 1995	
1 1 MAY		
05. OCT 90	D1350053	
23. NOV 9		
11. JAN 91		
26. MAY 92		
23. NOV		
09. JUN 93		
3 1 MAR 1995		

PUBLISHING BY MICROCOMPUTER:
ITS POTENTIAL AND ITS PROBLEMS

EDUCATION AND HUMAN COMMUNICATION SERIES

Publishing by Microcomputer:

Its Potential and its Problems

by

T.F. Carney, Ph. D.,

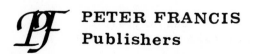

PETER FRANCIS
Publishers

686.22544

CAR

© 1988 T.F.Carney

Peter Francis Publishers, Orchard House
Berrycroft,Soham.Ely.Cambs..CB7 5BL. UK.

Lasersetting by MacTypeNet, Livonia, Michigan. USA

British Library Cataloguing in Publication Data

Carney, T.F. (Thomas F)

  Publishing by microcomputer:
  its potential and its problems —
  (Education and Human Communication).
  1. Publishing. Applications of
  microcomputer systems
  I. Title II. Series
  070.5'028'5416

  ISBN 1-870167-04-X
  ────────────

  Printed and bound in Great Britain by
  Biddles Ltd., Guildford and Kings Lynn

10102574

30 1 90

The Education and Human Communication Series

There is a growing need for all teachers, lecturers and those concerned with the planning and administration of education and training at all levels to be well informed on the variety of educational techniques and methods now available; to learn about information handling and communication skills; and to be kept aware of developments in information technology and its growing influence on education, work, leisure and society in general.

This series is designed to fulfill this need. Written by specialists, these books provide up-to-date perspectives on these developing areas, deal with practical aspects of the subjects, and include bibliographies of key works for those who wish to read further.

This book, *Publishing by Microcomputer: Its Potential and its Problems*, has been written by Tom Carney, Professor of Organisational Communications at the University of Windsor, Ontario, Canada. The book sets out the implications of desktop publishing for writers and publishers and for organisations in general. It is also a practical book: it contains detailed guidelines on layout and design in desktop publishing, the use of graphics, formatting and control of quality in content.

The book concludes with a survey of market forces in microcomputing technology, especially in production and distribution. The aim of this is to give those who have to make purchasing decisions some understanding of the marketing strategies behind developments in this fast-growing new computer specialty.

The implications of desktop publishing are considerable, not only in the production of learning materials at all levels of education and training, but also in the communication of information in government, professional, industrial and business organisations. This book will prove invaluable to anyone in these fields who wishes to learn the basic guidelines of desktop publishing.

P.J. Hills
Cambridge

To Barbara,
without whose help,
at the computer and in editing,
this book would not have been completed.

Preface

This book was written with three kinds of readers in mind: writers, publishers and managers responsible for their organisations' publications (some readers will fall into more than one of these categories). The book addresses the concerns of all three groups, and combinations thereof:

- It shows how writing and the position of writers vis-à-vis publishers are changing as result of the empowering of writers by desktop publishing technology.

- It sets out guidelines for layout and editing, in case you've been promoted into a position of in-house publisher for your organisation.

- It indicates how much an organisation can save by having such a publisher, and how the savings are effected.

- For those who have to decide what kind of computer to buy, the book sets out the pros and cons of the marketing strategies of the leading manufacturers of microcomputers. (This is the best way I've come across of making sense of the otherwise bewildering variety and pace of developments in this market niche.)

You don't have to know anything about computers to read this book with profit. On the other hand, many of its readers will already be converts to word processing. I've tried to write (and re-write, and re-write...) for both sorts of reader. Earlier versions of what are now parts of the book have been well received. I've built on these, going by what related audiences and readerships have found most helpful.

On the subject of help, I have a special word of thanks for Frank and Susan Lee and Jeff McCarty of MacTypeNet, the leading lasersetting company in the Detroit area. Over the years, Frank and Susan have helped me gain a deeper understanding of what's involved in desktop publishing; and Jeff laserset the book to a tight deadline. Thanks also go to Phil Hills for contributions beyond the call of a publisher's duty. There would have *been* no book without the support and help I received from my wife Barbara: hence the dedication.

Tom Carney,
Windsor,
March 1, 1988.

Contents

Contents

Contents

Chapter 7: Developments in Computing:
Their relevance for desktop publishing

Chapter 8: The Desktop Publishing Revolution
The logistics of the microcomputer production and distribution process

Contents

List of Diagrams and Tables

1 Print Culture in Transition:
The Impact of the Personal Computer on Writing

Historical Background

With each major development in communications technology that affects the written word there are at least five other changes in regard to:[1]

1. How one goes about writing. This involves techniques for getting ideas into writing as well as technology with which to do the writing.
2. The way the written word is formatted. This changes dramatically, and brings with it changes in diction and syntax.
3. The kinds of illustrations used with the text. A picture –a well-thought-out chart or graph, for instance– can reveal at a glance what it would take pages of writing to explain. Hence developments in picture- and/or diagram-drawing usually accompany developments in transmitting the written word; the two are closely connected.
4. The production process. This undergoes changes, becoming more complex.
5. Views about the ownership of ideas expressed in words.
   (See Table 1.1 for an overview.)

The changes brought about by the personal computer differ significantly from those brought about by previous major changes in communications technology, namely: development of pictographic scripts; the alphabet; the printing press and the high speed press (see Table 1.1). These changes all have the characteristics of a revolution in communications:[2]

- each makes it easier to gain access to better records of its society's knowledge and expertise;
- each increases the amount of information available for sharing;
- each expands its users' capacity to discover and develop interests which they have in common;
- each alters the environment in which its society's economic system is set, opening up new ways of developing that system.

However, the first four major developments concentrated upon ways of making writing easier to read, while the changes brought about by computer assisted publishing involve ways of heightening consciousness of how one goes about

Table 1.1: The development of writing:

	Pictographs	Alphabet	Printing Press
Writing Techniques Technologies	Model shapes for pictographs Stylus and clay tablets	Grammar and syntax Literary genres emerge From stylus, ink and papyrus roll, to quill and parchment book	Punctuation and spelling Moveable, lead typefaces
Format	Lists	• Capital letters • Page • Undifferentiated text block, sometimes with commentary in margin	• Paragraphs • Uniform text block with headers and footnotes • Contents, appendices and indices
Illustrations and art forms influencing them	The pictographs themselves Line drawings	Illumination Plays	Woodcuts Chamber music with written scores
Production	Scribes make longhand lists Only scribes can read and write	Author writes his own manuscript Copyists copy, also by hand Readers recon-stitute incorrect-ly copied or aged texts	Publisher's team reconstitutes and/or sets up the text Team: editor, typesetter, maker of woodcuts, scholar/author
Rights of author	Authorship unrecorded	Authorship often disputed	Publisher owns the literary property Author identified

Techniques of, and technologies for, writing

	High Speed Press	Computerized Printing
Writing Techniques Technologies	• Readability formulae, receiver orientation • High speed press, typecasting machine • Pen, pencil; typewriter; telegraph and telephone	Spoke diagrams, scenarios and story architecture: cognitive scripts/schematics as aids Personal computers: word processors; outlining programs; editing and page make-up programs
Format	Newspaper Multi-column page layout, with text flowing round pictures and diagrams	Magazine or specialist journal Visually informative text with lots of graphics
Illustrations — and art forms influencing them	Half-tone photographs Radio and film	Computer assisted design • Photocopying • Television and interactive computer disks, and, increasingly, • CD ROM
Production	Newspaper editor has a team of editors, journalists, printers and illustrative artists, maybe even a stable of writers Mass readerships	• Writing involves much interaction: with computer data bases, networks of peers, programs and user groups • Authors recover control over form of their work setting their own text
Rights of author	The heyday of copyright	Producer or director as model for writer

writing. They involve planning aids –cognitive 'scripts', schematics of the deep structure of a particular story form, and the like. That is, the changes are internal, affecting the author, rather than external, affecting what is already written.

This is necessarily so when the writer's tool is a computer. Working in electronic space, rather than with pen and paper, he or she has a new kind of 'pathfinding' problem. It's necessary to find his or her way round the texts and programs stored on disks so as to plan or even format work. These feats, along with that of recognizing what the problem is when the program 'hangs' (becomes immobile, not responding to standard commands), call for metacognitive strategies: ways of thinking about thinking or writing.[3]

These changes in the technologies for reproducing writing don't all have the same kinds of results. For example, pictographs and the printing press resulted in 'fixed' text; the reader couldn't change it. But owners of manuscripts in the High Culture of Greek and Roman literature brought about by the alphabet did change their manuscripts. They had to: quick commercial copying by hand of texts consisting of an endless column, composed of row after row of letters, without breaks between words or punctuation, resulted in frequent errors. Word processed text, likewise, is always being changed: it goes through numerous revisions ("massaging", in the jargon).

There was relatively little art in the manuscripts of the alphabetic age, apart from "illuminated" capital letters inset into the text at the start of chapters. And there were virtually no diagrams. Neither could be accurately reproduced. Art and diagrams were costly and difficult to reproduce in the print age, too. On the other hand, computer graphics have produced an efflorescence of art and artistically presented diagrams which can be accurately and cheaply introduced into text.

SPECIFIC CONSEQUENCES OF DESKTOP PUBLISHING

Possibly the greatest turnabout, however, is that the author has been given back control over the actual production of his or her text. Desktop publishing puts a printing press on the desk of a personal computer user for a few thousand pounds. Personal publishing hasn't been possible since Ben Franklin's day, in the eighteenth century. And nowadays hackers (computer users who habitually modify their own hardware and/or software) are making their own typefaces. It's the first time that typefaces have been constructed locally since the mid-nineteenth century.

Another major shift, again reversing a long-standing trend, is towards joint authorship. The printing press set teams of experts to produce an author's work after it was written. Computer networks, databases and user groups are now drawn upon by the author to get his or her work written. The interaction occurs during the writing; the author may subsequently publish the work almost single-handed, by getting it to the camera-ready stage on a personal computer, then having a printer run it off.

It would appear likely, then, that computer assisted publishing is resulting in major changes in the culture of printing: what gets printed; who does the printing, and the extent to which writers control what's in their text and how it's presented. After all, every other major development in the technology relating to written communication has produced such changes, and there are clear signs that print culture is in transition. Let's look more closely at what's going on.

Summary of Changes Currently Occurring
IMPACT OF PRINT ON MANUSCRIPT-MEDIATED CULTURE

Any major technological development that affects the way we store and transmit data also changes the way we write and the way we think about writing. For example, print, impacting on a manuscript-mediated culture, changed the following practices:

1. *How people remembered*: word perfect quotation replaced the capacious, if rather general, thematic memory of manuscript culture.
2. *How data were accessed*: contents pages, footnoting and indexing were impossible on papyrus rolls and little practiced, if not actually impossible, on parchment.
3. *How pictures were transmitted*: woodcuts –a development that was as important as the invention of movable type– made the transmission of accurate diagrams possible for the first time, without artistic license. Accurate diagrammatic representation of mechanical contrivances became possible, and machinery emerged from the world of magic.
4. *Thinking about intellectual property altered too.* Rewriting an aged, worm-eaten and carelessly copied manuscript involved creative interpolation that was usually beyond the capabilities of the average, imperfectly literate scribe. Authorship was often disputed, as opening pages tended to be particularly prone to loss or damage; and few copies of any given work were produced, so cross-checking was difficult. Literary property came into its heyday only with the advent of the printing press, when the publisher's team of scholars, artists and printers made major contributions by reconstituting definitive editions.

IMPACT OF PERSONAL COMPUTING ON PRINT-MEDIATED CULTURE

> Computer-assisted writing and recording of data is currently introducing extensive changes in print culture and in the ways we mentally and aesthetically relate to that culture.

We tend to be oblivious to these changes, because they are so many, so apparently unrelated, so diverse and have come in so gradually and naturally. Not seeing them as a whole, we tend not to appreciate their cumulative effect when they interact on one another. At least four major shifts are involved:

1. *Text has become subject to frequent revision.* In consequence, it's looked on as 'in process' rather than as 'cast in stone' –an essentially unalterable typescript. Also, it has become much more visually informative, shedding its 'monolithic text block' appearance.
2. *Composition is now seen as a highly interactive process.* This interaction may be with 'tools of the mind' as well as with co-authors.
3. *There's a changed visual sense.* This change involves much more than just importing lots of graphics into the text. Writing is increasingly coming to be thought of in terms analogous to 'scripting' or film directing.
4. *Attitudes towards literary property have changed enormously.* Collaborative writing and public domain authorship are now common.

Changing Views on What Text 'Is'

TEXT AS PLASTICENE/PROVISIONAL/'IN PROCESS'

Probably the commonest use of the personal computer is for word process-ing. With word processing comes a new way of thinking about text: the 'text as plasticene' concept –hence the common expression, to 'massage' a text (into any shape you wish):

- When you're using a batch word processor, you only have to change a few initial macros (shorthand programming com-mands, inserted into the text) and the typefaces and formatting of the entire document change throughout, in a flash.
- Import a text, formatted by one program, to run formatted by another program, and similar massive changes can occur.
- You can, very quickly and easily, make changes in detail: addi-tions, alterations (for instance, of the typefaces used, or of par-ticular expressions, throughout a text), deletions, emendations and insertions (which may require automatic renumbering of footnotes), for instance.

And these are only some of the possibilities.

A typescript text is a *static* entity –a structure. Only minor changes can be made without retyping the whole piece. A word processed text is a *provisional* entity. The average 'hi tech' manual goes through from eleven to thirteen ver-sions before arriving at its 'final' (for this year's edition) form. Word processed text is text in process; so it's thought of in process terms.

VISUALLY INFORMATIVE TEXT

Most of us think of serious books as containing pages with solid text blocks, possibly with the occasional diagram. But books are set out this way largely to suit the convenience, and for the economic advantage of, the journeymen who reproduce them. It's easy to print text in this format. Graphics and unusual for-matting, on the other hand, are beyond the capabilities of the average electronic printer's batch text-editing program. Mathematical formulae, for example, con-stitute "penalty matter": they send printing costs soaring, simply because they're difficult to set using this technology.

Yet monolithic text blocks can make for difficult reading. The ideal number of characters per line is from 50 to 70 –if you're employing a typeface that's easy to read (a Roman typeface, with serifs –like the one you're reading now). Long lines of text, set in solid paragraphs, with no means of emphasis or section headings, hide key points in a mass of undifferentiated text.

Authors and academics tend not to notice these disadvantages, because 'writ-ing' for most of us, given our educational conditioning, means writing letters or essay-like proposals –that is, use of solid text blocks. But you wouldn't write a résumé in one of these solid text blocks if you were job hunting. You'd write a 'qualifications brief' (or at least an 'executive summary' as the first page of a womb-to-tomb, standard, everything-but-the-kitchen-sink-type résumé, with its page after page of densely-packed typing).[4]

Such functional résumés contain a main heading in a display typeface and running heads in standard size.But they also contain bolded, typefaces; hanging indents (or tabbed lines to produce mini-tables within the text; point form state-ments introduced by bullets, and so on.

This is the standard, easy-to-skim-read format that any good word processing program will easily produce –and that business writing now demands.

Such a layout is called 'visually informative text' (henceforth VIT: see Table 1.2)[5]. In VIT, the layout itself emphasizes important points, sets out special sections in the text and so on. An undifferentiated text block (henceforth UTB) does none of these things.

> Undifferentiated text blocks are the equivalent, in text, of speech without any body language. Visually informative text is the equivalent, in text, of the body language that accompanies speech and enhances (indeed, presents the greater part of) its meaning.

When business people say that "students can't write", what they generally mean is that students don't know how to write visually informative text. This is because there are considerable differences between the kind of writing that goes with UTBs and the kind that goes with VIT (and the latter isn't usually taught in the schools). Let's review these differences; you may be surprised at what they add up to (Table 1.2 refers).

1. **VIT sets out its text in highly visible divisions.**

This is its most striking feature: it has running heads to indicate major points, and bolding, italicizing or changes in typeface to emphasize major concepts. UTBs have to do all these things by choice diction and syntax, since their text has to go in a continuous, undifferentiated flow.

So you have to read it, all of it, and read it closely, to get the sense; you can't skim read, as you can with VIT. Yet few people read books from start to finish, nowadays.

2. **Subordination and coordination of ideas are also managed differently.**

VIT helps you perceive subordination by using a smaller typeface and by indentation, perhaps with altered leading (spacing between lines). UTBs have to manage these things syntactically, employing subordinate clauses that make for complex (hence difficult-to-read) sentences.

Similarly, VIT handles coordination via bullets and point form statements, or by tables, whereas UTBs have to use parallelism in sentence structure. To tie things together, VIT can use simple 1, 2, 3 sequences, whereas UTBs have to make much use of language gadgets such as conjunctions.

3. **The overall vocabulary structure is different.**

VIT uses KISS (Keep It Short & Simple) English. It can make good use of sentence fragments (those point form statements) and dingbats (informational graphics –bullets, boxes, etc.) to express a complex, lengthy idea in simple diction and simple 'sentence' structure.

UTBs have to use multisyllabic words and complicated sentence structures to get the same idea across. So they're much harder to read –and they look it, too. The spirits sink when confronted with UTBs, whereas VIT layout can be designed to be attractive to the eye. VIT sends the message 'highly organized', whereas UTBs send the message 'wordy'.

Table 1.2: How Formatting Affects A Text's Intelligibility

Visually Informative Text	Details of Format	Undifferentiated Text Blocks
Visual cues provided by page layout indicate the page's priorities & content at a glance: this is punctuation at the level of the page. A pre-planned framework is involved: relationships between text blocks are thought out in advance. Sidebars can adjust spacing to make content fit the page, in an attention-getting layout, with positioning used to give selected items high visibility (and making them easy to remember —and find, when hunting through the text).	*Overall Page Layout as Informational Design*	A large type mass (a pageful of paragraphs, each with long lines of small type) tires the eyes. A solid block of text isn't readable or memorable: it's the equivalent of speech without nonverbal messages. The typesetter's convenience obscures the writer's plans: a unit of thought may not fit on its page (e.g. the conclusion may come atop the NEXT page). With no purchase for the memory, it's hard for readers to access specific parts of a text. As with the committee in small group communications, UTBs are used constantly, and inappropriately, where special-purpose VIT formats are required.
Chunking: partitions and divisions are immediately evident; different kinds of divisions are visually distinct at a glance, making skim reading easy. Sequential reading of the entire text is not required. The text can be read at a number of levels (main points; argument in full; details on specific topics).	*Within-page Content Units or Subdivisions in Text*	The text flows in an unbroken stream, with only paragraphs to indicate divisions. There's no type of text block unit intermediate between paragraph and chapter (or chapter division). So the whole text must be read in detail, with frequent back-checks to keep readers on track (a reading style that's no longer common).
Highlighting of key points is by **typographic contrast** (by use of larger fonts &/or bolding or italicizing), or by informational graphics (boxes, rules, screening/grey scales). **White space** is used to make headings stand out. '**Out-quotes**' (passages in the margin) indicate special emphasis. A policy re emphasis must be developed for the whole document prior to writing and uniformly applied (using a '**style sheet**').	*Means of Emphasis: different technologies impose different organizing logics*	Emphasis is achieved by semantic means: choice diction and intensifiers. Rare words are apt to result, making for difficult reading, being unfamiliar to many readers. Alternatively, **topic sentences** may be employed, to signal in advance what the paragraph that follows them is to be about. Thus the entire burden of indicating emphasis must be borne by the words alone.

Continues.....

Visually Informative Text	Details of Format	Undifferentiated Text Blocks
Managed by indentation, using **outlining** conventions, or by a 'headings family' of graduated sizes, indicating degrees of importance in headings.	*Hierarchical Relationships*	Managed by syntax: much use of subordinate clauses. Complex, formal and lengthy sentence structures result. Readability suffers: too much work has to be done by words: graphics & positioning are underemployed.
Managed by **tables**, or by **pie-charts, bar graphs** or **bullets & point-form** statements, or **hanging indents**, parallel to one another, inset under the themal statement to which they refer. Long sentences result; but both their structure and language is simple.	*Co-ordinate Relationships*	Managed by **tropes** —stylistic forms: parallel sentence structure and literary figures such as **anaphora.** There's much use of coordinating language (usually in the form of repetitious phrases). Long and complex sentences, and some repetition of phrases, necessarily result. These sentences may be perceived as sprawling.
May be managed by sequentially numbered hanging indents, or by **informational graphics** (arrows, or even, when necessary, **algorithms**, or **flow charts**, beside the text related to them).	*Sequential Relationships*	Has to be managed by diction: there's much use of connectives and parallelism of phraseology. This too tends to result in lengthy, complex sentences.
Used with **K.I.S.S.** (Keep It Short & Simple) English, written with a **readability formula** in mind. Much of use point-form sentence fragments. Terse & high impact expression results. It's usually perceived as that of an expert or of an authority figure ('power speech').	*Sentence Forms and Overall Style*	Formal, grammatically & syntactically correct diction and sentence structure are essential, as the text, without the help of visual clues from the layout, must convey all nuances of meaning on its own. Diction (usually involving qualifiers [e.g. "quite"]) and sentence forms are perceived as pedantic/bookish ("powerless speech").
Detailed discussion of complex issues requires simple language (and usually graphics) to be well understood. Visually informative text is designed for the reader's convenience: it's meant for skimming & selective reading. It's generally perceived as 'getting straight to the point', and as 'clear and well organized'.	*'Between the Lines" Impressions Generated*	Essay-type organization of writing leads to generalities: it's difficult to focus sharply on technical details. Close reading of the entire document is necessary. This assumes a captive reader and is perceived as wordy or 'not business-like': UTBs may be taken as 'trying to impress'. Basically, it isn't possible to talk about complex things in complicated language and be easily readable.

Follows S.A. Bernhardt, "Seeing the Text", *College Composition and Communication* 37 (1), 1986, 66–78.

> Wordiness in our 'come as you are' culture tends to be ill-regarded. The combination of hyper-correct grammar, use of intensifiers, and a plethora of adjectives has been termed "powerless" speech.
>
> "Power" speech is blunter, less grammatically correct, more to-the-point.[6] UTBs, necessitating very careful use of language, produce a written message that closely resembles powerless speech; VIT produces a written message that closely resembles power speech.

4. Writing VIT normally means using a 'script':

A set of formatting concepts and guidelines (on these, see more below). There's a growing variety of VIT scripts available, for cover letters, job guides, 'playscript' memos, position papers and so on. Scripts normally come in clusters. For instance, the 'qualifications brief' type of résumé comes with subscripts for providing a 'reader orientation' and 'positivity approach'.[7]

Basically, then, you don't have to design a VIT layout from scratch; you use a set of proven guidelines. This set, or script, lessens the cognitive load, as does the simplicity of the language you can use with the VIT. This lessened load in turn allows you to design in other, script-guided features.

5. VIT can be designed for a variety of readers;

Readers can pick and choose –because they only have to skim read– from the several, easily distinguishable themes or storylines that you can build in. UTBs, on the other hand, are restricted to one target reader. They're so complex in their linguistic structure, and must be read so closely, that a presentation in UTBs can only address (one storyline and) one interest group. More targets would so compound the complexity of UTB as to make it too difficult to follow.

The consequences of this development:

Use of VIT has increased enormously with the advent of personal computers, which make it relatively easy to do the complex formatting involved. The new electronic layout programs are more flexible (and certainly far easier to use) than the batch processing programs of mini-computer-using publishers.

Together, these new programs give writers the capability to set out their text as they want it set out –rather than as it's convenient for the printer to set it out. So writers are no longer alienated from their own product. In fact, they can even publish their own books, something that's not been possible since Ben Franklin's times.

There's little likelihood that this trend will be reversed. VIT is a much more effective and convenient way of presenting ideas than are UTBs; so anyone who has to do a lot of reading of complex, detailed or technical matter will opt for VIT over UTBs.[8] This means that business and government will continue and extend their use of VIT. After all, it was largely they who developed VIT, and they're lavishly equipped with the computers necessary to produce it.

Together business and government produce more pages per year than all the publishers of books, newspapers and magazines combined. So use of VIT will spread, to become the norm. By now even the UTB-fixated world of academe is altering: take a look at its textbooks. When ease of reading is critical, VIT becomes the presentational form of preference.

Changing Views on How to Write
WRITING CONCEIVED AS AN INTERACTIVE PROCESS

As we've seen, computerized text is perceived as text in process: unlike a typescript, it's not seen as something static; text processing is thought of in *interactive* terms. This kind of perception results from two causes.

1. To get your manuscript or notes on disk, you're likely to be interacting with a variety of computer programs.

Some combination of the following is common: an idea processor; charting-making and drafting programs; a 'paint' (drawing) program; a spelling-, read-ability-, sexist language-, and/or cliché-checker; a keyboard enhancer (this enables the keys on your keyboard to activate various programmed commands), and various desk accessories (such as outliners).

2. You may take material from (someone else's) database to substantiate the case you're making.

Or several other persons may be working with you, on a local area network, or a wide area network, or through an electronic bulletin board (if you're working on an electronic journal, for example). Or, if you're developing a 'dungeons and dragons' type of adventure game, a group of people may be serially but interactively developing the content, format, graphics and pro-gramming. (This type of game produces the equivalent of a novel with multi-ple storylines, which each reader constructs into his or her own unique version as he or she works through it).

Either way, you're composing the text interactively.

Besides this, research into how writers actually go about writing (rather than reconstructions of this process from their finished products or from their memo-ries of this process collected after they've finished writing) has revealed an extraordinary amount of interactivity.[9]

Possibly the best analogy is to a gigantic switchboard, with the writer as operator making connections here and there all over the place, constantly bom-barded by incoming messages. Typically, planning, putting ideas into words, and correcting what's been written are all going on at the same time. Effective writ-ers have a wider range of planning frames –scripts– and use them more flexibly.[10] This characteristic, more than any other, distinguishes them from less effective writers.

This discovery has led to designing interactivity into the writing process, as follows. To facilitate interactive planning, a brain-compatible planning frame has been devised. This is a presentational format that works the way the mind does during a brainstorm. (Taking notes during such an event is the literary equivalent of shooting yourself in the foot.)[11]

This idea has been –rather imperfectly– converted into the idea process-ing program called *ThinkTank*, bringing a new genre of program, the outlining program, into being. If you've tried an outliner, you'll know how addictive they become.

Idea processing has led to "larger vision" writing –a computer program for writers that exploits the idea processor's capabilities. It lets the writer, while outlining his or her plans, move up and down and around and about among the levels of a complex and lengthy piece of writing in a way that would result in cognitive overload without the assistance of an idea processor.

Combined with this are a set of guidelines on how to write up the plans thus outlined.[12] These guidelines are adapted to the way the mind is known to flit around during writing. A new, computer-assisted writing technique has thus been developed that extends a writer's capabilities. Writers are likely to need some such help to cope with the task of writing, because it's becoming much more formidable as a result of technologically inspired changes in what and how we write.

COMPUTER USERS' NEED FOR SOCIAL SUPPORT

But there's more to interactivity than this, where personal computer users are concerned. It goes bone-deep for heavy users of computers. It's drilled into them by some very basic, primal experiences. Most adults aren't prepared for the trauma associated with acquiring computer skills. All the worst experiences come right at the beginning. The worst of all is deciding how to get started. What program should you learn? What hardware is needed?

You can't answer either question without a lot of knowledge, which you can't have at this stage –and your decision involves momentous consequences in time, money and payoffs. In such a situation, the range of software that your friends have, or are familiar with, will most likely turn out to be critical. You'll have to try different programs out to see what they actually deliver and what they'll be like to learn and use.

Moreover, you soon begin to realize that the educational system has conditioned you to be taught, but that now, suddenly, you must become a self-directed learner –the hardest (and most rewarding) form of learning that there is. And you begin to realize what being in a learning society means: you're going to have to become a self-directed learner for life, for involvement in computers entails continuous upgrading of your learning.

Besides, most of us start on a word processing program, and these are among the more difficult programs to learn. The early stages of this learning curve are horrendous; you have to learn the technology and a user-hostile program –quickly, too, usually.

This is why user groups are essential for computer users; they are social support groups for mutual aid, as essential as Alcoholics Anonymous is to would-be escapees from alcoholism.[13] They're repositories of experience and knowledge, freely and cheerfully given. And they're for life, because you've embarked on lifelong learning (and effective self-directed learners each operate with a backup group of about ten people[14]). Everybody going through the early learning curve of acquiring computer skills requires the help of a support group.

It's help that's vitally necessary in these early days of ego-destroying inability to cope with, or understand, the technology. For this is a technology that introduces you to a new kind of psychic trauma, when a trifling error can irretrievably erase, in an electronic flash, work that has taken you hours to produce.

As a result, you bond very strongly to your support group. It fills a basic need that's otherwise poorly provided for in our competitive, careerist-filled organizations. As you were –are– helped, so you in turn will help others on request in their need: this is the basic 'hacker ethic'.

This bonding is strongly reinforced by other experiences which commonly accompany heavy computer use. You can't time-budget computer learning. You can't anticipate when you'll meet with a glitch (a mistake of your's , or the program's –often you can't tell which kind it is) that can take hours to deal with. Such a block can stop all progress at a task that has to be completed for an imminent deadline.

Non-essentials get dropped, when you're into computers: there's no time for frills. First to go is TV, that great inductor into the mass culture. Meanwhile you're learning an in-group language, computerese, that admits you to the technological wave of the future; and a common language is one of the most powerful group bonding factors known.[15]

Besides, self-directed learning is an incomparably liberating phenomenon (which is why people get hooked on it, for all its arduousness). You're making your mind over –changing your cognitive processes– while realizing how the educational system has been training you to be a passive consumer of information and a cog to fit into the prevailing socio-economic system. You're undergoing intensive counter-enculturation (deprogramming the values of the mass culture), though you're usually not aware that the transformation is so profound.

NETWORKING

Meanwhile you're likely to be involved in networking. Networking is possibly the single greatest exception to the normal top-down communications practices common in our society. Each node in a network is equal; all interact freely; information is 'out there' for the taking, often authorless, unowned and non-proprietary.[16]

Electronic Bulletin Boardsand Electronic Mail:

The prime example of computer networking is the electronic bulletin board; a network of these boards, including many 'pirate' boards and 'safe houses' spans North America, from New York to California and from Texas to Alaska, freely sharing information. A newly 'broken' program (a program with its copy protection removed) is usually available throughout this immense area, through pirate bulletin boards, in a matter of *hours*. Anyone with a modem (a device for communicating with other computers over 'phone lines) can access (contact and get data from) any of them.

Potentially, networking is a revolutionary phenomenon.

Local Area Networks

Less anarchic is the LAN (local area network), through which the group in which you work may be involved on a joint project, or the WAN (wider area network), which you may be involved in for another work project, or because of some hobby or special interest group, entailing people at some distance. Again, however, differences of rank or status tend to vanish in an atmosphere of anonymous, interactive sharing. Here is an example of the changed attitudes to composition produced by this conditioning in interactive sharing.

Computer Gaming Networks

In a discussion of 'How to build the world's best adventure game', a leading developer said the following (I've paraphrased his words):[17] "I won't hire the top experts to make it. I'll get my programming team to produce a really superb game-making program."(*World Builder*: this program contains a graphics module with a variety of drawing, painting and animation packages; a sound editor and a library of digitized sounds, and a number of editing programs –and it requires some programming skills on its user's part.)

"This program will encourage thousands of gaming enthusiasts to collaborate and compete to develop games, to improve the system itself, to change the concept of what a game can be... In short, I'll make gamers active creators rather than passive consumers of games, then let their combined efforts develop the genre and the system to levels not currently imaginable."

In many ways now, largely under the influence of films (more on this below), certain types of composition are becoming thought of as a group process, rather than as an individual effort. The new kinds of computer adventure games are the equivalent of a new kind of novel: a novel with many story lines, catering to many perspectives –and learning styles. In practical terms, it takes a team to put together a game, or an instructional simulation, or a business case. (These genres are becoming less easy to distinguish from one another.) You need a set of specialists and a director.

The Instructional Design Team Mentality

All these genres are growing in use, becoming more a part of the fabric of our lives. They constitute very powerful learning experiences, and they accustom those exposed to them to interactivity. Moreover, they blur the distinction between (text)book and rôle play/socio-drama. Such blurring occurs elsewhere, too. Telematics has led to a melding of film/TV and computing; and the VIT approach to writing is further blurring the distinctions between what were formerly the domains of print and of film. Again, this trend is on the increase, as the next section will show.

To sum up:

networking powerfully reinforces all the conditioning in interactivity and sharing that you've experienced since becoming involved in computing. The next two sections will show how this interactive sharing is reshaping fundamental aspects of traditional print culture. The book, after all, produces the solitary thinker and goes with an ethic of individual ownership of intellectual 'property'.

A Changed Visual Sense

THE PROLIFERATION OF PICTURES AND DIAGRAMS IN SERIOUS WRITING

Underlying the shift to VIT is a changed visual sense. Most people nowadays put far more hours into film and TV viewing than into book reading. We're picture drawers before we're writers of alphabetical letters. A picture –a graph or a diagram– gets its message across much more quickly, easily and powerfully than do the pages of text required to express that same message. So most of us –printers with their inhibiting batch processing programs excepted– prefer pictures to text.

Click Art:

The computer has 'paint' (picture drawing or retouching) programs, and 'click art' (ready-made graphics, the equivalent of print's 'clip' art). Some companies publish collections of drawings, produced by professional artists. These are sold as periodicals, at regular intervals, for copyright-free use (including adaptation) by the purchaser. Such art is known as clip art. Click art is the computer equivalent: collections of drawings on disk, sold for similar purposes.

> Click art has emerged as the equivalent of clip art, in the computer milieu.

Newspapers have huge collections of such computerized art work, which they have recently released onto the market. Much computer art consists of adaptations of such drawings.

Business Graphics

Also available for personal computer users are business graphics: programs which turn matrices of numbers into a wide range of graphs and charts at the touch of a button. There are also peripheral devices (attachments for your personal computer) –digitizers, frame grabbers and scanners– that capture drawings and pictures and store them on disk. This technology has given us the ability to put sophisticated graphics into our texts, and adapt it to our purposes.

Recent developments (c. 1980 following) in computer assisted graphics constitute, in historical terms, the fourth major development in our capacity to reproduce graphics in text. So we've just come through a watershed development. To go by past experience, major changes are likely to result.

Electronic Layout Programs

Combined with these graphics programs there are now electronic layout programs –another major, complementary development in computer technology– which allow you to put pictures into your documents and 'flow' the text around them. In consequence, text is becoming more and more populated with graphics. Writers' styles are changing, as they take advantage of this new capability to get their messages across: their work is becoming more visually oriented.

Flipperships –formerly readerships– have changed, too: many readers now skim material, going from one informational graphic (chart, diagram, graph or table) to the next. 'Infographics' –graphics packed with information– is the new buzz-word among newsletter editors.

ALGORITHMS AS AIDS TO VERBAL PRESENTATION

There's another way in which computer graphics are changing our modes of representing our ideas in text. It has become evident that one can't make complex regulations easy to understand merely by expressing them in simple language.[18]

For instance, regulations which stipulate that 'you are eligible if you've done this and this, but not that and that, providing you come within these classifications (but only within this time frame [except for the following two categories of exceptions])' are likely to be understood only if set out via an algorithm with a running commentary in words. That is, the thought must be expressed diagrammatically, with words as back up to the diagram: of the two, the visual element is the more important.

Thinking Diagrams

This primacy of diagrammatic representation is not an isolated phenomenon. Flow charts and decision trees are other types of schematics –thinking diagrams– that help organize our planning. You can do the relevant types of thinking *without* these schematic aids; but it's much easier (and less error-prone) if you do it *with* them. Hitherto such diagrams have been prohibitively expensive. But now that there are computer programs that enable them to be easily and cheaply drafted and represented in text, they are beginning to appear more frequently.

THE FILM DIRECTOR AS MODEL FOR THE AUTHOR

The influence of films and television can be seen in the fact that we don't nowadays always think in terms of print's single storyline. Rather, we sometimes think of our presentations much as a TV or film director would.[19] A story has to accommodate itself to many viewpoints; it has multiple levels, with several different tracks of action, each with persons with different perspectives moving along them.

Such movement requires a master framework, with several subsidiary frameworks, and often includes means by which readers can assess whether they're getting the message or not (self-inventories or other questionnaires; cases and other self-testing devices).

Writing to accommodate this type of consciousness *can* be done –but hasn't, traditionally, normally *been* done– in print, where a single storyline is preferred. To write with this multi-level complexity, you have to do as film directors do: think in terms of scripts –scripts in the sense of thinking tools. Think of the formula novel, for instance (Haley's *Wheels*, *Hotel*, *Airport* and so on –the exploration of a system in systems terms).

Instructional Design and Writing Teams

These scripts are planning frames or schematics, often nested one within the other, which help you to manage the complexities of such a text.[20] You may contract out some of the research work, or the graphics, or the development of cases, interacting with a team to get the writing done when you're involved in one of these multi-level projects.

Developments in the publishing of social science textbooks –in particular the phenomenon of multiple authorship– provide an even clearer illustration of the need for such a team.[21] There's a new awareness that there will be a range of learning styles, among readers, and that these styles have to be accommodated.[22] So a textbook requires a design team, with a range of expertise in teaching as well as in content specialties, for the following reasons.

1. The main characteristic of the new, computer-generation reader is a 'What if..?' approach.

Such readers want to interact with the subject matter, to manipulate it so as to see for themselves how things work. They won't simply accept someone's word from on high. So the book will need cases, puzzles, self-inventories and the like. (Increasingly often, it comes with an interactive computer disk.) The instructor who's using it will need a back-up manual, containing guidelines on running the exercises it contains.

2. Designing these exercises calls for specialized expertise.

The design and layout of the text is important, too. A skillful editor is needed to control the reader's eye-movement and facilitate the reader's co-orientation. The editor can do this by outlining; by provision of multiple tracks in the account (so that a reader can go back over material at a deeper level once initial overall comprehension has been attained), and by attention-getting layouts.

3. Complex as it is, such a book is provisional:

it will go through a series of upgradings, unanticipatable at the outset, in response to formative evaluation by reviewers *during* the writing process.

Such textbooks represent a genre of writing that reflects the new mentality of current readerships and the new realities of our changing print culture. They also foreshadow a new attitude to copyright.

A Changed Attitude to Copyright
THE HACKER ETHIC

Amid all the changes so far discussed, there's also been a change in the way that ownership of literary property is viewed.

Such changes have been usual when there have been major shifts in the technology of the transmission of writing. Copyright only came with the printing press, for example: authorship is difficult to establish where pictographic texts are involved, and was sometimes disputed when manuscripts were concerned.

Some technologies make literary ownership easier to pin down than others do; and attitudes to the sanctity of literary property change as a result. 'Xerox morality' has long since led to casuistry about the ethics of copying: photocopying is just so easy and convenient.

The computer has furthered this change to an astounding degree. Software, circulating on local area networks or electronic bulletin boards, is even harder than print to protect against copying. The emergence of a whole new set of terms indicates how far things have gone: the 'hacker ethic'; piracy; public domain software; freeware; shareware; the 'grey market', etc.

Emergence of a semantic field usually indicates that the topic lexically elaborated in this way is important to a major group, or groups. To see why a changed attitude to copyright is important to heavy computer users, let's consider what the new attitudes to interactivity involve.

A computer program –a word processing program, an 'idea processing' program (as the outlining programs are sometimes called), or a 'decision support' program (one that provides you with a range of options, and with evaluations of each one of them, as you go through each stage of a decision process)– is a kind of electronic skull cap.

'Getting into' such a program admits you to the thought world of a brilliant design team. Their thinking affects your thinking, as their program becomes part of your everyday way of expressing yourself: it adds new reflexes to your thinking patterns. Indeed, one may learn to use a program to remedy one's deficiencies in certain skills. A spread sheet or charting program, for instance, can make up for weaknesses in accounting or statistics.

The program, like your text, is a process. An upgrade will alter it, sometimes extensively. New peripherals can change your hardware, thereby altering the capabilities of the program you're running on that hardware; in short, the program changes its nature somewhat.

So the program is in a state of flux –just as you are yourself, as you strive to extend your cognitive grasp to keep up with the new insights and problem-attack strategies built into the upgrades– even without your doing anything to it.

But you **do** do things to it: you 'customize' it to suit your own needs, as follows:

But you **do** do things to it: you 'customize' it to suit your own needs, as follows:

1. You may add typefaces to the program that drives your computer –you may even create special characters for the typefaces resident therein. This extends your word processing program's capabilities: it now has more typefaces to use

2. Likewise, you may add ancillary programs that have been specially designed to 'reside in' and expand the program that drives your computer (usually outlining or paint programs). These programs can be used within your word processing program; you call them down and use them while you're using that program.

3. You may 'enhance your keyboard' by adding a capacity to use macros (usually for use in your word processing program).

4. And you've likely built 'templates' into your word processing program itself by this time. (These are skeletal formats for common types of letter or report or whatever.)

Whose program is this word processing program by now? It's your program: no one else could use it without your explaining how to use the changes you've made. Somewhere along the line, you've become a hacker (someone who changes a program by making little 'hacks' at it). From here to the hacker ethic is no great distance.

Something similar is apt to happen to your graphics library:

• Some of your artwork comes from clip art disks that you've bought –and subsequently changed, using "fat bits". (This is a sub-program within your paint program, allowing you to re-draw a picture by turning its 'pixels' –picture elements– on and off.)

• Other pieces of artwork may have been given to you: a line drawing, say, read to disk by someone's digitizer, and then customized using fat bits.

• Not you, but someone else might have captured graphics while using another program (a game or the like), using an 'art grabber' ancillary program (which takes a kind of snapshot of the screen and saves it to disk as a picture).

• People swap text files of Christmas or anniversary cards that they've designed.

Somewhere along the line here, someone has strayed into piracy.

PIRACY

The term personal computer (PC for short) has many levels of meaning. Personal computer users tend to be different from mainframe users, for instance. The latter accept what they are given by the system's mainframe. PC users insist on making their hardware and software over till it's theirs : specially configured to their particular needs.

As the heavy computer user sees it:
• TV is chewing gum for the mind;
• a car is wheels;
• but a computer is a "second self", as Turkle puts it.[23]
    The computer mirrors the self: what you make of it reflects your creativity and imagination. Interacting with its programs teaches you about your consciousness, intelligence and learning abilities.

It's an "evocative machine", in Turkle's words. The "first psychological machine", it easily becomes addictive, coming to be regarded almost as another person –a disembodied intelligence. The trauma resulting from making an error that your user-friendly machine
executes (as when you close without saving, instantly and irretrievably losing hours of work) is analogous to betrayal by a friend.

Personal computer users tend to be anarchic individualists. As TV use typically
drops off by 80% if you become seriously involved in computing, PC users tend
to be subject to different socializing influences from the rest of the population
–less steeped in the TV-culture and less passively consumerist. They drop out of
the print culture (which tends to encourage solitary individualism) too.
Computing wreaks havoc with your time budget; you have time only for survival reading –and for computer manuals and journals.

So here you are, heavily involved with a user group, with which you are, by
this time, bonded. This group is linked, by its bulletin board, to other such
groups: you're in a subculture with its own language and norms. Those norms
require the giving of assistance to a fellow user at need.

Suppose someone in the group is trying to decide which word processing program to start on. A major commitment is involved; most people
don't ever quit the word processing program that they start on (that's
how some of the earlier, less user-friendly programs survive). There's
the initial cost of the program; the hardware that it ties you into; the
constant relearning of its updates; all the ancillary programs that
enhance it; the peripherals that you'll need to run them, and so on. And
you can't trust the advertisements for a program –or even some of the
reviews. 'Try before you buy' makes a great deal of sense under these
circumstances.

When your cult member asks you for a copy of the program, so that he can see
whether it's really what it claims to be and what he wants, are you going to
refuse? If you assist him, however, you're definitely a pirate.

PUBLIC DOMAIN AUTHORSHIP

The Source and *Compuserve,* America's huge 'information utilities' (gigantic, information-packed databases which also provide electronic meeting
grounds and electronic 'mail boxes' for special interest groups of all kinds),
have literary soap operas running on their bulletin boards. Here writers, banded
into a literary group, each take it in turn, one person per day, to write the soap.

Everyone monitors and makes electronic comments. You write up your
day's worth of the soap, advancing your ideas on plot development, characteri-
zation or the like, when your turn comes. Who owns the end product? Such
soaps can't be classified in terms of traditional authorship. Neither can electronic journals, where writers interact at long distance, via modems, to jointly produce a multi-authored end product –which any non-participant who's electroni-
cally monitoring them can copy as it's being produced.

Changes in the print culture are associated with changing views on how people communicate; there has been a major rethinking of how persuasion comes
about, for instance.[24] Persuasion is no longer conceived of as a top-down, one-
to-many influencing process that changes the public's views on this or that
issue. Rather it's seen as inherent in the interactivity and mutual influencing

that's ever-present in our everyday interactions with other people; it's something that changes the persuader as well as those whom he or she is influencing.

Also, a deeper understanding has recently been achieved of how professionals think in action. Investigation has shown that they think in terms of complex schematics which are case-like in nature. They hold several of these patterning devices provisionally in mind, trying them out for fit on events as these events unfold. The schematic/case that best accommodates unexpected developments in this flow of events is the causal framework that is eventually accepted.[25] Provisionalism again.

But perhaps the most striking illustration of our emerging sensitivity to phenomena like provisionalism, interactivity and 'public domain' authorship comes in the discovery of the importance of group-developed narrative. It's becoming apparent that humans are, essentially, story telling animals.[26]

We make sense of the complex organizations we live in via 'dramatizing narratives': by interactively developing group 'fantasies' –stories, to which all members of the group contribute, which explain pivotal events in the organization's life. Participating in the developing of such narratives is what gives us a shared symbolic consciousness –somewhat like a myth. By subscribing to this we gain a shared, multifaceted understanding of, and feeling for, the events that occur in our complex organizations.[27]

These narratives form a 'meta-code', a means for constructing, with the help of those around us who matter, the social 'reality' of our lives. Film scripts, and interactive, 'hacked' programs, are analogous to this type of narrative and our participation in it. The literary ownership of such a narrative is also somewhere 'out there' in the public domain –or maybe it's 'shareware'.

What of cases where someone's talents are 'institutionalized'? This can happen in the development of an 'expert system':

• You identify a number of highly effective experts in a given field.

• You set a surveillance team to watch how these experts perform some complex decision-making procedure.

• The team gets the individual experts to talk about what they're doing as they're doing it; then, afterwards, gets them to reconstruct why they did what they did.

• Then you cross-compare your investigative team's findings from all the experts studied.

• Finally you create an algorithm of the deep structure of the decision process underlying the regularities you find.

• Turn the result into an interactive computer program, and anyone who can afford the program can train him- or herself to operate at the level of these experts by putting on this electronic skull cap.[28]

Meanwhile the experts have been automated out of business, and the person who financed the expert program 'owns' the expertise. There's no name for such a financier –who may well have become a multimillionaire in a few short years by running a software development house. But if you lend the expert program that you bought to a friend, so that he or she can try it out before paying the stiff price involved, you are a pirate. You can imagine what hackers think of the ethics of this situation.

The technology is going beyond traditional ways of thinking about intellectual property, as always happens in times when technology changes the ways we store and transmit information. Our views on what a book should look like, on what and how one should write, on what genres should be presented in books (as opposed to other means of transmitting ideas), on the relationship of graphics to text, as well as on copyright –all of these have changed, probably irreversibly. Print culture is in transition.

CD ROM: The Shape of Things to Come?
A MAJOR INCREASE IN OUR CAPACITY TO STORE AND RETRIEVE DATA

Convergence of computer, video and audio technologies has resulted in a new medium, a disk that provides the personal computer with the capacity to store amazing amounts of data cheaply. This disk has a thousand times the storage capacity of a floppy disk, yet costs about the same amount:[29]

- from computing has come the optical disk, which allows immense quantities of data to be stored and quickly accessed;
- videodisks have been developed for interactive training manuals or display exhibitions;
- compact audio disks now store high fidelity music.

Combining these technologies on a laser disk produced CD ROM: Compact Disk Read Only Memory (550 megabytes –million bytes, MB for short– of data on a 5.25" disk; 4,000 MB on an 11" disk).[30]

So far, these disks have been mainly used for distributing large amounts of information (550 MB allows storage of five encyclopedias), or compressing archives to save storage space and retrieval time. But the crossover point has been passed. CD ROM disks are less expensive, financially and environmentally, than the books that they store –and they permit much more rapid and convenient recovery of data from those books. And erasable disks are in the offing.

THE MOST INTERACTIVE COMMUNICATION TECHNOLOGY TO DATE

CD ROM is a new, interactive supermedium –the most interactive medium yet to be developed. To the personal computer's static text, numbers and graphics, it has added full motion video, animated graphics and high fidelity audio. Entirely new forms of communication and art, currently unimaginable –to judge by what happened in the development of the movies– are likely to result. Here are some of the things that we already have:

- The full Library of Congress catalog, on one disk.
- The animated book, so far mostly used for training mechanics. This allows parts installation to be viewed as a movie, with zooming in (to look at parts of an engine or a schematic in fine detail), replays (of the steps in an assembly procedure) etc.
- Then there's the "Aspen Movie Map". This allows you to drive through Aspen (a noted resort town in Colorado), taking whichever route you wish, with the town unfolding before your eyes. You can switch from summer to winter, or touch a building represented on screen and have a voice tell you what's inside as that 'inside' comes on screen.
- Or there's the roller coaster ride in EPCOT Centre, Disneyland's fellow showplace. A computer allows you to design your own roller coaster track, then ride it, experiencing the trip you've just designed.

The potentials of this medium for the presentation of case studies, novels and simulations are mind boggling. It's a technology that permits you to participate interactively in the activity that you're watching and listening to. You can view your own movie as you direct it.

For this technology to become widely accepted, there has to be a mass of software; and this in turn requires a mass of software developers; distributed production is necessary to maintain a major market.[31] So we're back in the situation, already discussed, which made the production of the authoring system *World Builder* necessary. Moreover, this technology, more interactive than any consumer product before it, cannot be produced by any one individual. It requires an interdisciplinary team, pooling a variety of skills from a variety of fields.[32] In short, CD ROM is based upon, and further promotes, exactly the kinds of attitudes and practices that have been brought about by the use of personal computers.

CD ROM is in its early stages currently: those 550 MB, which store five encyclopedias, provide only twelve minutes of full-featured video. New means of enabling people to use the complex programs on which the disks run, and to find their way around within the vast amounts of data stored, will have to be developed. More important, new visions of what this new technology can be used for will have to be developed. Here writers and artists have a critic-ally important rôle to play. Those of them who are already using personal computers are likely to be the vanguard in exploring the potential of this new medium.

We aren't making use of the accumulating information stockpiles that we now have. Few of us ever really use the resources of our libraries, because the methods available for consulting them are outmoded and inadequate. Indexing, our heritage from print, is largely to blame. On the track of an idea, our minds work by free association, not by tracking through hierarchies of category systems: knowledge and learning is a seamless carpet with no frames or boundaries.[33]

HYPERTEXT

CD ROM offers us this seamless carpet in the shape of hypertext, which *InfoWorld* defines as "a non-linear way of tracing various aspects of a concept or feature, with multiple options at each step". Programs such as *Guide* provide non-linear access, in single-step moves (but with a retraceable return path), to related texts or graphics or sounds, at multiple levels and at multiple sites.

The reader or viewer or listener or experimenter can easily, and at electronic speed, skip from one document to another, as free association prompts. Most problem solving comes through exploration –discovery learning, rather than by a linear process of acquiring pieces of information under direction. And, when society is undergoing rapid, technology-driven change, there's continuous demand for problem solving.

Thus CD ROM can radically alter education, as well as the structure of knowledge on which it's based. "The micro revolution is on the same level as the Copernican revolution" claims Gabriel Ofiesh. It gives us new ways of thinking about thinking, as well as opening up new ways of learning. Researchers in artificial intelligence, for example, are revealing new vistas of the way our minds work. Think of Marvin Minsky's "society of mind" for a view of the brain as a structure –a society of different minds– whose key characteristic is that it changes itself.[34]

2 Impact on Printing, Publishing and Readerships

Our Changing Information Environment

CHANGES IN THE MIX OF COMMUNICATION TECHNOLOGIES IN USE

A new communication technology, such as the computer, impacts on all the other communication technologies in use, altering their share of the mixture used by consumers of information and entertainment. It usually takes time for this impact to become evident. But indications are that, among people who are seriously involved in using computers, a major shift in communication media use has occurred.

There has certainly been a major shift in the reading habits of the serious reader, who is also, usually, involved in using a computer. Computing defies time-budgeting; it requires on-going, discovery learning, involving unanticipatable holdups. So it wreaks havoc with use of other media. TV tends to suffer most heavily: viewing drops off by 80%. Radio survives: on-the-move listening is possible. There's a drop in the amount of newspaper reading: the serious reader does not care for scatter-gun, brush-fire-fighting coverage of important events. He or she relies on specialist journals, newsletters and manuals –of necessity, because the rate of job-related change is now so great that it requires continuing learning to keep up.with it.

As will emerge, specialist newsletters and manuals are at the very core of the new computer technology of desktop publishing.

CONTINUING LEARNING: WHAT IT TAKES

'Keeping up' generally means self-directed, discovery learning –a very demanding form of learning. More highly educated readers generally have more demanding jobs; so, being under more pressure to do survival reading, they try to read more material. They have less time for any one item. So they skim. They want the essence, early. So specialist journals, focused on one area of prime interest, become the most critical item in their intellectual input. The signs of resulting changes in media use patterns, to take North America as an example, are as follows[1]:

1. By 1980, specialist magazines grossed $7.8 billion to TV's $5.1 billion.
2. By now, 94% of adult Americans read a magazine at least once a month.
3. Professionals have come to rely on specialized magazines/journals for their survival reading.
4. A new type of presentational format has evolved to seize and hold the attention of readers of these specialized publications.

Continuing learning requires a very special kind of support group, one that few of us are able to put together. So these new specialized magazines do it for us. Their editorial boards gather together the different kinds of information purveyors required for the diffusion of innovations:

- Innovators (quick to adopt novelties with potential).
- Opinion leaders (knowledgeable about developments of concern to the groups in which they are influential and about the acceptance of such developments in these groups).
- Liaisons (those who trade significant information between persons and groups).
- Cosmopolites (conference goers: early in getting information on developments important to their industry or specialty).
- Specialists (up to date in regard to technical breakthroughs).
- Gatekeepers (knowledgeable about information flowing within their organizations, and about items in that flow that are of special importance).[2]

The journal *MacUser* is a good example of a specialist journal that has such a mix of information purveyors on its editorial board and among its stringers.

This is the mix of expertise you need to consult, if you're thinking about embarking on any important venture. Your specialist magazine provides it for you –while functioning as an early warning system, on an ongoing basis, about developments in your area of interest.

The Technological Breakthrough

A NEW CAPACITY TO PRODUCE PRINTABLE GRAPHICS EASILY

In the '80's, driven largely by demand from the US military-industrial complex, there was a quantum leap in the technology of producing graphics in print –only the fourth such great leap forward since the introduction of printing.

It has become easily possible to produce engineering drawings, business graphs and charts, photographs and line art, via computer, in camera-ready form. The computer programs involved were originally produced for 'high end' (very expensive) page-making systems running on mainframe computers or minicomputers. But they were soon, as will appear, 'ported' to (designed in forms that could run on) the more powerful micros that appeared by the mid-80's.

A PRINTER THAT PRODUCES CAMERA-READY COPY FROM A MICROCOMPUTER

Then came two more developments in 1985. One was the development of *a (relatively) cheap 'intelligent' printer*. This was Apple's LaserWriter printer, *which originated the 300 dpi (dots per inch) printout*. This printer gave microcomputer-users printout that looked like print (most people can't tell the difference between 300 dpi and real print, which begins at 600 dpi): no more ugly dot matrix printouts! Besides this, the LaserWriter produced graphics that look like those you see in print (300 dpi is shorthand for 300 X 300 dpi: *90,000 dpi*).

There were two major innovations built into this printer. One was a 'page-description language' –*PostScript*– that converted text and graphics sent to the printer by a microcomputer into a 'language', which described the positions and shape of all items on each page, in a fashion that the printer could read and print. Second, built into the printer's huge rom (Read Only Memory), were the original Times and Helvetica typefaces (used under license from the International Typographers' Corporation). So the characters printed by the printer were actual print typefaces to which readers were accustomed.

The LaserWriter printer made camera-ready copy (copy that a printer can simply make a photographic plate out of and then print), cheaply, quickly and easily. This printer has made Apple the largest seller of typesetting equipment in North America.

PAGE MAKEUP PROGRAMS FOR MICROCOMPUTER USERS

The other development that came in 1985 was *the 'low-end' (inexpensive) layout program*. These electronic layout programs 'poured' word processed text and computer graphics into page layouts. Their text, which came in all kinds of formats and typefaces,.simply flowed round the graphics Printers' bugbears, such as multi-column tables and math formulae, could also be set via these programs. And this page makeup could also be done cheaply, quickly and easily.

This last feat was possible because this technology had separated the creation of (1) text and graphics, (2) page makeup and (3) printing into three separate operations (see diagram 2.1):

1. Text and graphics were first prepared using word processing programs (which could involve a preliminary operation of importing unformatted characters via a modem or by using a scanner on a typescript) and paint or drafting programs (which could involve a preliminary operation of importing photographs scanned by a digitizer).
2. Graphics were put on a page, and the text then flowed around them, by a page makeup program.
3. The results were then turned over to a page-description language, residing in the printer's rom, for the actual printout.

A chain of technological developments was thus integrated into a new, and amazingly powerful, combination.[3]

Because of the separation of these three stages, the individual programs used for each one of them, being focused only on one task (and having the advantage of running on the new, more powerful micros), became individually more powerful. 'High end' electronic layout programs, which formerly ran only on workstations (minicomputers), are currently being ported from their workstations to run on the new, more powerful micros.

> These are the third-generation micros that appeared in 1987.
> Initially, micros were 8-bit machines: the Apple II line, the Volkswagen of microcomputers, is an example (initially, this had 64,000 bytes of ram). Then came the 16 bit machine: IBM's PC originated this increase in power (initially, 128,000 bytes of ram). Then, in 1987, came the 32-bit micros: Apple's Mac II (initially, 8,000,000 bytes of ram,) and the IBM PS/2 and its clones.

These page makeup programs were formerly restricted to professional printers because of their price and complexity and the cost of the machinery on which they ran. Their complexity, however, has been dropping because worksta-

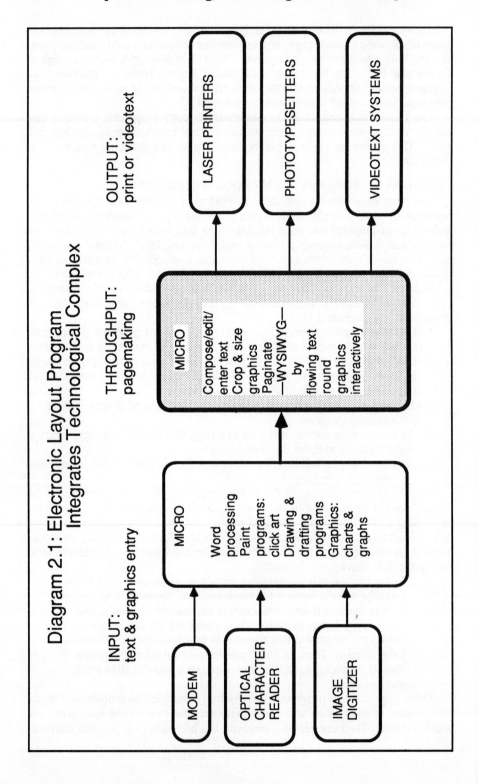

Diagram 2.1: Electronic Layout Program Integrates Technological Complex

INPUT:
text & graphics entry

THROUGHPUT:
pagemaking

OUTPUT:
print or videotext

MICRO

Word processing
Paint programs:
click art
Drawing & drafting programs
Graphics: charts & graphs

MICRO

Compose/edit/enter text
Crop & size graphics
Paginate —WYSIWYG—
by flowing text round graphics interactively

MODEM

OPTICAL CHARACTER READER

IMAGE DIGITIZER

LASER PRINTERS

PHOTOTYPESETTERS

VIDEOTEXT SYSTEMS

tions allowed on-screen previewing of the results of the codes entered into text (so formatting no longer had to be done 'blind'). Their prices, given the much larger number of micro users, could well drop to about one-fifth of what they originally were. Thus a further increase in the potential of the micro for personal publishing is in the offing.

> Business & government in North America publish far more pages than all its book, newspaper and magazine publishers combined.

Changes in In-House Publishing

WHO'S THE BIGGEST PUBLISHER IN THE LAND?

Xerox reported over 2.5 trillion pages copied in 1984, for instance. Large corporations generally spend from 6 to 10% of their gross revenues on various kinds of communications on paper: Boeing spent about two billion dollars in 1984.

RESULTS OF THE DROP IN COSTS OF PRINTING

As indicated, the electronic layout programs created pages containing text, engineering drawings, graphs and charts, and line art and digitized photographs. The resulting paginated documents could be fed into laser printers and phototypesetters such as the Linotronic 100 and 300. (The latter, whose output consists of photographic prints ready for printing from, provides a resolution of 2,540 X 2,540 dpi. This is a better output than any standard printer produces.) No second-best technology this.

The technology had two other major advantages, too:

1. The new publishing systems were no longer expensive or hard to use. Printing equipment dropped in cost to about one-tenth of its original prices (besides being much more convenient and less messy to use). This price reduction made it economical for many organizations to own their own print shops.
2. People could be fairly easily trained, in-house, to use this new technology. The 'machinery' was familiar and easy to use: microcomputers. The page makeup programs were simple and easy to use (the most popular program, *PageMaker*, is a splendid illustration of this. There was no need for all the knives, wax, and the other paraphernalia of the page makeup person: all were incorporated into the page makeup program.

In-house publishing can mean enormous savings: up to 70% in time and from 30–70% per page. The new equipment could pay for itself within a year, in many cases. Consider the following:

1. An in-house report can cost £7 per page, and take considerable time, if sent to an outside publisher. For a short run of 5 to 25 copies, it's not worth the cost, when a LaserWriter version can be produced for 25p per page in house, quickly (fast turnaround time is important when there may be last-minute updates of the document).
2. A company can produce forms to its own specifications, and in the quantities needed. No more making do with out-of-date forms because the over-ordered inventory is too expensive to junk; modification and publishing on demand of short runs is easily possible on a LaserWriter.
3. This is the ideal technology for producing manuals, which require frequent revisions and up-datings, so are otherwise very costly to produce.

4. It's likewise the ideal technology for producing newsletters, which involve a complex mix of text and graphics, and usually have to be produced at short notice, so are very costly if done by an outside publisher.

So the new equipment pays for itself in short order, while providing an added facility: an electronic publishing system constantly available in house. The LaserWriter, in practice, runs every day of the week –and for long hours on most days. Besides, the publishing centres mentioned below have found ways of turning themselves into *profit* centres. They sell disks containing graphics produced by their organizations as click art; and they run off extra copies of manuals produced for successful in-house training programs, to facilitate selling those programs out-of-house. And, of course, the micros can be used for ordinary business uses, such as spread sheeting and database management, when they are not being used for page makeup.

CONSEQUENCES OF CENTRALIZING AN ORGANIZATION'S PRINTING

The high costs of the publishing being done by organizations only became evident with the advent of this new technology, for the overall cost of their publishing activities was previously often hidden:

1. Only actual *printing* costs were generally considered under the heading of 'publishing costs' –and printing costs are only a fraction of the actual costs of any published document (they're about 10% of the cost of a technical document, for instance).
2. The average technical document undergoes thirteen revisions per page (and technical manuals are constantly updated once published). As such work is done in discontinuous pieces and different departments, its cost was generally going unrecognized.
3. The costs of the different operations involved in getting a manual to camera-ready form were scattered across many individual departmental managers' budgets, nowhere combined under one heading.

Once a centralized publications department had been set up for an organization, however, management took a systematic look at the overall cost of *all* aspects of publishing activities. Here's what tended to happen.

The publications centres didn't relish the prospect of being categorized as service departments,'overhead', or 'cost centres'. So they instituted charge backs for all their services, based on what it would have cost to have had the work done outside. Reciprocating, other departments charged back to the publication centres all work done, in document preparation and the like, for these centres.

So overall costs –previously hidden in a multitude of individual managers' budgets, where their overall, cumulative cost was not readily evident– now became evident. Organizations thus came to realize that their total costs for publications were *much* higher than they imagined: as stated, a staggering 6–10% of gross revenue.

Computer assisted publishing (CAP) has thus emerged as the means of cutting the time and expense of publishing a wide variety of materials –a significant saving to any organization. Hence the large growth in corporate expenditures on CAP, making it the fastest-growing market segment in electronic publishing. The corporate preference is for micro-based, single-user desktop systems, especially now that micros are becoming as powerful as minicomputers.

By developing this way of automating in-house publishing in a highly cost effective way, vendors of these layout systems thus created a new use, and a new market, for their technology.

ORGANIZATIONS BECOME PUBLISHING HOUSES

Large organizations publish a surprising amount and variety of printed matter via desktop publishing:

1. The bread and butter items are business forms and mass mailings plus their enclosures.
2. The big money-savers, after business forms, are manuals.
3. Public relations releases, often required at short notice and in short runs, are another large outgoing: bulletins and flyers come under this head.
4. Prestige publications are annual reports, to shareholders and to staff. Posters and brochures are other display items that come under this head.
5. The company newsletter has come to serve as a prime means for keeping organizational members, and sometimes the organization's clientele, up-to-date with important events relating to the organization.

   The volume of newsletters published is generally not realized: currently, in North America, three times as many people are in receipt of newsletters as are in receipt of daily newspapers. Newsletters, then, are important publications for organizations.

It's convenient, as well as being much cheaper, to have newsletters produced in-house.

It's crucial that the newsletter editor is perceived as being 'one of us', and as 'caring about us', by readers within the organization.[4] The newsletter gives members of an organization a sense of belonging and of being in the know. It tells who's done what, and what the significance of this action is for the organization. It's quick to tell what's going on, and why, speaking with the voice of someone who knows the business and whose fortunes are tied up with those of the organization. So an outsider won't do as editor. Besides, with the trend towards participative management, especially where employee stock option programs are in effect, it's essential to have a very proactive and quickly responsive newsletter.[5] This is yet another reason why the organization must find its editor in house. And the desktop publishing technology makes it easier to develop organizational members into in-house editors.

SPIN-OFF EFFECTS

Even those businesses and groups with relatively modest financial resources can now afford print. Print has an impact that xeroxing and multilithing don't, and a small print run is no longer prohibitively expensive. So there's a lot of demand for the personal publisher, from a new clientele –small businesses and relatively small groups– who want camera-ready copy. The advent of the copy centre with a Macintosh, hard disk and a LaserWriter marked the advent of a new type of printing service, the small typesetting service, which turned captured keystrokes into camera-ready formats.

> The 'authority of print' is now available to any small business and special interest group.

Meanwhile, as small printers an **increase** in business (materials that weren't printed before, now are), a new kind of small business has appeared: lasersetting. A lasersetter prints computer text files, sent by mail on disk or by telephone via a modem, on a laser printer (or a Linotronic phototypesetter, if requested). Lasersetters will also take word processed text files and lay them out in book form, camera-ready, using page makeup programs.

Some even provide an advisory service to their clients, when the latter can't get a program or a micro to do what it's supposed to do. Desktop publishing, as explained above, involves a system. No seller of any piece of software or hardware is responsible for this system or can advise on it in its entirety. Lasersetters have to make it work: they receive text files from a variety of software and hardware and have to get it to run on their printers. So they've become the experts on integrating the system in its various configurations. Such advice-giving requires formidable computer expertise.

In another new trend, manufacturers of 'low end' (less expensive) typesetting equipment are discontinuing their product lines. This is because a microcomputer plus software can do the same job at a fraction of the cost, so the equipment is no longer selling. These manufacturers are now selling their software (see the discussion of the *MacMat* book in chapter 3), to run on in-house microcomputers for desktop publishing. This software was previously only available as part of the package which came with such manufacturers' typesetting equipment.

At the same time, more corporations than publishers are buying microcomputers for publishing purposes. Corporations bought 62% of all computer publishing systems sold in 1985; predictions are that they'll be buying over 90% of all such systems sold by 1989. Low-priced desktop publishing systems and software are accounting for an ever-increasing amount of sales of personal computers, for use in desktop publishing. It's estimated that, by 1990, these systems will account for 97% of all computer sales.

Overall: a new environment, and new opportunities for personal or in-house publishers, has been created in 'low-end' (small) publishing by the above changes.

Impact on Book Publishing
THE SPECIAL PROBLEMS OF BOOK PUBLISHERS

It was the newspaper industry which developed the technology for creating a page on the computer's screen. In consequence, computer assisted publishing has, to date, been of most assistance to newspapers and magazines.

> Newspapers and magazines are produced by an in-house staff, all of whom are in daily contact and in close proximity. These publications are short in length, with a high ratio of graphics to text. They're got together very quickly, without use of off-site reviewers. This is a perfect work environment for the new technology –not surprisingly, as it was developed primarily with such users in mind.

High end book publishing –the publishing of lengthy books (or learned journals) involving complex layouts (tables, diagrams and mathematical formulae)– is still struggling to develop this technology to cope with the special problems of book publishing. These problems mainly centre on automating its 'copy flow', the complicated and long-drawn-out editorial and production process.[6]

Publishers of books –as opposed to the publishers of newspapers and magazines– have to deal with a lot of 'wordsmiths' (editors, authors and assessors of manuscripts), who are widely (often internationally) scattered. They call such dealing 'marking up'. *Marking up* involves a protracted cycle of securing assessments of, then editing, manuscripts; coaxing authors to rewrite, and overseeing several lots of page-proofing. Notes are kept of all this, in an *audit trail*, to guide the final makeup (and chargeback) process. Marking up also entails '*trafficking*': sending large volumes of text back and forth among all these wordsmiths. Finally, as few publishers have their own printing presses, they have to '*buy print*': to find a printer to print the book they've at long last made up.

MARKING UP

Marking up involves several problems for a publisher. As stated, a book's text may involve many authors, in several countries. Comments on that text are usually detailed and may involve several editors. Comments always involve one or more assessors. Besides all this, the authors are actively involved throughout, usually by mail. They rewrite and go over the page proofs –as do the editor(s)– right up to the end.

This copy flow process, with all its marking up and trafficking, commonly goes on for over a year. Clearly, a system is required to keep track of all this. Penta, a high end editing and page-making house, has developed software that keeps all versions of a book on file, creating an audit trail which shows all additions and deletions, as well as who made which changes. This system enables injudicious revisions to be undone and authors' alterations to be billed (authors' alterations to galley proofs can easily cost more than the galley proofs themselves).

MEDIA CONVERSION

Many authors word process their own manuscripts nowadays; some can even input their own graphics. Hence another problem: media conversion. Effectively, publishers can exercise little control over the programs that their contributors use.

Computer users tend to get locked in to software and hardware, because the punishment involved in learning an 'unfriendly' program is such that few of us can face learning another. So, whatever instructions they're given, writers submit their work using the word processing program that they're familiar with –usually the golden oldie that runs on their trusty old home computer.

The editor has to get the text files that come in, via disk or modem, to run on his or her own micro and page makeup program and/or to print on his or her own printer. Inevitably, the editor is confronted with problems of incompatibility between his or her software and that of the writers. For instance:

1. Drive operating systems differ (CPM and MS-DOS, for instance).
2. Word processing codes differ (as with the aged *Wordstar*, now at version 3.1, and the brilliant newcomer *Word Perfect*).
3. Machine languages differ, especially when writers are using the older, 8-bit machines (there are 7-bit codes –ASCII[7]– and 8-bit codes –*Gutenberg*, for instance).

4. Phototypesetting codes can differ.
5. Different modems, relaying different programs from different computers, may send in different codes to that of the host modem.
6. Data entry and formatting errors are common in writers' material, especially when batch processing programs have been used.

It takes very expensive technology and expertise to read a wide variety of programs into the one master electronic layout system. So a new type of typesetting service has sprung up, with commercial editors undertaking to get the material submitted on disk by writers into a uniform format specified by the periodical's editor.

TRAFFICKING

Besides this, the trafficking itself –the sending of text back and forth– involves problems. The authors' and assessors' hardware and software are rarely compatible with the expensive systems that the publishers have to use. So they have to be mailed hard copy –printed page proofs. (Printed, because a dot-matrix print-out encourages the recipient to make all kinds of further changes, which are very costly, whereas a LaserWriter's print-out, which looks like print, is treated with more respect.)

Mailing is also necessary because not all computerized telecommunications systems (which are far from cheap, when large volumes of data have to be sent or stored) can cope with the sending of hundreds of pages of elaborately formatted text. Errors creep in. As a result, book publishers are still involved in labour-intensive checking and emendation of page proofs by hand, which slows down the turnaround time.

THE POTENTIALS AND PROBLEMS OF BATCH PROCESSING PROGRAMS

You don't normally make up a book of 300 or more pages interactively, one page at a time. It takes too long, and you can't make instant changes if you need to reformat the end product. You have to use batch pagination programs.

> These require you to insert lots of macros (foreshortened commands that call down elaborate sub-programs in the batch program), and use plain text. What you see on the screen is not what you'll get when you print out. It's just characters (not even in the various typefaces, styles and sizes that you're using), interspersed with computer jibberish –the macros. And you're programming blind: one error in one of these macros can result in chaos. So you have to print out your handiwork to see if your own programming –all those macros– was properly done.

It's rare that you won't make some mistakes on your first few tries, because batch programs have to do so many complicated things. They have to check for widows and orphans, gutter flipping, automatic footnoting, and indexing; they have to change running heads and footers; see that tables and diagrams aren't split when you make corrections to the text, and make sure that chapter and part openings come on the right pages, and so on.

Such programs aren't easy to learn: they usually take three months of constant use before competence is attained, six months before expertise is evident. They need to be constantly used if you're to retain your expertise. Besides, they usually require powerful computers. (Until the new micros arrived, they usually needed minicomputers –and were *very* expensive.) Effectively, only full-time printers use these complex and demanding programs.

THE PROMISE OF THE TECHNOLOGY

Finally, when the publisher comes to buy print, he or she will find that not every electronic printer is compatible with the editing and page make up technology that he or she has been using. Standardized page description languages should end this problem; but complete standardization hasn't yet been achieved.

As we'll see, the technology for automating copy flow, making electronic trafficking possible and providing user-friendly pagination programs, is gradually coming together. ('User-friendly' in this case means batch programs that allow interaction and provide for 'WYSIWYG' screen previews: previews where what you see –on the screen– is what you get –in the printout.) As yet, however, this sector of the publishing business is still beset by difficulties as it tries to streamline its operations via computerization.

Things are moving faster where desktop publishing is concerned, however. Under pressure from business, the makers of hardware and software are now trying very hard to make their equipment and programs compatible. Users are *demanding* that what's produced on one set of hardware and software should be able to run on another set. Training staff on new computer programs costs eight times as much as the programs; so constant changes in programs (required whenever there's new hardware) are prohibitively expensive. The battle for universal standards is being won: business has clout.

Background Changes in Electronic Publishing
A NEW KIND OF COMPUTING, STILL IN ITS INFANCY

In 1985, then, there was an epochal development in electronic publishing. The advent of the electronic layout program and the laser printer provided a new type of use –personal publishing– for the personal computer. This development was analogous to the advent, earlier, of the spreadsheet, which made the 8-bit machine into a business machine instead of a hobbyist's plaything. Similarly, the electronic layout program has made the personal computer into a printing press as well as a business machine.

To exploit its potential, the personal computer has had to be enormously developed. 1987 was another epochal year for the micro: the 32-bit machines arrived. They're as powerful as the minicomputers of yesteryear. New programs, with many new features, have been written to exploit this additional power. This is a new, pioneering generation of software. All such new generation software is faulty: it takes years of use to find the 'bugs' and work them out of it. So using the new software is rather like driving a high-powered sports car on a busy motorway –the M1, for instance– with the vehicle sometimes responding unexpectedly to the controls. You need to have your wits about you.

EMPOWERING THE PERSONAL PUBLISHER

The computer on your desktop gives you the equivalent of a team of printers. Its programs can do the following:

1. *Text entry*: outlining programs which feed into word-processors make for

rapid, legible text entry (and massive changes can be easily made without great bouts of retyping). There is now provision for style sheets, as well as automatic footnoting, contents generation and indexing, and some limited capability to insert graphics in text.

2. *Typesetting*: advanced on-line word processors provide a range of typefaces (including display typefaces and symbol sets), in a variety of styles and sizes A range of different alphabets and scripts is also available, along with the capability of printing right to left as well as left to right.

3. *Proofreading*: utility programs can now check spelling; enrich vocabulary (they have thesauri built in); hyphenate automatically, and check for clichés, some forms of grammatical and punctuation errors, readability level and sexist language. They'll also insert "strike through characters" to show editing changes made.

4. *Graphics*: utility programs allow the manipulation of a rapidly expanding library of click (ready-made) art; statistics can be rapidly turned into a variety of charts and graphs, and you can now digitize photographs, and crop and size pictures.

5. Page makeup and copyfitting: interactive electronic layout programs allow you to play intuitive 'what if' games with your page makeup problems, as you set pages individually. They also allow you to do kerning and letter spacing, as well as set headers and footers in body text, as you set large blocks of text. Some batch processing programs with on-screen preview capabilities now exist.

Note: No one program can do **all** of these things.

You can now produce a sophisticated publication on your personal computer, if you buy a little time on a LaserWriter printer.

THE TRAINING GAP

Meanwhile, apprenticeships have, effectively, ended, for printers. You can no longer compel a person whom you have trained through an apprenticeship to work for you as a printer. So it doesn't pay you to train him or her. Anyway, the requirement to acquire (and keep updating) computing skills, coming on top of all the other skills required of a trainee printer, has tended to be too heavy a burden.

So trainees are harder to find, as well as harder to keep. Electronic publishing is having much the same impact on printers as CAD/CAM (computer assisted design/computer assisted manufacturing –based on computer programs for three-dimensional engineering drafting) has had on draftspersons. A long, proud tradition of apprenticeship, going back to the earliest days of printing, has come to an end. It has left a skill shortfall in an area that's critical to our society –the area of production of printed material.

A new style of editing has come into existence, for all but high end printing (where professional printers still hold sway). Desktop publishing combines editing with printing activities. This type of editing requires the ability to continuously generate quality text, edit it, and set it out aesthetically and without errors. A personal publisher is apt to have to act as a graphic designer, typographer, layout designer, writer, copy editor, and production manager (costing stock and generating subscription lists), as well as a content editor.

The savings in time, cost and flexibility promised by the new technology come at the expense of the new breed of editor, who has a more demanding job than editors in the past. For a newcomer to personal publishing without some background in traditional publishing the learning curve will be steep and arduous. The superstars at desktop publishing come from typesetting or editing, bringing their professional expertise with them. In practice, what generally seems to happen is that an editorial team builds up round the new technology: together, the team has the skills required. Failing this, drudgery can be the lot of personal publishers.

Skillful instruction is needed to train this new type of editor. It's beginning to look as though it's easier to train a person to handle the computer technology of personal publishing than it is to develop him or her as a personal publisher type of editor. The rapid development of workshops and specialist journals indicates that this problem is being met; but formal training programs are as yet not widely available. Still, given what's now known about facilitating self-directed adult learning, this should not be an insuperable difficulty (especially if the team concept is adopted as the norm).

New-Style, Desktop Editing
CUTTING COSTS BY PUBLISHING JOURNALS VIA DESKTOP PUBLISHING

Changes are occurring for most editors as a result of CAP. Rising publishing costs have moved most editors from wondering "Can the new technology cut printing costs?" to "How can I effectively use computer assisted publishing to cut costs?" In the case of editors of Canadian academic journals, for instance, with 50% of their governmental subventions to be lost over the years 1986–7, and printing costs going up by 20–30% a year, this is a critically important question.

Typically, costs are transferred to the editor and the writer. The editor increasingly has to input at least some of the text into the computer. The writer may soon be faced with page charges for material not submitted on disk; elaborate graphics –diagrams and the like– already have to be paid for by the author in many cases. Soon graphics-intensive papers may be affordable only if submitted, with their graphics already in place, on disk.

In the case of learned journals, however, this solution rarely works, because their editors must deal with many of the problems facing high end publishers, mentioned above. The problem that they talk about most is that of media conversion. The new typesetting services can produce superbly typeset, camera-ready text out of a hodge-podge of variously programmed on-disk material. But the cost of the service eliminates any savings gained by having authors submit their material on disk (particularly as authors' errors in entering text to disk can rarely be automatically rectified, thus necessitating expensive reprogramming).

NEW ROLES FOR EDITORS OF JOURNALS AND NEWSLETTERS

Currently, changes are occurring for editors of learned journals. Most of them end up entering text from hard copy to disk. As they report it, an academic saddled with the task of editing his or her discipline's journal becomes an overworked hack typist. Moreover, as most of these editors –who can't afford media conversion and professional editing services– are using *Word Perfect* on an IBM PC or clone without access to a local area network, they can't, as of now, easily use Apple's LaserWriter to produce print-quality hard copy.

This problem hasn't disappeared with the advent of the open-architecture, IBM-compatible Macintosh capable of running *Word Perfect*. This micro is too expensive for most such editors, or their associations, to be able to afford. The advent of a version of *WordPerfect* that runs on the Mac, with the ability to read *WordPerfect* text produced on the IBM PC should cope with the problem (except that most of these editors have IBM PCs, not the [much more expensive] Macs).

A 'solution' that requires computer users to purchase new and expensive micros and learn new and expensive (and sometimes difficult) software may not be a real option for those outside the business environment (or even for many within it, for that matter). Economic considerations seem likely to keep many editors in the rôle of hack. They have to do what was formerly the work of several people. It's the *organization* which gets the savings in time and costs, generally at the expense of the editor's 'private' life.

Changes are likewise occurring where in-house publishers of newsletters are concerned. The rôle of the in-house publicist has been redefined. He or she is no longer the 'hired gun' of

> The hard fact is that, for many desktop publishers, their job —which replaces the jobs of several other people— involves a great deal of drudgery.

management. Gone, too, is the in-house publicist as muckraking journalist. What readers want to know is whether they'll have a job a year hence. Currently, in-house publicists are more like continuing educators, developing among their coworkers a sense of what the issues, alternatives, and likely technological futures are that face their organization. This role for an in-house publicist is one with which an able and socially-conscious person can readily identify.[8]

3 The Art of Desktop Publishing:

The Concerted Effort to Make Page Makeup Learnable

What *is* the Meaning of the Term "Desktop Publishing"?

THE RANGE OF PUBLISHING ACTIVITIES ASSOCIATED WITH THE TERM

'Desktop publishing' is one of those trendy terms, like 'systems' or 'environment' that are so overused as to lose precision of reference. Presumably, however, the term wouldn't get so much play if it weren't giving its users *some* advantages that the other, related terms (like 'computer assisted publishing' or 'electronic publishing') don't give. Let's consider what these advantages might be.

Basically, the term 'desktop publishing' is currently used to mean that you can create text and graphics, compose the results into pages with the text flowing round the graphics, and produce camera-ready copy for either a laser printer or a phototypesetter. You can't reproduce this copy en masse by this technology: you have to get a traditional printer to do that. Distribution may well be done by someone else, too. So the 'publishing' part of the desktop publishing term means something rather different from the word 'publishing' when it's used on its own. (Let's not go further into the range of meanings associated with 'publishing' here.)

THREE BASIC CONCEPTS UNDERLYING THE TERM

There seem to be at least three basic concepts implicit in the term *desktop* publishing, as it's currently used:

The first is that you can do page makeup with a microcomputer

–that you can publish a document (a pamphlet, a newsletter or a book) by using your microcomputer (which is usually positioned on your desk). You don't need a mainframe computer or a minicomputer or 'workstation', the computers associated heretofore with the terms 'computer-assisted publishing' and 'corporate electronic publishing'. Your personal microcomputer will suffice.

With the micro that you've got sitting on your desk, you can set type, produce graphics and make up pages, flowing the text round the graphics.

You don't need all the paraphernalia –drafting board, special lighting, glues, "razor blades, waxes and paste pots"– that are traditionally associated with making up pages for a publication. You simply produce a text file, on a computer disk, containing the made-up pages.

Next, still at your desk, you send this text file, via the LAN (local area network) or, via a modem over the telephone, to a printer. If it goes via the LAN, it usually goes to a laser printer that you and others share in-house. If it goes by phone, you're usually sending it to an outside lasersetting house or –more likely– a computerized typesetting shop. The latter prints it out, generally on a phototypesetter.

A laser printer such as the LaserWriter (which is the printer most associated with desktop publishing) produces a resolution of 300 (X 300) dots per inch (dpi). This is camera-ready copy: at 90,000 dpi, it looks like print to most people. A phototypesetter produces densities of over 1200 dpi (the Linotronic 100) or of over 2400 dpi (the Linotronic 300), turning out photographic plates, which a printer prints from The Linotronic 300 gives better results than many printing processes used to print expensive books.

Running off the made up pages accounts for about 10% of publishing costs (if distribution costs aren't included therein); so you've just produced a 90% saving in getting your document printed. As desktop publishing is so quick and easy, you've usually cut at least 30–40% off the time taken by traditional printing. Maybe your graphics took longer than your graphic artist would have taken to do them. But, with desktop publishing, you've now got a set of graphics (which can be easily and quickly adapted for other purposes), for future use or for sale.

The second basic concept is that of interactive page makeup.

Desktop publishing is strongly associated with use of a WYSIWYG computer. WYSIWYG means that you don't have to become expert in the programming –the coding or tagging– associated with batch processing, which is done 'blind' (you can't see the results of your programming till it's printed out) and which requires considerable expertise and training.

Moreover, desktop publishing programs can now easily do things (such as flowing text round irregularly shaped graphics) that traditional page makeup programs had great difficulty with. With very little training, nearly anyone can make up a page using an interactive WYSIWYG page makeup program. It's this ease of learning and use, combined with the cheapness of the technology, which has made desktop publishing so popular.

The third basic concept has to do with the term 'desktop'.

The desktop metaphor is basic to the Macintosh's user interface (which it uses in place of the PC's command-driven operating system) and so to desktop publishing (the PC has had to appropriate most of the Mac's desktop features to do desktop publishing).

This 'desktop' (an image of a desktop is what you actually see when the Mac's screen comes on) consists of a graphics-based micro, with much use of icons to represent visually the operations to be performed; a point-and-click 'mouse' to activate them; 'windows' that open to enable you to have several 'pages' open on your desktop at once; and 'desktop accessories'.

The latter are the electronic equivalents of the paraphernalia found on a desk. They're there in the background as you work, for you to pull out and use while working on your 'pages'. Desktop publishing is publishing using *this* 'desktop'.

The facts are that 70% of all desktop publishing is done on the Macintosh and the LaserWriter, generally using the page makeup program *PageMaker*.

This was the combination that made desktop publishing feasible. People don't talk about 'PC publishing' because the term 'PC' is associated with the IBM PC and its clones. You can't do desktop publishing on a PC/PC clone unless it's been considerably upgraded. You really need something like an AT –and even then it's easier to do interactive page makeup involving lots of graphics on a Macintosh.

Consequently, desktop publishing isn't primarily associated with the PC in most computer-users' minds. Rather, it's associated with the Macintosh *and the latter's easy-to-use 'desktop'* –the chief metaphor of the Macintosh, and what most distinguishes its operating environment from the command-driven, MS-DOS environment of the PC.

So the term desktop publishing is a very convenient expression. It carries a considerable freight of implications and associations. None of the other terms, such as computer-assisted publishing and the like, carry precisely this penumbra of associations. It will be interesting to see if the expression 'desktop publishing' stands the test of time. Meanwhile, I propose to use it in the sense set out above.

Who and What is a Desktop Publisher?
DESKTOP PUBLISHING AND STRUCTURAL UNEMPLOYMENT

Basically, desktop publishing is part of the trend to eliminate costly, labour-intensive (and sometimes unionized) operations by introducing machinery that cuts costs by doing jobs these people.once did. It's part of the replacement of skilled operators by sophisticated computer software that we know as de-skilling, a phenomenon accompanying structural unemployment. The desktop publishing technology gives its operator the equivalent of a team of printers, thus doing away with the much of what is needed from a small print shop with its printer's team.

The person chosen to operate this technology is usually already on staff. She or he –let's make it 'she'– is generally employed at a job which is below her abilities. Maybe she lacks the paper qualifications obtained via higher education. Appointment to head the desktop publishing 'unit' (initially, at least, comprising only herself) offers the chance to make it to managerial status, an otherwise unlikely prospect. Find a workaholic in a situation like this and dangle a lure like desktop publishing in front of him or her, and management can get prodigies of work done.

There's one difference from the usual situation involving de-skilling as a result of structural unemployment, however: desktop publishing involves massive skills upgrading for whomsoever is chosen to do it. This fact is not generally appreciated.

HOW A DESKTOP PUBLISHER DIFFERS FROM A TRADITIONAL EDITOR

In the first place, publishing is a demanding craft. Acquiring competence in the group of computer programs required for electronic publishing is the easiest part of it (unless batch editing programs are involved), as the Macintosh and its programs are so easy to learn. Learning the editing skills is the hard part. Normally an editor gets appointed only after a form of apprenticeship which has taught him or her, over a period of years, the tricks of the publishing trade. Computer software can't replace this kind of know-how and experience.

In practice, many an in-house desktop publisher has to learn the editor's trade while also learning the computer skills required for desktop publishing. This is a formidable task. As indicated above, most successful desktop publishing editors generally come from a background in editing or printing, bringing publishing expertise with them.

In the second place, an editor who's a desktop publisher has to be a Jack of all trades, whereas the publishing house's specialist editor (normally supported by a team containing specialists in page makeup and the like) is a specialist in magazine or book editing or what have you. So the desktop publisher has to have acquaintance with, though not in-depth expertise in, an unusually wide range of publishing activities. Such broad competence is usually acquired by some form of apprenticeship.

In practice, the major difficulty currently being encountered by organizations which are starting in-house publishing ventures is precisely that of training desktop publishers, who are usually newcomers to publishing, in editing and publishing skills.

Typically, an editor has a different job to do than has a desktop publisher. A specialist editor is normally primarily concerned with maintaining standards in content and form, being guided in both cases by set policy.

1. As to content, the editor secures this via specialists. First she identifies specialist writers who can produce work of the nature and quality desired. Then she goes to her panel of assessors, from which she identifies assessors, likewise specialists in the field, to appraise the competence of the writers' work. The editor then supervises the interactions of writers and assessors so as to develop a quality product.

2. As to form, the editor will follow a house style which dictates formatting, typography and so on in minute detail. Layout is largely determined by the manufacturing process and the typographer, illustrative artists and paste-up person.[1] Much of the detailed work is done by these specialists. The editor flowcharts the work to be done, and monitors it to see that it's done to specifications.

An in-house publisher who is a desktop editor often has a far more demanding rôle: it's proactive, not reactive.

First, content. Here the rôle of the in-house publicist has changed. Once this rôle was simply to act as spokesperson for management: to make the official line attractive or palatable. Then there was a phase when in-house publicists saw their rôle as that of muckraking journalists, calling attention to the organization's shortcomings.

Currently the rôle of an in-house publicist is more like that of a continuing educator: they have to inform members of the organization of upcoming developments in the field in which the organization operates. They must set out, in scenarios and in advance of events, what the organization is going to have to do to stay competitive.[2] ESOPs (employee stock option programs), which seem to bring greatly heightened organizational growth and flexibility, can't be operated without a very skilful in-house publicist to arouse their members' awareness in this way.[3]

These last two rôles involve the in-house publicist in policy setting. They're proactive and call for scanning the future and the creativity of an editorial writer/commentator on an industry and its economy.

Secondly, form. The desktop in-house editor generally has to function as a publisher rather than as an editor. Publishing in-house is done precisely so as not to have to send work out to a printer with his or her expensive editors, illustrative artists, typographers and paste-up persons. So the desktop editor has to become familiar with what these specialists do. Moreover, the desktop publisher has to become a designer. This is the first time that publishing has been attempted in-house on a microcomputer. So there is no established way of doing it, no house-style to serve as guide.

For example, if an army marches on its stomach, an organization advances on its forms. In-house production of forms makes short runs and frequent redesign at short notice possible –a big money saver (especially with the new computer programs for designing forms).[4] But such design involves highly creative work. The in-house publisher has to work with the relevant organizational specialists, getting them to function as a design team. And forms are only one –though admittedly an important one– of the many kinds of documents that he or she will have to create formats for. In many cases this will mean establishing or adapting house style, rather than conforming to it.

So again the in-house desktop publisher will be involved in policy setting; creativity will be required where format, as well as content, is concerned.

NEED FOR FORMAL TRAINING FOR DESKTOP PUBLISHERS

In such a situation, there isn't time for apprenticing. What's needed is a crash course in publishing lore. This is reinforced by the acquisition of computer programs which, embodying the expertise of a publisher's team, themselves educate and train the person who uses them. This is, after all, how transitions between cultures are managed.

In these circumstances, it's good to know that some people can learn from well designed instruction with surprising speed. This is particularly the case for those who have a print orientation –a natural feeling for good layout and interest in the details of typography. There have always been such persons: they appeared as soon as books did. The Greeks, who produced the first book trade, had a name for them: bibliophiles.

This book aims to be a textbook for such formal training. Specifically, the aim of this part of the book (chapters 3–5) is to survey the lore of typographers, graphics artists and editors. What this chapter aims to do is to provide a summary of the principles behind page layout and typographical design. The next chapter will consider graphics; and the one after that will look at quality control over content. This survey should provide a synopsis of the basics of publishing, so that a novice can straightaway form an integrated picture of what's involved.

Layout Principles

FORMATTING

In these circumstances, the rapid development of a body of concepts and well articulated general principles on the subject of layout and design is a welcome feature of the specialist literature pertaining to computer assisted publishing: see Table 3.1.[5] It's now possible to state fairly concisely what constitutes the principles of a good layout. The main concept seems to be that of formatting.

Formatting a page of text adds meaning to its content, visually emphasizing points which are cognitively important. A solid, unbroken text block sends a crossed message. In words it says that certain points are more important than others, but in layout and positioning it says that everything in the text is equally important. Formatting –visually informative text, punctuation at the level of the page– makes the main points on a page visible at a glance.

Likewise, the absence of diagrams and pictures makes for much easier layout procedures. But pictures are, some claim, twenty-six times quicker to comprehend than printed text. And diagrams make the relationships they present far easier to understand. A diagram can say in half a page, understood at a glance, what it may take five pages of print to explain.

The personal computer has made it easily possible to format a page and add graphics.

> A feature of desktop publishing is its use of designer formats.

Designer formats are formats designed by experts in page design. These are most often the front cover page of a newsletter or the first page in the chapter of a book.

These formats are available as text files on disk. You simply make a copy of any of these master formats and use it as a template, replacing its contents with your own. Some page makeup programs even contain designer formats, for chapters in books or for newsletter layouts, as their default formats (that is, as what the program will have you do unless you program it to do something else). Using such work is a form of apprenticeship. By the time you know enough to be able to change the default settings, you know enough not to want to do so.

Readers have acquired the taste for layouts which reinforce the meaning of the words in the text.[6] In fact the specialist journals played a prominent role in introducing such reader-oriented presentational formats: they had to, to build readership in competition with TV.

There can be no going back from reader-oriented layouts now. The development of the electronic layout, and the laser printer, ensure this. The principles of a reader-oriented layout have been worked out, and a set of terms for talking about them has been developed. It takes a speech community to produce such terms, and the terms in turn guarantee the continuing existence, and further development of, that community.

What follows presupposes that a newsletter is being published. Publishing a newsletter is a very demanding task, both as to content and format; it's possibly the most demanding task given to an in-house publicist. Also, it's a task that's very commonly given to him or her. Essentially, if you can produce a newsletter, all lesser assignments should pose few difficulties. Hence its choice as a vehicle for presenting the editing know-how outlined in this chapter.

Table 3.1: Guidelines for Page Makeup

DESIGN PRINCIPLES	LAYOUT CONCEPTS	LAYOUT ELEMENTS
Harmony	• Grid	Columns: number & structure of modules and rules
	• Font family	Integrated, uniform series of font sizes and faces
	• Headings family	Heads, sub-heads, running heads, caption heads, photo credit lines
	• Departmental unity	Standardized headers, (screened or shadowed) boxes, rules, dingbats
	• Unified treatment of graphics	All graphics appropriately sized in a set of sizes & similarly enhanced sizes, and similarly enhanced
Emphasis	• Contrast	'Busy' vs 'empty' formats: boxes, bullets, rules, sunken capitals, use of colour and white space
	• Legibility	Variety of typeface; point size; leading, measure
Movement	• Controlling eye movement	From dominant visual element, large to small, colour to black & white
	• Traffic flow	Model page
	• Directionality	Depicted eye gaze; centre of visual impact; pictures/diagrams in series; arrows
Balance and Proportion	• Vertical and horizontal axes	'Heavier' items closer to balance point on axes than 'lighter' ones
	• (A)symmetry	Spreads & packages; (no) 'tombstoning'
	• Alignment	Graphics across columns; bleeds; 'Dutch wrap'

THE GRID

The grid is a basic organizing concept, providing possibly the major means of introducing order into one's layout.[7] A grid establishes a matrix that organizes typography, pictures and diagrams. It organizes the presentation of content while maintaining a uniform set of proportions that unify the whole publication. A grid lets you group related elements together so that their interrelationships are immediately and intuitively evident to the reader. (This is important when you've got 3 seconds to get the reader's attention at the point of sale at the magazine rack.)

If anything 'makes the page', it's the grid. And it's easily teachable; there are grid templates available on disk; grids are even storable, as a 'style sheet', on some computer programs.

Grids set out:
- the number of columns to be used;
- how these columns are to be broken horizontally;
- the size of page margins and gutters (spaces between columns, and at the edge of the page which is to be bound);
- whether the columns should be ragged (unjustified on the) right or justified;
- the use of rules (lines dividing up the page);
- body copy font(s);
- size and placement of headlines.

Essentially, a grid enables you to visualize the page as a set of modules, the building blocks of your page planning. The grid allows for considerable variation, while subliminally —as far as the reader is concerned— maintaining a uniform underlying presentational format. Grids now come in nine different standard forms, each form developed to serve specific presentational purposes. These grids embody years of experience, gained by generations of editors. They can be quickly taught.

BASIC CONCEPTS AND FINDINGS UNDERLYING THE USE OF GRIDS

Each different type of grid is designed for a specific purpose, and the effects of its main variations have been empirically established. Let's consider how the grid you use affects what you can do on a page. Let's assume that the page involved is the first page in a newsletter and that you're choosing between the two commonest types of grid: the two-column and the three-column varieties.[8]

What you have first to decide is how many stories you're going to have on the page. This is largely determined by your *'jump' policy*, that is, to what extent you make a habit of 'jumping' to later pages to continue stories. Jump starts allow more stories per page. But readers don't like page jumps, and only about half of your readers actually will follow when you make a jump.

You also have to decide what will be your *major display item* (the element that will be most visually striking) on the page. Then you have to decide what your second major display item is going to be: see Diagram 3.1.

If you only have one major display item, there will be nothing to attract your reader's eye to the bottom of the page, in all likelihood. So you won't be able to direct your reader's eye around the page, and he or she is likely to skip to the next page, leaving the bottom of your first page unread.

Diagram 3.1: A Model First Page

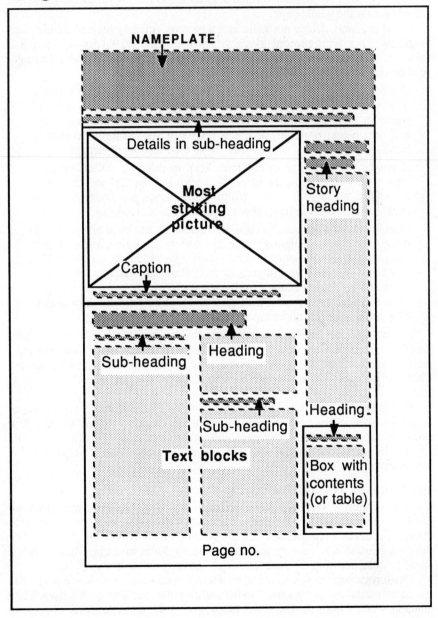

THE STANDARD, TWO-COLUMN GRID

Suppose that you decide on a standard two-column grid (both columns being of equal width). This will give you a page containing your nameplate at the top and two columns running downwards below it. Pictures and diagrams don't go too well with this layout; one column's width is too narrow for them, while two extends across the whole page.

You'll probably decide not to include a picture; you may include a little chart or graph. This arrangement gives you a page dominated by two vertical columns, which allows you to get a lot of material in. You might be able to get your two lead stories in on this page.

The ideal line length for legibility is 50–70 characters (giving a length of 6" or more), *but only if you're using a highly readable font* –about12 points in size (for details on point size, see below). A single column, 6.5" text block, however, produces lines that are too long to read. It results in pages filled 'wall-to-wall' with type that put readers off.

If you're employing short columns, keep in mind the following findings: with 9 point type, the ideal line length is from 2.5" to 3"; with 10 point type, it's from 3" to 4". Within these ranges, the longer lines will cause readers' eyes to jump about less, so are more readable.

Double columns are usually each 3.1" in length. So you'll be tempted to make your columns slightly wider. You can do this by making your side margins and your gutter (the space between the columns) narrower. This could free up space for columns of 3.5". But such widening of the text block and narrowing of the margins should be avoided: readers will perceive the page as crowded with print and will be disinclined to read it. More on this below, under typography.

The two-column layout is usually perceived as rather formal. (If you fully justify the text in your columns, the layout will appear even more formal.) Austere and uncluttered, it conveys the impression 'professional and reliable'. Chartered accountants, banks and research institutes use it a lot in their newsletters.

This is an easy layout to compose, as you don't have to make any breaks or unusual shapes in your columns. But it's boring –daunting, even– to read. You can cram more letters into your page with this format than with any other. And printers in years gone by did just that. Hence the traditionalist image that this format gives.

THE 'MODERN' TWO-COLUMN GRID

So a –currently very popular– variant of this two-column format has been devised. This involves two columns of unequal widths. The narrower one is wide enough for about twenty characters (in practice much of it is left blank). Then there's a hairline rule –a very thin line– running down the page. Then there's a broad column, allowing 50 characters or so –an ideal width for legibility.

This format permits you to construct a much more visually attractive page. You can have 'outquotes' or 'sidebars' in the narrower column. Out-quotes feature key quotations taken from the main text block, giving the main thrust of its content. Sidebars are actually running heads. They extend down the narrow column, giving the gist of what's in the text block beside them.

Besides this, the broad column easily admits pictures –big ones, over half the width of the page– and diagrams. Also, it can be divided by a **horizontal** rule into two or more modules, for horizontally-running stories.

This grid is a 'modern' layout. Broken up into its component parts, it's easy to read. The outquotes and side bars make skim reading easy. It's often used in technical writing: it's frequently found in computer developers' newsletters –and in their manuals, for that matter. But it does still convey that 'vertical page with a mass of writing' impression. Besides, some readers find outquotes and side-bars distracting (they perceive them as breaking up the flow of the text), and regard unused space as an extravagance.

THE THREE-COLUMN GRID

The three-column grid allows a lot of variety:

1. You can run a graphic –a picture or diagram– across two of its columns and place two columns of text beneath it, the whole making one unified story package. Another story can run down the long single column beside this 'package'.
2. You can run stories as modules horizontally across all three columns, dividing each such story off from the others by a hairline (or thicker) horizontal rule.
3. Alternatively, you can insert a large picture extending vertically downwards –introducing a vertical element on a page of otherwise horizontal modules.
4. You can even wrap the text around the picture in an 'L' shape –two short columns beneath the picture, and a long narrow one running down beside it.

When you use a three-column grid, each of your pages can appear different from the next one. Yet the underlying uniformity of format causes your pages to be perceived as somehow similar (most readers won't be consciously aware of your grid). The three-column grid is probably the best one for achieving variety in presentation. And it has a modern, news-magazine-like feel about it.

MODULAR DESIGN

Modular design allows you to construct a page with high visual impact. You can have several headings, and graphics of a variety of sizes. This makes it easier to construct an informally balanced page (on this, see more below), and to insert a second major display item on the page. Besides, thinking in modules requires you to group items (headings, graphics and text) or related stories together.

Such groupings make it easier for the reader to see the logic behind your presentation; modules stand out distinctly from one another. Also, as we read from left to right, a story running across the page is perceived to be shorter than the same story running down the page, then starting at the top again and running down again.

Modules make for more convenient packaging than do downward-running text blocks. If you have to cut a module's contents out, it's relatively easy to insert another module, adjusting the size of its graphic component. Cut out a story that's contained in downward-running text blocks and you generally have to re-organize the entire page. Modular design is 'in', and studies show that readers prefer it in print.

This horizontally-structured page has a 'modern' look. You'll see it in many different newsletters that emphasize getting information across quickly. Modules don't go well with page jumps, however; each should contain an entire story. So you've got to plan the contents of your newsletter very carefully, page by page, in advance of laying out page one (especially as the contents of each module have to be grouped). Also, these complicated page layouts are harder to construct, initially, than the simpler two-column layouts. And the three columns make for too few characters per line for ideal legibility. Besides, your page may appear cluttered and 'busy' if you've got too many rules, boxes, headings and graphics.

In general, the more complex the format, the more power it provides –and the more restraint is needed in using it. But the more diverse the material (and a newsletter typically has many departments, with a wide variety of material), the more flexible your grid needs to be.

THE MODEL PAGE

A 'model page' acts as a kind of 'ideal type', to help new editors understand how these principles should be applied. Readers read from left to right, and from the top down, generally. Consequently, the top right of the page is likely to get most attention, the bottom left least. So you put highly salient items top right, in a 'grouping' (on this arrangement of headings and graphics see chapter 4). A 'model page', embodying ideal sequences has been evolved to help visualize this kind of page layout: see Diagram 3.1.

This layout normally features a large graphic (a photograph or chart) as its major display item. The caption, sub-caption and column(s) of body text immediately below make up the major display package. The secondary display item and its package are usually placed in the opposite quartile of the page, below. This arrangement moves the reader's eye over the page. It attracts attention to what would otherwise likely be a dead zone at the foot of the page.

As with the grid, this model page embodies generations of practical, tested (by gains in readership) wisdom. The principles and rationale underlying its design are readily teachable; and examples to serve as templates are readily available on disk (the format templates mentioned above are generally model first pages for chapters in books).

SOME OF THE MAIN USES OF BOXES AND RULES

Boxes and rules are key components in page layout. Guidelines for their use have been developed and empirically tested. It pays to know them. Then you can develop a consistent editorial style (the hallmark of an experienced editor) in your use of them. Basically, rules break the grid's columns up into modules, and boxes either emphasize or de-emphasize items within the grid. The following are some of the main uses of boxes and rules:

1. Emphasis:

A box may highlight one part of the text, calling attention to it by setting it off from the rest of the text.

A '*call out*' is a particularly dramatic way of doing this. Normally consisting of a quotation from the body of the text and giving the main thrust of the argument adjacent to it, this short extract is bolded and put in a screened (shaded-in) box. Because of the size of its typeface (a bolded typeface is larger than the regular one in the text block proper), the call out 'bleeds' across into the margin, with the greater part of its box inside the text block, which flows around it.

A variant of this means of highlighting is the *'sidebar'*. Sidebars are usually used in the modern two-column grid. The sidebars are situated in the narrower column, which is otherwise empty of text. Such a sidebar will contain text that runs down beside the main text block, giving an abstract of the points made therein.

Call outs and side bars function as a kind of 'aside', commenting on, or summing up the thrust of, the text adjacent to them. They enormously facilitate skim reading. The objective of using these formatting devices is to increase readership of the text thus emphasized. They provide the editor with another means (as well as the headings) of attracting attention to this particular item. They are often used where otherwise the spread would only contain solid text blocks on its two facing pages, to give more visual interest to the layout.

2. As a means of cross-reference:

Here a box singles out a text block which contains some illustrative material. This might be a synopsis of a book or an article, or a brief outline of a case. The heading within the box is numbered, allowing easy cross-reference to, or comparison of, such synopses or cases.[9]

3. *De*-emphasis:

You may want to de-emphasize 'housekeeping' materials such as a masthead or indicia (details of address, postal arrangements, and so on). If so, you can tuck them away, in a small font, beneath a rule at the foot of a page.

Alternatively, you may want to keep a table of statistics, or some other background material, from interrupting the flow of your main text block. In this case, you tuck this ancillary material away, inside a box with hairline-thin border, in a non-salient area of the page (such as the lower right quartile on a left-hand page).

4. Making a text flow more smoothly:

A series of solid, undifferentiated text blocks, page after page, makes a daunting prospect for many readers. Breaking up such pages into smaller chunks will make them more inviting. Two hairline rules running across a three-column page make the text within the rules appear far less than the same amount of text going up and down the page and filling one and a half columns.

Reading can also be made easier by breaking a text up into its component parts. These can then be set out with the main thrust in a side bar, the body of the text in the main text block, and background materials boxed in and away from the main flow of the text, so as to invite fast reading.

5. To make a unit out of a page's subject matter:

After placing a complete story on a page, you may find that you've got space to spare at the bottom of the page. Yet there isn't enough space to get another piece or story well started; and, anyway, to do so would distract from the unity of your page. You may not want to add more details to your completed story. If you increase the size of your typeface or the leading (space) between the lines, you'll only make this page look odd compared to all the others.

This is a situation where a box running across the bottom of the page, or a call out somewhere on the page, will fill up your page and retain –indeed enhance– the unity of that page.

DISADVANTAGES OF THE USE OF BOXES AND RULES

If they are frequently used, rules and boxes produce 'busy' text –text that's all chopped up by lines.

Boxes are a nightmare if you're using a batch processor (if you change the typeface, your boxes are apt to split between pages or bleed –unintended by you– across columns). But boxes are easy to insert, if you're using a WYSIWYG page makeup program. So they get overused by desktop publishers bent on using all the heady potential of their programs. Hence overdoing the use of rules and boxes is a common fault among beginner desktop publishers.

The basic problem is that too much emphasis means that nothing is emphasized: readers are either bewildered or distracted. Unless infrequently and carefully used, boxes are particularly apt to break up the flow of the text.

The Basics of Typography
TYPEFACES

A typeface is one particular 'face' designed for a 'set' of type. A set consists of the letters of the alphabet in upper and lower cases, the numbers from 0 to 9, and some punctuation and other symbols. *Times* is one such typeface (it's the one used for this text); *Helvetica* is another. Typefaces come in three categories: those used for 'body' text (the mass of the text in the text blocks); those used for display (in headlines –*Helvetica* is much used for this purpose), and decorative fonts (used for special purposes: see below).

1. For body text, the best typefaces to use are the Roman or serif ones.
English Times (used for this text) is a serif typeface. Serifs are sometimes sub-classified into old style (this means 'traditional' rather than 'designed long ago'), such as *Garamond*; modern, such as *Century*, and transitional (midway between the two), such as *Baskerville*.

Serifs are the small strokes at the end of the basic letter form: the downward-running end pieces on the bar of a capital T, and the horizontally-extending end pieces on its stem, for instance. Typically, the vertical 'strokes' are thick, and the horizontal strokes are thin. These conventions add legibility, as well as character, to the typeface. They provide a lot of clues, making it easier for the eye to recognize a letter

The little footings guide the eye along the baseline, where it runs along the line of print. We read *groups* of words, not individual letters. So we need to be able to make out the individual letters quickly and easily, to facilitate this reading of whole strings of letters at a glance. Legibility is thus critically important for body copy text, because it is densely packed.

Sans (= without) serif characters don't have these little eye-catchers at the ends of their basic letter forms, and all strokes are of the same width. This gives the letters a clean, 'modern' look. But the eye has to make more effort to recognize sans serif letters, and you'll tend to read a word, rather than a phrase, at a time. This makes reading a lot of text set in a sans serif typeface tiring, and is why such typefaces aren't recommended for body text.

2. Display text is used for short passages which are meant to catch the eye.
Typically, headlines, headings and captions. Impact is the primary concern in such cases. As only a few words are involved, and as they stand out clearly in the white space surrounding them, legibility isn't a problem. 'Square' serifs (such as *Clarendon Book*), or sans serifs (sometimes called 'Gothic' typefaces, for example, *Helios* or *Helvetica*) are suitable for this purpose.

3. Decorative typefaces are meant for limited, special purpose use.
You don't use these very often; but you have to have them when you *do* need them. The problem is that they come in so many varieties, and you never know when you may need some exotic or rarely-used variety. *Examples:*

- *Old English*, for the menu of an Elizabethan banquet or a notice of a Shakespearian play;
- a cursive script, such as *Murray*, for a wedding invitation;
- an oriental-looking typeface for a flyer about a visiting exhibition of Chinese art;
- a 'sunken capital' (an enlarged capital letter, inset in a 'box' of white space) at the beginning of a particularly important paragraph on an otherwise featureless page of body text.

For most desktop publishers the critical question will be: "What typefaces are available on the LaserWriter?" These, after all, are effectively the only ones that a desktop publisher can use. There's good news: the dearth of typefaces is over. A recent upgrade has added seven more to the original three (all licensed with the International Typeface Corporation).

This selection should be sufficient for most needs But, just in case it isn't (typically, where decorative typefaces are concerned), other typefaces have been developed for the LaserWriter. These can be 'downloaded' (that is, the LaserWriter will add them to its resident of fonts just while it's running your textfile).

Font-making programs are also available; you can make your own personal font(s) with (relative) ease. You simply scan a text printed in the typeface that you wish to computerize, then convert the dot-matrix scanned letters that result into the characters of a computerized typeface. From now on, computer typefaces will proliferate. We are, in fact, on the verge of the biggest expansion of the stock of typefaces since the nineteenth century, when the first major surge of typeface development occurred.

FONTS

A typeface comes in many varieties:

- It may vary in width, ranging from condensed through regular to expanded (condensed and expanded are not available in all typefaces).
- It may vary in weight, ranging from light (not available in all typefaces) through regular to bolded.
- It may vary in style, ranging from italic through regular to underlined and to shadowed.
- It can be bolded, underlined, italicized and shadowed (use sparingly).

- It will also vary in size. This means that there are a series of sizes for each of the above versions of the same typeface, ranging from 6 points (there are 72 points in an inch) to 72 (720 on a computerized typesetter).

A complete set of type (upper and lower case type, punctuation marks and symbols) containing one set of the above characteristics is called a font. For instance, Helvetica 10 point regular is one font, and Helvetica 10 point bolded is another. Thus a typeface has many fonts (think of it as a face with many expressions).

About 80% of your newsletter is made up of body text. This text is what determines the legibility of your newsletter. In fact, the kind of typeface you use determines the 'personality' of your newsletter. Readers attribute to typefaces much the same characteristics as publishers do: *English Times* is perceived by both parties as conservative and traditional, for example.

The sheer quantity of body text causes a problem. If the body text is all the same, your page will lack visual interest. If you use a variety of typefaces (a common fault of beginning desktop publishers, who can have a hundred typefaces and use twenty of them in a document), your page looks like a jumbled mess. What should you do?

THE 'FONT FAMILY'

You should use a font 'family': a number of fonts –sizes, widths and weights– all from the same typeface, each used uniformly for a clear purpose. An example follows:

Body Copy and its Headings
- All fonts are from the typeface *English Times*, and are regular unless otherwise specified.
- Headings: see below, under *Headings*.
- Sub-headings: 12 points; allcaps (all capitals).
- Sub-sub-headings: 12 points; italicized.
- Body text: 10 points (use 'small cap[ital]s' for emphasis and italics for book titles).

Headers and Footers:
- Running heads: 12 points, bolded;
- Footnotes: 9 points (readers aren't exposed to this kind of text in quantity).

Headings: Book and Chapter Titles and The Like:
- Book titles and chapter titles are a special case: they're likely to need a decorative typeface or a really large font.
- Employ a display (sans serif) typeface for headings within chapters. Choose a typeface that's complementary to that used for body copy. For example, *Helvetica* complements *Times* (that's why they're so often used together).
- Headings: *Helvetica*, 14 points, bolded and upper and lower case

  Note: Bolding is very emphatic: you won't need to increase font size if you bold. But don't use it much, as it's difficult to read (see below). Readers don't like condensed and expanded varieties of a typeface –and not all typefaces have them, anyway; so they're best avoided too.
- Captions (titles for diagrams): *Helvetica*, 9 points.

If your reader becomes consciously aware of the appearance of your typeface, it's because something's wrong with it. Most readers of a text set out as described above won't notice the differences in font sizes, or even the difference in typefaces, since the two chosen complement one another. What they will notice, but only subliminally, is the uniformity of the body text and headings.

A pair of font families provide the different font sizes which unobtrusively make the text visually attractive. It's this subtle, underlying, carefully thought out consistency and integration that's the hallmark of a professional editor. It gives variety, but without creating the jumbled effect that a variety of typefaces would create (they would inevitably produce non-uniform heading and leading [see below] sizes).

LEGIBILITY

Underlying the above advice are some findings on legibility –the ease and speed with which text can be read and understood. In reading, we recognize letter forms, and take in words, in groups. So it's best to observe the following guidelines:

1. **Choice of typeface:** serifs are easier to recognize than sans serifs; they make a small, bodycopy-sized letter easier to identify. So avoid lengthy passages of sans serifs.

2. **Size of font:** letters in the 9 to 12 point range are easiest to read in bulk; and older readers, who constitute the majority of serious readers, prefer the larger of these sizes. So keep 9 point fonts for footnotes. 4 point fonts are used for giving credits for photographs or graphics. Look at the edges of photographs in a magazine, and you'll find them there. (They've always been there; you've just never noticed them.)3. Width of line (called '*measure*'): 50–70 characters per line is the optimal length for legibility only if your typeface is easily readable.

   Bookman is a typeface that has been specially designed for readability. *Times* was designed for newspaper-reading readability: the bowls of its letters don't fill up with ink when it goes through the offset printing process.

   Keep your intended font sizes in mind when deciding on your grid.

3. **Space between words:** beware of fully justified text. With most current page make-up programs, especially where short lines are involved, full justification leads to occasional unduly large spaces between words. Such spaces occurring roughly below one another on successive lines are known as '*rivers*'. They're most distracting to readers.

   These irrational spaces cause the reader to read individual words rather than groups of words. As words only have meaning in context, this makes the sense harder to follow. Full justification also leads to lots of hyphenation. This produces odd, and initially unintelligible, word part-forms, which again slow down comprehension.

   There's no evidence that justified text is easier to read than unjustified text. Hence many magazines and newsletters use "ragged right" text: text flushed up against the left-hand margin but with an unjustified right-hand edge –as in a typescript. This convention avoids undue white space between words and involves only occasional hyphenation.

Multisyllabic words tend to go on the following line causing very ragged right endings, if they aren't broken between lines by hyphenation. So some hyphenation occurs, in what is known as modified ragged right text.

Bear in mind, however, that fully justified text has a very official, precise look, while ragged right appears rather more relaxed and informal. So choose the format that fits the image desired for your publication.

4. **Space *within* words:** with fully justified text you're apt to need to alter the spaces between letters within words (as well as between words) to avoid irrational white space. If you make your alterations by tiny increments but uniformly, they won't be noticeable –and the undesirable white space will be eliminated.

   Making alterations in this way is called '*negative*' (when you subtract) or '*positive*' (when you add) *microspacing*. It can be done in one-thousandths of an inch, either automatically (called '*tracking*') or manually, by the second generation page makeup programs.

   For certain combinations of letters, such as 'To' and 'ry' in 'Tory', you'll need to make the 'o' creep back under the arm of the 'T' or the 'y' slide under the outreach of the 'r'. If you don't, at font sizes above 12 points, an unsightly white space –a break– is produced between these letters. Crimping the letters together like this is known as '*kerning*'. Again, it can be done either automatically or manually.

5. **Space between lines ('leading'):** a moderate of space –9 on 10 or 10 on 12; see below, under typesetting– makes for the most legible body text.

6. **Shape of letters:** it's the space in the 'bowls' (the rounded portions) of letters that makes for legibility. This is why boldface type, which almost fills these bowls in, and italics and condensing, which distort the shapes of the bowls, aren't easy to read in bulk: they make the letters difficult to identify. So lengthy passages of text in either bolding or italics or condensing (or a script typeface, for that matter) are best avoided.

   Text which is all in capitals is also difficult to read: the shapes of the letters become too uniform. The ascenders and descenders are what make letters easier to identify.

   The 'x height' is the basic size of a letter –the central mass of a lower case letter which sits on the baseline, such as an x. Ascenders are the strokes of the letters which go up –as with an h– from the x height. Descenders are the strokes which go down below the baseline –think of a p.

   So upper and lower case (capitalized first letter and the beginning letter of all following proper nouns) makes for much easier reading, and should generally be used in preference to 'all caps'.

7. **Contrast effects:** black type on a white background is easier to read than is white on a black background. Colour or screening (dots which appear as shading, on LaserWriter text) overlaid on text also makes for difficult reading, and is best used only for small amounts of text, which should be in large font sizes.

TYPESETTING

Typesetting largely revolves around four basic elements:[10]

1. **The typefaces used.** Experience indicates, as observed, that you should use only a few typefaces: two, preferably; not more than three. For variety, employ a family of fonts, using a uniform set of font sizes (for headings and so on, as indicated) throughout.

2. **Point size:** measurement is in '*points*', of which there are 72 to the inch, or sometimes in '*picas*' (there are 12 points to the pica).

   The following terms are used for spacing letters. First, there's the '*em*' space. This is the space that would be taken up by the capital letter M (the biggest size of letter in the alphabet): a square, each side of which is the length in points of a capital M in that typeface. Next there's the '*en*' space. En stands for N(umber). The numbers in a typeface are the size of its medium-sized letters, so the en is half an em space. Then there's the *microspace* or *skinny space*: one-tenth the size of the em space. Micro-spaces are negative as well as positive: you can take them off a letter or add them to it.

   Microspaces, as explained above, allow you to add or remove spaces from between words so as to justify a line without having undue white space between words. Microspaces also allow you to 'kern'.

3. **Leading:** the space between the lines.

   The name comes from the strip of lead –it looked rather like a wafer of chewing gum– inserted between the metal typefaces (lead blocks, each with a raised letterhead).

   Leading is closely connected with legibility. If there's no leading, the letters crowd together, with the descenders from one line abutting closely on to the ascenders of the next. This crowding makes letters more difficult to identify. If there's too much space between the lines, this too makes for difficult reading; you'll read word by word, at the ends and beginnings of the lines, rather than in groups of words.

   Hence guidelines such as '9' (points) 'on 10' (points) –9 points for the font size and 1 point of leading, making a total line space of 10 points– or '10 on 12' –a 10 point font on 2 points of leading: total line space 12 points. (These are the two standard configurations for footnotes and for body text respectively.)

4. **Measure:** the width of the line.

   This determines the number of letters on the line. You can have as many as 50–70, if you're using a very legible typeface. Reduce the line length if the typeface is small or hard to read. What makes a uniform text block such daunting reading is that it can have 60 or more *small* characters per line (as in a cheap paperback).

   If the leading is meagre, to save space (say 10 on 11), readers will often go to the wrong line when moving to their next line, or will double check to see that they have moved to the right line. In either case, reading is slowed down, becoming more difficult.

SETTING UP THE TEXT BLOCK

If you're employing a batch processing program, you, rather than the program, will have to plan your page. The elements listed above enable you to do this, as follows:

1. An 11" X 8.5" page with margins of .75" top and bottom, and 1" at either side gives you a 9.5" X 6.5" text block.

   If you're printing on both sides of the paper, make the left and right margins alternately 1.25" and .75", to allow for binding. This is known as 'gutter flipping'.

2. 6.5" across, at 72 points to the inch, gives you 468 points.

   How many letters you'll be able to get into this depends on the size of the typeface that you're using. *English Times* is smaller than *New York* (*Times*), for instance: 12 point *English Times* will fit into the space occupied by 10 point *New York*. So you'll fit more letters in using the former. (There are font tables that tell you how many characters per inch you'll get with each font.)

   You may well have too many letters in a 6.5" long line if you're using a small typeface. If so, you could break it up into two columns, each of 3.1", allowing a gutter of .3" between them. 3.1" gives you 223 points per column, which is a suitable length for a small-sized font.

3. 9.5" down at 72 points per inch gives you 684 points.

   With single-spaced lines (12 points –remember '10 on 12'?), this gives you a maximum of 56 lines. One-and-a-half spacing (18 points) gives you 38 lines; and double spacing (24 points) gives you, obviously, 28.

   Actually, you'll have to allow space for the page number and possibly for a running head and a heading somewhere or other, so you won't ever have these maximum numbers of lines to use.

COPY FITTING

It's possible to work out how much body text you can get into a given number of pages by performing such calculations, a procedure known as copy fitting. When you have to allow for headings and sub-headings (each with special leading), graphics and empty space (a new chapter must start on a fresh page, preferably a right-hand page), this gets to be a very complicated set of calculations. It's one of the main reasons why computerized page make up programs were developed.

A 'high end' publisher (one using an expensive press) nowadays sets up 4 or 5 different batch programs, each involving differently sized typefaces, and each with different spacings for headers, headings, graphics, footnotes and page breaks between chapters.

The computer is then programmed to run the text of a projected book (which could be of 500 or more pages) through each of these batch programs, one after the other, overnight. Next morning, the publisher has the specifications of overall page- and chapter-lengths for each of the 4 or 5 different book-length layouts.

Close control over the size of the text block is what enables a printer to get so much text on a page. For instance:

- with ten characters –this comes to two words, on average (each of four characters, plus an inter-word space)– per inch,
- using proportional spacing (which allots an 'i' or an 'l' only a third of the space it gives to an 'm' or a 'w'), and with kerning and microspacing of letters,
- and employing two columns (involving short, easily readable lines, thus saving space by allowing use of minimal leading and a small typeface)

–a printed page contains almost twice as much text as a typewritten one.

Up to now, only batch text processing programs gave this kind of fine control over text layout. These programs aren't easy to learn or to use. What you see on screen –plain text with strings of programming commands embedded in it– bears no relation to what appears in the printout (especially if you get a command wrong!).

If you're involved in publishing text intensive, lengthy manuals (that is, manuals without lots of diagrams, pictures and tables), these batch text processing programs give excellent results. You can reconfigure an entire text merely by changing a few macros at the beginning of the book. Versatile desktop publishers know how to use batch programs.

Some of the second-generation WYSIWYG page makeup programs –Quark's *XPress*, for instance– now provide similar capabilities running on micros (I'm using *XPress* to lay this book out). These second-generation page makeup programs mark a giant step forward for the infant technology of desktop publishing.

Principles of Design
WHAT YOU HAVE TO WORK WITH IN DOING PAGE LAYOUT

Information consists of both content and form: form is part of the message, not mere decoration. Design is as important as content: information that people won't read doesn't inform them. Basically, the designer of a newsletter has five elements to work with: body text; headlines; rules; photographs, and graphics (line drawings, charts and so on).

A word-oriented editor will concentrate largely on the first two, unconsciously regarding pictures –and still more dingbats and rules– as add-ons. This is a serious error. Print is a visual medium; humans are picture-drawing (rather than alphabet-writing) animals; TV-habituated readers expect pictures to accompany text.

Graphics are what makes a text visually interesting. You design your text around them: they're what highlights the text. Thus the design process is crucial for a desktop publisher, who, working alone, must be both editor and designer. The price of freedom from the pre-cast formats that the illustrative artist, typographer and paste-up person impose on an editor is the need for unending creativity.

The first thing that a designer has to do is to decide what is the most important, or the most visually interesting, element in the newsletter. Designers need courage above all else, because this element has to dominate the design. Having *several* 'most important' items –being unable to determine your priorities– results in confusion for the reader. And it's the items featured on page one of the newsletter that indicate what its editor regards as important. So a decision on priorities has to be made at the outset.

Once this decision has been made, design principles serve as guidelines for carrying it out. The acronym HEMP refers to these principles (see Table 3.1), as follows:

HARMONY

A good newsletter has a 'recognition factor': something about it that tells you that you're reading this particular newsletter. This recognition factor is produced by the house style, which gives a feeling of unity to it. All its parts are perceived as fitting together (no small feat with a publication that's as multi-faceted as a newsletter). Most readers are only subliminally aware of this unity, because it's produced by four design elements which are so subtle and pervasive that most readers aren't consciously aware of them.

1. The first of these is the grid. The grid provides a uniformity in column structure (all columns ragged right, for instance) and modules. Underlying considerable variation in the layout of individual pages (as when a three-column layout with horizontal modules is used), this uniformity causes the newsletter to be nonetheless perceived as an integrated whole.

2. The second design element is the 'family' concept. A *font* family provides overall uniformity of typeface and a consistent set of sizes and conventions for heads and captions. A *departmental* family requires that all 'departments' (sections –usually two-page spreads– dedicated to particular topics) in the issue commence with similar section-identifiers, and have similar logos for their feature columns.

3. The third design element is a unified graphic theme. This requires that most, if not all, of the newsletter's graphics relate to the 'centrefold' graphic. The latter may not be an actual centrefold; but it's the most arresting graphic element, and all the other graphic elements are chosen to relate somehow to it.

It follows from the above –and this will be reinforced by the rest of this discussion– that the desktop publisher should make a 'thumbnail' or dummy (a rough outline sketch of text blocks and graphics boxes, each with an indication of its contents) for *each* page before starting to set text.

EMPHASIS

Secondly, emphasis: a general policy on emphasis –on format as well as on individual elements– underlies any systematic plan for an issue. Each page will entail hard decisions, if this policy is being well executed. The basic policy issue is whether to have an 'empty' or a 'busy' page. Emphasis is largely a matter of use of rules, boxes and dingbats (those little symbols that mark the end of an article) and suchlike.

• At one extreme, there's the austere, two-column, fully justified layout, containing the occasional chart or graph: the uncluttered look.

• At the other extreme is the three-column, 'three-ring-circus'. Ragged right layout, with horizontal modules separated by rules and boxes, each item terminated by a customized dingbat, all accompanied by lots of splashy halftones and line drawings: the busy look.

The basic problem, one that calls for hard decisions, is that for maximum effect, means of emphasis have to be sparingly used. Used too frequently, they generate confusion, rather than emphasis. But the austere look only suits certain topics and readerships.

Each page requires decisions on:

- what is to be its major display item and related package of heading(s), caption(s), text and graphics;
- what its secondary display item and package are to be;
- how each of these two display sets is to be emphasized so as to maximize the impact of the other.

The model page format, and, still more, the collections of page formats (such as those provided with the *PageMaker* page makeup program) will help here. If modules are to be an important feature of the grid, their overall pattern of rectangular shapes has to be considered, so that the major display item and its package stands out among them (see further under proportion, below).

MOVEMENT

Here we're dealing with 'page traffic': how the reader's eye will be led to move around the page. In general, a reader's eye goes first to the major display item. This, the centre of visual impact, is usually a large graphic, that is, one that's more than half a page in width.

Other common eye movements are:

- from the larger to the smaller items (a typical sequence is picture ->caption ->sub-caption ->body text);
- colour, then to black and white, then to the white space;
- from the top left to the bottom right (we're accustomed to reading from left to right, and from the top to the bottom of a page).

Graphics are the eye-catchers: they're the best means of controlling a reader's eye movement. The direction of the gaze of a person or persons depicted in a photograph sends the reader's eye, too, in that direction: to the centre of visual interest. A text block is usually positioned in the targeted spot.

A busy layout will have to employ arrows to direct the reader's eye. A series of pictures or diagrams (generally in a sequence running down the page, paralleled by text giving a running commentary) will tend to carry the reader's eye along with them.

So a sense of movement can be gained by laying out a series of pictures, or some other graphic element, so that it is clearly repetitive –as a narrow column down the page, for instance, with a running commentary in the text block beside it. Manuals exploit this tendency, showing a series of successive technical adjustments with commentaries in a series of side bars paralleling each diagram.

In any event, the sense of direction is achieved through the positioning and integration of a number of elements on the page.

PROPORTION AND BALANCE

The general principle here is that formal balance is boring. Asymmetrical balance is what piques readers' interest. Unconsciously, a reader will think of the page as having a vertical and a horizontal axis. For balance, the 'heavier' items (those that are larger, blacker [or more colourful], or more irregularly shaped) should be nearer the centre of this axis than the 'lighter' items. Asymmetrical balance counterposes different types of item: a photograph against a heading set in ample white space, for instance.

Readers unconsciously align heading and text: they don't like a heading that extends beyond the text relating to it. The opposite –a heading shorter (covering one and a half columns, let's say) than the (two columns of) text beneath it– is fine. This layout is called a '*Dutch Wrap*'.

Readers also dislike a row of headings in a line across a multi-column page: three headings, let's say, each at the top of its own column, at the head of such a page. The natural tendency is to read this line up as one composite heading. There's confusion till the reader sorts things out. Known as '*tombstoning*', this layout is to be avoided at all costs.

Readers expect what's under a graphic (rather than what's beside it) to go with the graphic. Readers also expect more white space between unlike elements than between elements that are alike. So there should be more space between (a) the final paragraph in one text block and the (unconnected) heading that follows it than between (b) that heading and the (connected) text which follows it.

EMPLOYING WHITE SPACE IN YOUR LAYOUT

How you handle empty space –'white space'– is very important. Readers don't consciously notice it, if it's well handled. But, if you *haven't* got a policy –if purposeless irregularities occur in your spacing– an impression of amateurishness quickly builds up. Then your argument won't be taken seriously, no matter how good it is.

You may have a simple policy (always to leave the same amount of space between all elements in your newsletter), or a sophisticated one (more space between unrelated items, at the top of boxes, at the bottom of the page, and so on). But what's essential is to have a policy. Without a policy, you can't use space in a discriminating fashion: to single out elements for special attention, for instance.

It's the planning that goes into these issues –issues that most people don't consciously think about– that characterizes superior editing. Rather like body language, these underlying consistencies in positioning are what determine how readers react to your words.

GUIDELINES FOR EMPLOYING RULES

Rules, like white space, cut things off, so far as readers are concerned. So the best sequence with horizontal modules is:
- last line of type in text block (for instance, in module 1, in a 3-column layout);
- rule;
- heading (for the columns of text in module 2);
- text (of module 2).

That is, the heading comes **after**, not before, the rule.

THE 'SPREAD' AND THE 'PACKAGE'

Possibly the most helpful concepts in connection with proportion and balance are those of the 'spread' and 'package'. A newsletter consists of two 'stand alone' pages (the first and the last) and a number of spreads (pairs of facing pages). Each spread should be thought of as a unit for design purposes, because the pages are seen as a unit, and have to be balanced as such.

It helps enormously if the contents of the spread can be planned so that they, too, form a unit: a package. Such packaging enables the two-page spread to have a unifying theme, related headlines, possibly its own special running head, differing slightly from the other running head(s) of the news-letter, and maybe even a heading in a special decorative typeface (if the subject matter warrants this). Often departments within a newsletter can be packaged in such spreads, thus avoiding page jumps.

There are a number of advantages to planning in spreads and packages:

1. Just under 50% of readers are 'backwards readers': they skim-read, flipping through the pages of your newsletter from back to front. A backwards reader's eye will go first to the top left quartile of the left-hand pages of your newsletter. Similarly, the (slightly over 50% of) 'normal' readers, flipping through from the front page, will eye the top right quartile of the right-hand pages first. So each spread has to be designed with major display items in these positions. And this determines the rest of the layout on these pages.

2. Secondary display items will be needed for the lower part of each page, usually the corner opposite where the major display item is situated. A diagram of a dummy two page layout spread is provided in Diagram 3.2. The advantage of designing in two-page spreads is that asymmetrical balance –mirror-image pages– is easy to plan for. Also, the two pages allow enough space for considerable diversity in modular layout and use of outquotes, boxes and the like. So you can have a variety of spread plans, which will nonetheless be harmonious.

Conclusion

Specific individual elements of the layout are consciously seen; but it's the underlying design principles which give a publication that intangible element, its 'feeling' of being a unity. Visually informative text requires careful planning. It also requires a writer to know as much about the principles of page layout and design as about the principles of semantics and stylistics.

Since the advent of desktop publishing, typesetting expertise has replaced typewriting expertise as a basic skill in a writer's repertoire. Writers now customize their pages, employing graphics, a variety of typefaces or fonts, and layout grids. It has become clear that expertise in graphic design, layout principles and typography is just as essential for a writer as for a printer if an attention-getting presentation is sought.[11]

Diagram 3.2: A 'Dummy' Layout of a Two-page Spread

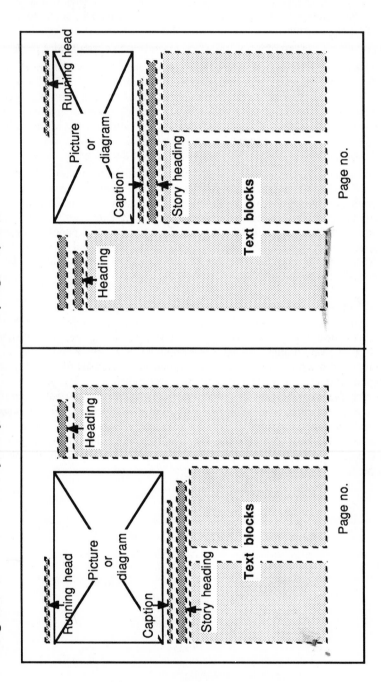

4 Graphics in Desktop Publishing:

The Increasing Use of Graphics in Text

Graphics: The Step-child of Desktop Publishing
WHY THE SLOW DEMAND FOR, AND UNIMAGINATIVE USE OF, GRAPHICS?

Basically, desktop publishing programs are utility programs that enable us to put graphics into word processing: they're designed to allow us to flow text round graphics. So why, when there's been such a demand to develop programs *precisely* so as to flow text round graphics, has demand for graphics been so weak?

The fact is that the demand for click art –professionally-drawn pictures on disk– has grown very slowly, whereas the demand for desktop publishing programs has grown amazingly rapidly. Far more 'business graphics' (pie charts, bar charts, and graphs) than picture-type graphics are produced and inserted into text. Likewise, there's been more interest in, and development of, laser printers and scanners than of graphics programs.

The advent of computer graphics was as major a development as the advent of computerized page makeup programs. Yet there's been little innovation in the way we use graphics. This compares strikingly with the spiralling innovations in the way we've developed desktop publishing programs. We haven't 're-invented' uses for graphics programs as we have for desktop publishing programs.

There seem to be at least five reasons for this state of affairs:

1. **Most of us have an arrested graphics capacity: we draw like five-year-olds.**

   The reason for this is simple: our drawing capacity was arrested at that age, when we were required to learn to read, in a matter of weeks. Since then, the schooling process has systematically and vigorously promoted verbal and numerical data analysis, at the expense of spatial, global data processing. Most males in our culture have become over-specialized in left-brain hemisphere development. Most of us aren't good at right-brain hemisphere tasks such as drawing, so we'll avoid them if we can.[1]

2. Connected with this arrested graphics capacity is our sense of competence in dealing with the experts who control the technology of print.

   Between the author and his or her book/article, the printer and typographer have interposed their expertise. As writers, we've lost control of what our work is to look like on the page. But we will, sometimes, argue with printers. After all, we're wordsmiths and we see printers as technicians. So we have the (sometimes misplaced) confidence that we can judge when we're being oversold on formats unsuitable for our work.

Things are very different when it comes to art work. There the art directors and graphics artists have interposed a much more formidable barrier between us and the presentation of our work. We're most of us *not* competent artists, and the technology of the graphic designer is generally a mystery to us. So we don't know when we're being oversold –or at least we don't feel competent to argue about our suspicions.

As a result, despite the new desktop publishing technologies, the designs and thinking of the old cut and paste graphics artists still determine what is done with the new technology.[2]

3. The graphics technology hasn't been very user-friendly: it lacks 'connectivity'.

The micro which most people use is an IBM PC or clone. This a character-based micro. It's meant for producing characters (letters and numbers), not graphics (details in chapter 6). True, you can upgrade it so that it can display and produce graphics. But the problem then is that the add-on devices required to do this, being produced by a host of third-party developers, aren't all compatible with one another –and neither are the programs which run on them..

Besides, they don't have a uniform graphics file format, which you need if you're to move your files from one program to another. Yet this operation is basic to desktop publishing. It's a task of daunting complexity to get one of these micros to do it.[3]

4. The bit-map barrier has put people off using paint programs for desktop publishing.

Now the Macintosh *does* have a uniform graphics file format; and most of the hardware and software that runs on the Mac allows files to be easily transferred from one program to another. Certainly the page makeup programs for the Mac support all its major applications programs. No connectivity problems here. So a huge library of click art is becoming available for the Mac.

But there's still a problem. Most of this art work is done by the Mac's paint program: it's 'bitmapped'. Bitmapped images (for details, see below), at 72 dots per inch (dpi), are like dot matrix printout: clunky and ugly. They don't look good when printed on the LaserWriter: 72 dpi translates into unsightly chunks when printed out at 300 dpi. There's just no point in wasting Linotronic printout (at 1270 or 2440 dpi) on them.

So the problem is that the Mac's got a library of graphics that it can't use for *quality* printing.

5. To date, you haven't been able to produce good colour graphics on micros

– or to *re*produce such graphics if you *did* manage to produce them.

So colour has been associated with high-end (expensive) printing only. Without colour, much of the attractiveness and impact of graphics is lost.

Signs of Increasing Interest in Graphics
HARBINGERS OF CHANGE

There are increasing signs of a recent upsurge of interest in graphics, however. Again, the reasons for this are both psychological and technological. (Discussion will be largely in terms of the Macintosh technology because this is at the leading edge of developments in graphics.)

1. **Graphics literacy is appearing among desktop publishers, largely as a result of increased familiarity with graphics programs and products.**

   Organizations are by now publishing documents that they wouldn't have considered publishing prior to having their own graphic arts and page makeup departments in-house: flyers and brochures with elaborate typography and graphics.

   The main new line, however, is probably the production of slides for overhead projection in presentations at board meetings and conferences. Fifteen billion of these are produced annually, it's estimated, in the US, only three million of them by computer. New programs available on the Mac promise to change this by making such slides easy to produce, in sophisticated forms, very rapidly *and in colour*.

   > This is the major current market opportunity. Developers are striving, with GREAT ingenuity and energy, to exploit it.

   Now it's clear that the high standards beloved of professional graphics artists aren't needed for this material. Besides, desktop publishers are getting used to using decorative typefaces, and emphasizing key elements in diagrams with special pictorial features for heightened illustrative effect.

   There's less subservience to professional graphics artists, and less judging by the standards of high-end print publications. Instead, *middle*-level publications, done by desktop publishers on the LaserWriter, are becoming the standard of comparison. This is a less daunting standard. It allows hope of attaining –even, on occasion, of surpassing– its level of achievement.

   As a result desktop publishers are acquiring some competence, and confidence, in handling graphics. They realize that one doesn't need high-end publishing for *all* documents. It's no longer easy to oversell them on graphics standards: they are acquiring graphics literacy (or, as the graphics artists see things, a lowering of standards is occurring).

2. **A move is under way towards greater connectivity –users are demanding it and hardware vendors and software developers are making strenuous efforts to comply.**

   a. Apple and IBM (the first and second largest makers of microcomputers in the world) are both bent on making it more easily possible to transfer files from one company's micros to those of the other. 'Slots' are receptacles for 'cards' –virtual computers on miniature boards, which can be inserted into the 'mother board' within the micro's central processing unit. The most recent Macintoshes, the Mac SE and the Mac II, have slots which are primarily designed to accept cards that will run PS DOS and OS/2 programs –PC software. There's a distinct possibility that both will adopt a common Nubus 'bus' to govern the central processing unit in their micros.

But it's easier to achieve connectivity by means of software. The hardware is already paid for, in place and in use, and it would cost a fortune for large organizations to change it. So let's see what's happening to the software.

b. Leading software houses are programming their best-selling programs to facilitate easy transfer between the two main types of hardware in use (the PC and the Mac).

   Microsoft's PC version of its leading word processor, *Word*, converts into its Mac version of *Word* at the touch of a button. Transfer of files between Aldus' PC version of *PageMaker* (the leading page makeup program) and its Mac version also occurs at the touch of a button. The same is planned for Microsoft's *Excel* (probably the leading spreadsheet program), Ashton-Tate's *dBase III* (probably the leading data base management program) and WordPerfect Corporation's *WordPerfect* (possibly the leading word processor for the PC).[4]

c. Programs have been developed that make it easy to link Macs and PCs in LANs (local area networks). Centram system's *TOPS* and West Dataviz's *MacLink Plus* seem currently to be the most effective at doing this.

d. a small library of disk transfer software has built up. This enables you to transfer files from a 5.25" floppy to a 3.5" one.

e. Adobe's *PostScript* is emerging as a standard page-description language for laser printers and phototypesetters. This means that, by including a "Convert [this file] to *PostScript*" program within any application program, that program can run on any printer.

f. Efforts are being made to achieve graphics standards for the PC.:

   • Probably Microsoft's Windows (close kin to the Mac's Windows) will emerge as the standard, on-screen display system.

   • Compuserve, one of America's gigantic electronic information utilities, has developed a graphics interchange format (dubbed GIF) that permits users of incompatible micros to exchange graphics files. Compuserve has put the GIF software in the public domain, so that graphics software developers can incorporate it in their programs.

   • Altsys Corporation has developed an EPSF (Encapsulated *PostScript* File Format) that looks like becoming a standard.

   If you save your graphics file in this format, you can see it on screen in a WYSIWYG page makeup program, and it will print on any laser writer that supports *PostScript* (this is likely soon to mean 'any laser printer').

   • TIFF (Tagged Image File Format) is fast becoming the standard format for all types of bitmapped graphics files, especially for those produced by scanning devices.

   Most page makeup programs will allow you to place TIFF files on their pages and will print them. TIFF also manages gray-scale images (on which, see below).

- Difficulties in sending data by modem −where hardware and software incompatibilities have long bedevilled information exchange− are being solved by increasingly more powerful and sophisticated programs. Currently leading in this area is *Blast*, produced by the Communications Research Group. *Blast* copes with noise on telephone lines as well as media conversion.

So the technology is becoming much more user-friendly. As a result, desktop publishers are making more use, and are showing more innovativeness in their use, of the various graphics programs. Accessibility (provided by connectivity) is the *father* of invention.

3. **The technology, and the desktop publishers, have broken through the bitmap barrier.**

We may be hesitant to draw, but we're *not* hesitant to tinker with the click art produced by graphics artists to adapt it to our needs. Computer graphics are, after all, wonderfully forgiving: we can play 'what if' games with it, keeping our successes and still having our originals in the event of failure. In fact, only computer graphics encourage an adult to learn to draw, in our society. And the second-generation graphics programs enormously enhance and encourage our artistic abilities in this regard:[5]

a. The new standard for paint programs is *SuperPaint* by Silicon Beach.[6] It's a huge advance on Apple's *MacPaint*. To be fair to Apple, *MacPaint* was put out to sell Macintoshes by showing what they could do, *not* to beat out all the other programs in the field. There *was* no 'field', or other programs: Apple invented this type of program. The same goes for *MacDraw*, the first object-oriented program for the Mac.

Superpaint allows you to edit your bitmaps at 300 dpi; to draw as well as paint; to integrate the results of the two; to rotate, slant, give perspectives to and distort your 'painting', and to print the results out in colour on your ImageWriter II dot matrix printer.

b. The new standard for draw programs, *Cricket Draw*, enables you to do things with object-oriented graphics (on which see more below) that are new: rotate high-resolution text and graphics; introduce gray-scales and 'fountains' (grays which range from white to black), and draw curves better, for instance.

c. Three dimensional drawing has now come to the Mac, so you no longer have to be an engineering draftsperson to do it[7] As you know from experience, three dimensional drawings are difficult to do (by hand, let alone on a computer). In publications, two-dimensional drawings look weak, but three dimensional drawings need such expertise that they have so far been produced by professional graphic artists or draftspersons.

Hence the development of '3D' drawing programs. These add an engineering draftsperson to the printer's team already resident in your micro. Some of these programs are meant for engineers (Diehl Graphsoft's *MiniCad*); but others are meant for illustrators (*Pro3D*, from Enabling Technologies).

These programs have impressive features: you can rotate an object; choose the viewpoint from which it's presented, and draw it in true perspective from that viewpoint. You can draw shapes with *many* surfaces, with a choice of sources from which light originates, to provide shading effects. You can draw a cross-section, then extrude the sections out from it, three dimensionally.

Most of these programs allow you to transfer their products into page makeup programs. Saved in EPSF, 3D programs produce spectacular graphics on a laser printer.

d. But, for drawing curves and producing shading effects, the new standard has to be Adobe's Illustrator.

This program enables a novice to draw like a professional illustrator. You choose any bitmapped graphic –a digitized photograph, for instance– and draw lines along those edges of the photo where you want lines. Illustrator makes the lines conform, smoothly, to these edges. You then remove the original underlying bitmap (off to one side, where you can still refer to it), and put in your own shading effects. You can now print the results *at the resolution of whatever machine is doing the printing* (for example a Linotronic 300 at 2540 dpi). You've produced an object-oriented graphic.

This program, and its likely future derivatives, will fundamentally alter computer graphics for desktop publishing. With a little practice in using this program, anyone can convert *any* photograph or drawing into a computer graphic that looks like the work of a professional graphics artist.

4. Colour printing has come to the micro.

a. The High (=expensive) End of Microcomputer Printing Technology

Colour printing is now possible via desktop publishing. The state of the art software and hardware appear, for the moment, to be Pixel-Craft's programs *Kaleidoscope* and *Heaven*, along with the Pixel-Craft workstation.[8] *Heaven* is a separator for colour-composite video displays. It can take any colour bitmapped image and separate the colours. *Kaleidoscope*, a tint-generator, can retouch the resulting colour separations.Essentially what happens is that the bitmapped image is colour-separated into the basic four colours of colour printing (blue, red, yellow and black). The image is then processed for sharpness of colour, colour correction and for the tones in its colour ranges. Each of the four separated negatives is then half-toned for gradations in image density.

The '*Kaleidoscope* to *PostScript*' interpreter sub-program then instructs *PostScript*, and thus the phototypesetting equipment, on how to print each separation. Each separation then goes through a separate run of a four-colour press: separation one goes through in colour one; separation two is then superimposed on separation one and colour two goes onto the superimposed separation two, and so on.

This technology, when used with a Linotronic 300 at 2540 dpi, makes a 260 lines per inch screen possible, employing a working pallette of 100,000,000 colours. It's a technology that goes beyond the best current high-end printing, which uses a 200 line screen. The new micros, the Mac II and IBM's PS/2, will run this technology.

b. Colour for The Rest of Us:

• *Colour-bonding Film*

Most of us may find the humbler technology of colour-bonding film more suited to our purposes and budget.[9] You need a special colour film and a bonding unit (to put the heat on the film, so as to bond it to the paper). You place the film over the page on which you're going to print or copy, using separate pieces of film, of different colours, if you want to get a multi-coloured printout. The toner on a laser printed or photocopied page causes this coloured film to bond to the page wherever toner (the black image) is applied to it. Once your page emerges from the printer or photocopier, you remove the film. You'll have the appropriate colour wherever you superimposed film over what was to be printed or copied on to the page.

This relatively inexpensive technology is useful for those special, one-shot presentations that need a coloured cover, or for preparing pages for colour printing by a printer.

- *Colour Printouts from Dot Matrix Printers*

It's possible to produce a multi-colour printout from a dot matrix printer; the problem is in reproducing that printout en masse for publication. A dot matrix printer's printout doesn't merit the use of four colour printing. It may merit the use (and cost) of a colour photocopier, though this, too, is likely to be technological overkill.[10]

Bitmapped versus Object-oriented Graphics

BIT-MAPPED GRAPHICS

Bit-maps, or 'raster images' as they are sometimes called, are the basis of the paint programs.[11] Here's a brief sketch of how they work.

The Macintosh's screen resolution is 72 dots per inch (dpi). Work-ing with a magnification of the true screen size, you can create a paint graphic, by drawing a picture as a pattern of dots, making each dot either black or white. You can also 'spray paint' dots on to, or fill with 'shade', the lines of your drawing. The result: a picture with shading.

To change the picture, you simply change dots from black to white, or vice versa, thus re-drawing the picture in minute detail –a laborious process, if major alterations are desired.

The snag is that the resulting picture is limited by the number of dots available to you at your original 72 dpi resolution. So when you print on the LaserWriter at 300 dpi, those 72 dots, now *clumps* of smaller dots, so much bigger, are individually visible. They produce the infamous dot-matrix jagged lines ('jaggies'): anything but a straight line becomes a series of square dots looking like a flight of stairs.

OBJECT-ORIENTED GRAPHICS

'Object-oriented' graphics produce far better results. These are constructed by using draw programs. You work with 'objects', such as arcs, circles, diagonal lines, ovals, and squares, not with the dots on your screen. The draw programs can enlarge these objects, fill with them with shading, and reduce, rotate and stretch them (in any direction).

To change the picture, you reshape the objects, using the tools provided by the program. This can generally be quickly done, with dramatic effects.

Such objects are not tied to the resolution of the screen on which they were produced, and print out at the resolution of the device doing the printing.

> The LaserWriter sets each of the dots involved in the lines of this type of art by co-ordinates. So the resulting graphics are very clean and precise: 300 dpi on a LaserWriter –and 1270 or 2540 dpi on a Linotronic 1 or 3 respectively. No jagged curves and diagonals.

To construct these draw programs, high end CAD/CAM software has been ported to (made available to run on) microcomputers. So object-oriented graphics produce sharply etched line drawings with fine-grained shading. More demanding to construct than bit-mapped graphics, object-oriented art collections have been slower to appear. But they're now appearing in ever-increasing numbers, and programs like Adobe's *Illustrator* should produce an avalanche of them.

Halftones

THE ADVANTAGES OF FILM TECHNOLOGY

Computer technology isn't well suited to creating halftones; film technology is.[12] A halftone is a simulation of a photograph. It consists of a grid of dots called 'grains'. A screen is laid over the photograph to produce the pattern of dots. A black and white photograph thus changes to a grey screen, called the 'grey scale'–hence the term 'halftone'. The number of dots can't be changed; it's determined by the screen. Hence the number of dots is called the 'screen size'.

Newspapers, using low quality paper, have to use a 65 to 85 lines per inch screen because more dots than this will result in blotches. Magazines, using better quality paper, can use a 133 to 150 line screen. Hence the grain in a newspaper halftone is visible to the human eye, but not that in a magazine halftone.

If you can't change the number of dots, you can change their size. A position on the screen can have no grain at all (that is, it appears as white), a fine grain (appearing as grey) or a large grain (appearing as black). The variation in size is what makes the dots appear to be more numerous (although they're merely denser), making darker patches appear in the grey scale of the halftone. This gradation of greys simulates the original photograph.

DISADVANTAGES OF COMPUTER TECHNOLOGY

As stated, computer technology isn't well suited to producing halftones. The reason is that it can't vary the size of its dots. Most computers simply put more dots where it's desired to produce a dark area in a picture. The 'Fat Bits' sub-program in the *MacPaint* program, for instance, does this by simply making each of its 72 dpi black or white –the 'bit-mapping' process described above. The resulting dots are fairly large; they create the familiar digitized effect: diagonals or curved lines suffer from 'the jaggies'; step-wise lines of dots, that can be seen.

The LaserWriter can vary the size of its dots. It does this by aggregating a number of dots into one 'dot' (= cluster), and darkening only a certain number of the dots within each cluster. Thus a cluster of 2X2 dots gives you 5 levels of grey (the extra one occurring when you don't darken *any* of the 4 dots making up the cluster); a 3X3 cluster gives 10 levels, and a cluster of 4X4 dots gives 17 levels. But this clustering decreases the number of 'dots' that you can get from your basic 300 dpi: clusters of 4X4 dots give you only 75 clusters per inch, for example.

So long as the Laser Writer can only produce 300 dpi, its graphics won't be very good. However, the Linotronic 100 produces 1270 dpi, and the Linotronic 300 over 2540. So these phototypesetters produce excellent graphics –depending on the bit-mapping (or, preferably, the object-orienting) ability of the software that created those graphics.

'WELLS': BACK TO RAZOR BLADES, WAXES AND PASTE POTS

Sometimes you can't find a suitable piece, or pieces, of click art for your newsletter. In such cases, the 'well' provides a way out of your dilemma. The well is simply a 'hole' or empty space in the text on your page. Into a well you can insert either a photograph, in the form of a velox print, or a piece of clip art work.[13]

A velox print is a photograph turned, by a photographic process, into a halftone dot pattern, described above, that a printing press can reproduce. This procedure will give you the halftone that you require, where you require it, on the page. When you've run the text off on a LaserWriter, you paste the print into the hole.

If you're using a halftone, it can be cropped before you put it into your text. You can cut it down in size so as leave only that part of it that's appropriate to the focus of your text. Or it can be re-sized: reduced in size to fit the well. It's best to calculate the size of the well from the outset with your art work in mind. So doing will enable you to arrange the most appropriate scale for the art work.

The same can be done with clip art. You can crop a picture yourself. But, if a picture (rather than a line drawing) is involved, sizing is better done photo-graphically (you use a pica stick and proportional wheel to measure the percentage enlargement or reduction). A halftone will give a good reproduction; photocopying won't. Photocopying will do for enlarging or reducing line art, however.

Disks of bit-mapped graphics are expensive, and disks of object-oriented graphics still more so. The labour and cost involved in developing a database for your library of graphics is also considerable. So it may well be cheaper, easier and quicker to insert the occasional velox print or piece of clip art into a well rather than try to build and catalogue an extensive library of click art.

From Clip Art to Click Art
THE NEED FOR A STANDARD GRAPHIC FILE FORMAT

So far as graphics are concerned, the Macintosh has an enormous advantage over the IBM PC: a standard graphic file format. This is the *PICT* format, also called the *QuickDraw* format because of the set of *QuickDraw* routines used to draw the graphics.

All graphics for the Mac are produced in either the *MacPaint* or the *MacDraw* formats (or compatible up-grades). Because of this standardized format you can transfer pretty well any graphic into any other program. You can paste a *MacDraw* graphic into a *MacPaint* graphic –or the reverse, then put the results into a word processing program or a page make-up program.

Each IBM graphics program, on the other hand, uses its own unique file format. The result, to date, has been incompatibility of end products. Because of this incompatibility, it's not been possible to accumulate a library of graphics art work for the IBM PC.

Obviously, this situation can't be allowed to continue. Hence the attempts being made, as indicated above, to achieve graphics software standards for the PC. Connectivity, which is coming, will mean that the latter will be able to draw on the library of software available for the Mac.

A standardized graphics file format is crucial because there's a huge volume of clip art work available for conversion to computer graphics. As a result, text is about to become more well illustrated by graphics –and more easy to illustrate– than it has ever been. Here's why.

THE GROWING CLICK ART LIBRARY

Clip art work is copyright-free art, camera-ready, for use by non-artists to explain or illustrate text. It has been accumulating for decades. It is avail-able in an amazing variety of forms. There are pictures of all types (including miniatures); diagrams (including reproductions of engravings by master craftsmen); logos, borders and abstract designs; decorative alphabets; dingbats to go into already finished art work, and so on: the list goes on and on.

There are many books containing collections of clip art: some collections are organized by theme, others by type of object depicted; there are historical archives (of engravings and suchlike); there's even an *Encyclopedia of Small Engravings*. Clip art now comes as a regular, on-going service, in the form of Dynamics Graphics' monthly magazine, *Clipper* (last ten years' back numbers cross-indexed). As services to these services, there are catalogues designed to enable potential users of these enormous art libraries to identify artfolios (portfolios) of material specifically suited to their needs.

This stockpile of art work is now being reproduced as computer graphics –for the Mac, because of the latter's flexibility with graphics and because 70% of desktop graphics is occurring on the Mac. The LaserWriter has effectively destroyed the market for low end typesetting equipment. Purveyors of that equipment are turning the clip art that once was available only if you purchased their equipment into click art for the LaserWriter.

> Thus the clip art library that newspapers use for their advertising graph-ics has now appeared as a multi-disk series for the Mac as *MacMatbook*, from The Electronic Publisher Inc. Dynamic Graphics , a leader in provision of clip art, has developed a computerized on-going art work service, reproducing its *Clipper* Art work as the series *DeskTop Art*.

Graphics Art Management Systems
PICTORIAL DATABASES ARRIVE

For many desktop publishers currently, the major problem is that of finding a specific graphic within their collection. A Mac graphics disk contains 400,000 bytes of graphics, often batched by general theme. A lot of individual pieces of art work are involved. Few need, or have, names. As a result, they may be memorable, but they're not easily locatable.

Suppose you've got ten disks. You know that the picture you're looking for is on one of them, but you're not sure which one or where. Finding it by search will be a time-consuming business.

To meet this need, Symmetry has developed a pictorial database program called *PictureBase*.

PictureBase enables you to copy any *MacPaint* or *MacDraw* graphic into a *PictureBase* library, providing each picture with a name and key words (a commentary of notes, too, if you wish). Each library consists of a collection of related pictures, grouped around a theme, such as 'dining out' (useful for preparing menus for restaurants). The key words denote aspects of the general themal idea (fine food, junk food, fast food –whatever). *PictureBase Retrieval*, a search program, can search all libraries for a specific key word. So retrieval of any graphic you desire takes only a few seconds.

Locating pictures and then putting them and their accompanying tag words into *PictureBase*, which is a database with pictures, is a time-consuming process. So some vendors are providing their pictures in the form of a *PictureBase* collection. This 'solution' requires you to purchase and use *PictureBase* –and requires other users of your system to familiarize themselves with *PictureBase*. There are other, simpler solutions.

Suppose you were to dedicate each one of a series of disks to one particular theme: for instance to Food, Drink & Dining, with sub-headings respectively: fine food; junk food; booze; non-alcoholic beverages; fast food; restaurants; banquets and the like. (Each disk's categories could be listed on its label.) You could set up your system as need arises.

Start with a couple of disks; then institute new ones –when you've got to find a certain kind of graphic in your collection of purchased master disks, for instance. When looking for this new kind of graphic, enter any items that you come across which are relevant to your established categories into those categories on separate disks.

This method takes more time than copying all your graphics across in one operation. But:

- I've never met anyone who has systematically copied his or her whole collection in one operation. In practice, no-one has days to spend just copying graphics files into a database.

- You can't be sure what themes and categories you'll need for your collection. No point in doing needless work.

- The procedure outlined cuts time spent on assembling a database to a minimum, and time spent can usually be non-prime time –you snatch an hour or so when you're not at your best for working.

Guidelines on the Use of Graphics
CONTROLLING READERS' EYE MOVEMENTS

Some guidelines have been developed governing the use of graphics.[14] A skim reader will flip through your publication, going from picture to picture, if you don't control his or her eye movements –and nearly half of these readers skim from back to front. So your graphics have to form a unified theme, enabling such a 'reader' to get the gist of the publication from the 'normal' sequence or from a back-to-front sweep.

You can control eye movement by putting captions under the pictures. Make these captions attention-grabbing but not self-explanatory (for instance, "Yuppy Puppies Go for Macs"). Then provide a longer sub-caption, in a smaller font, to explain the caption ("Teenagers in wealthy/professional homes form a disproportionately large proportion of purchasers of the Macintosh"). Next comes the body text, which gives the evidence for this contention. This succession leads the reader into the body text, by an orderly progression, in the text, of font sizes and levels of meaning.

As graphics are so striking for a reader, you have to choose them carefully: for their photo-journalistic qualities, not merely because they're all you've got available, or because they're visually attractive. What's needed are strong visual elements, that contribute power-fully to the body text while being able to stand by themselves. This applies whether you're employing the graphic to explain a point in your text or as an illustration to enliven it. Inappropriate or only marginally relevant illustration (and they are common) are worse than useless: they cause puzzlement and distraction.

Combining a typeface with a picture adds to the power of them both. You edit, 'crop' and 'size' your graphics, to indicate their importance and in keep-ing with your grid.

'GROUPING'

Integrating a striking graphic –a photograph, let's say– with its text isn't easy when that graphic is the major display item and must be positioned at the page top, as leading item. The obvious place to put the heading is above the photograph. But then the caption will run beneath the photograph. So the eye won't jump to the caption (and, from there, to the body text); instead, the reader will skip to the next graphic.

As this is a problem which occurs frequently, a way has been found of dealing with it, called 'grouping'. This technique works as follows (see diagram 4.1). Suppose you're using a three-column grid, with a photograph that's to be cropped to the width of two of these columns:

- the heading runs across (all three columns of) the page, flushed left;
- the photograph comes below the heading, extending across the centre and right columns;
- the sub-heading comes as a side-bar to the photograph, in the left column, flushed right, against the photograph;
- the direction of gaze of the persons in the photograph is left –into the text;
- the left hand column of body text commences below the sub-heading, but part way up the side of the photograph;
- the remaining two columns of text, continuing this left hand column, align with the photograph, extending downwards below it.

The photograph is now an integral part of the text. Heading, sub-heading and (direction of gaze in the) photograph form one complex, which leads inexorably to the body text of which this complex is clearly an integrated component. Thus the reader will be unconsciously led deeper and deeper into the story about (and physically around) the photograph.

Besides this, subliminally, grouping makes the combined text and graphic highly memorable to readers.

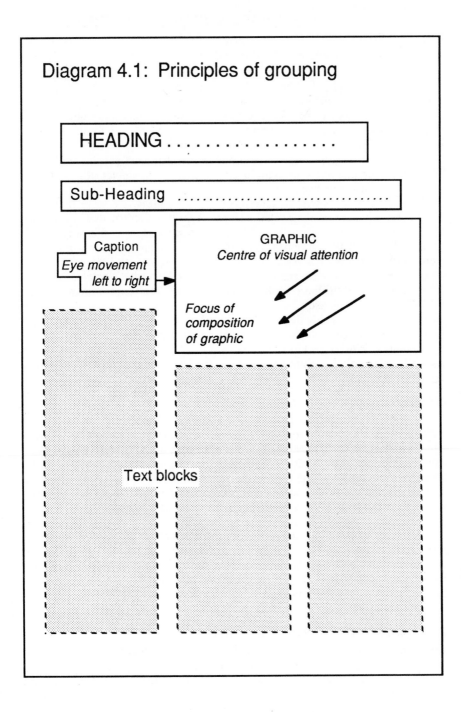

Diagram 4.1: Principles of grouping

HEADING . . . .

Sub-Heading . . . .

Caption

Eye movement left to right

GRAPHIC
Centre of visual attention

Focus of composition of graphic

Text blocks

From Graphics to Graphs: Visual Display of the Relationships Between Numbers

WHY BUSINESS GRAPHICS ARE SO POPULAR[15]

Visual layout and display has immediacy and impact: "a picture is worth a thousand words". Graphs show the relationships between numbers, quickly –visually. Visual presentation of statistics makes more sense to most people than do columns of figures. We take in the meaning of a picture more quickly, and remember it longer, than we take in the meaning of the same information when it's expressed in blocks of text and banks of numbers.

Besides, the picture saves the thousand words that most people won't read. They prefer the intuitively meaningful graph, fitting in a quarter of a page, that they understand at a glance.

This is because, when we remember complex ideas, we store them as a Gestalt, as a picture of their relationships. (You'll remember that Buzan [see Bibliography], exploiting our pre-disposition to store ideas in this way, developed the 'mind map' mentioned in chapter 1, as a means of recording a brainstorm during its process.) We don't re-member sentences, or lists, or unrelated points –especially when several criteria are involved. So what's wanted is:

- a depiction of the basic components of the idea (each expressed in one word or phrase);
- restricted to showing their relationships (via arrows);
- set out in a Gestalt (that is, with everything connected to something else in the picture).

As we'll retain only the outline structure of the idea, this skeletal representation is all that's likely to be remembered.

GRAPHS AS 'GEOMETRIC METAPHORS'

A graph is a blend of mathematics and art: a "geometric metaphor" in Bertrand Russell's terms. It's your view of what the most important relationships within a set of figures are. You have to work out *very* clearly what these relationships are. The basic organizing logic behind any graphic should be apparent to its reader within five seconds or less, if you've included captions, a few identifying terms, and some numbers. (If you can't graph or chart the relationships between a set of concepts, you won't be able to make those relationships clear by using text alone.)

Effective presentation of the relationships which you consider important requires that you follow a specific set of procedures. After all, you're dealing with a combination of mathematics and art, both of which involve disciplined thought and presentation. So graphics help you to set out the logic of your thinking, because they require you to work out very carefully what the main points of your argument are.

GUIDELINES FOR CONSTRUCTING GRAPHS

1. You must decide very clearly what is the question that the graph answers. This forces you to determine which are the relationships on which you're focusing. You should be able to sum up what you're doing in a short phrase or sentence: four to eight words.

2. Then you select the kind of graphic format that's likely to be appropriate from what you know of your readers' experience with graphs and considering the idea that you want to get across.

Graph-construction programs provide a wide variety of graph types to choose from. Apart from the standard Bar, Column and Pie Charts, there are Area, HiLo, Line and Scatter Graphs, as well as other, more exotic ones.

Different graph formats serve different purposes: the much-used pie chart, for instance, is particularly good at visually cross-comparing a limited number of variables at different points in time or place.

3. Now work out your problem in terms of numbers. For example, how many people chose item No. 1, and how many chose item No. 2 (or whatever), in January as opposed to December? Then work out how to set the resulting figures out so that trends will be evident at a glance: see Table 4.1. Next, do a rough sketch of what your graph is going to look like, turning your matrix or table of figures into the appropriate graph format.

4. You now set the graph up:

- Put the independent variable along the horizontal axis (called the X-axis, or abscissa, or category axis), generally: see Diagram 4.2. (The computer program will usually decide what the independent variable is, depending on the kind of graph you choose.) The dependent variable goes along the vertical axis (called the Y-axis, or ordinate, or value axis).
- By convention, the X-axis should be about 1.4 times the length of the Y-axis.
- Time lines should run from left to right and from the top to the bottom.
- Use the KISS principle. If you have to use a complex systems box, use the 'hold and build' technique.

This involves a series of boxes, appropriately interspersed through your text. The first box shows only the basic variables or factors or whatever –four of five items. The second box shows one or two consequences of each of these (so box 2 holds from eight to fifteen items). The third box shows one or two main consequences of each of the latter consequences (so it holds from 16 to 45 items).

When the display builds progressively like this this, readers are intrigued and follow its progression with curiosity. But if you present them with the third box at the outset, they'll regard it as too complicated to follow, and probably won't try to do so.

- Credits: always give your sources. By convention, they are placed in the lower left-hand corner of the box around your graph.

GUIDELINES ON GRAPH PRESENTATION

Now you can move the chart into your paint or draw program and enhance it with special effects. You have a range of fill patterns, line thicknesses, 3–D effects and typefaces (for labels); and you can paste in appropriate click art. See Diagram 4. 3. Besides, when you import your chart into a drawing program, every item on it comes over as an individual 'object' that you can manipulate by expanding, contracting, rotating or inserting text or art.

Table 4.1: Gotcha Company:December and January Sales

	December	January
Gizmo 1	731000	2900
Gizmo 2	853000	76000
Gizmo 3	152000	12300
Gizmo 4	51000	203000

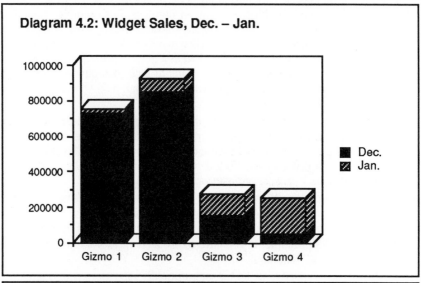

Diagram 4.2: Widget Sales, Dec. – Jan.

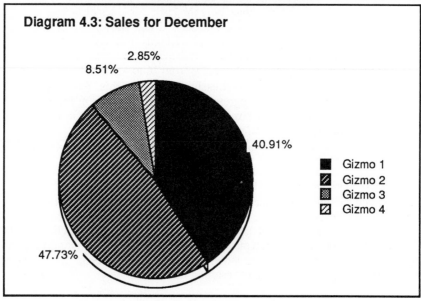

Diagram 4.3: Sales for December

A lot of things have to be considered in presenting your graphs if you wish to cover all contingencies and achieve a consistent house-style. You need something rather like the stylesheet set out in the HEMP diagram (see diagram 2.1). The following features must be taken systematically into account:

1. Typefaces: Style and Sizes

- Wordage is kept at a minimum in graphs and it's almost all headings or captions. So use display fonts and plenty of white space: Helvetica 14 point bold for headlines (depending on the overall size of the graph), Helvetica 9 regular for captions. For credits, the nearest thing to body copy, use Times 10 point regular.
- Keep captions to a minimum, writing them horizontally if possible, and, if your program allows it, centred on their respective axes, as in Diagram 4.2. (Neatness is critically important, as so much information is packed into a graph.)

2. Borders

- To ensure that the graph stands out distinctly and as a unit from its background, put a box around it.
- The box should be a hairline or slim line one, so as not to call attention to itself.
- There should be a policy on white space within boxes (for instance, more at the top of the box than at the bottom).

3. Screens

- As with typefaces, beginners tend to overuse the resources of the technology: a plethora of shadings and fillings is used, with no two graphs the same.
- The experts recommend restricting shading to five tones, and point out that any *one* graph rarely needs more than three tones.

4. Continuity and Emphasis

As with typography and page makeup, experienced editors exercise strict limitations on the features that they use. Their aim is to attain a disciplined and restrained house style for all graphs throughout their publications. To be effective, graphs have to be clear and simply laid out. Busy or unfocused presentation is counter-productive: it confuses, rather than clarifies, the issue. The pay-offs from having such a policy are:

a. You don't have to re-invent the wheel every time you have to compose a graph. Instead, you go through the check-list. All the graphs you produce or edit have a uniform house-style, and you don't forget things (such as credits).

b. Your special effects are few but choice, and consistently and discerningly applied: lift-outs (those wedges taken out of pie-charts for special effect); 3D shadowing effects (when a black shadow underlies the graph, 'raising' it from the page); arrows (when a pie slice is too small to contain its caption); dingbats (emblems identifying the items tallied in a bar graph or whatever).

c. Use of borders and screening is consistent and restrained.

5. Positioning

Your graph is another graphic or picture. So you'll have to position it on a two-page spread so as to maintain the balance of that spread, and it's apt to be the main feature of a 'stand alone page' (the first or last page).

PROCEDURES FOR BUILDING SKILLS IN COMPOSING GRAPHS

Standard recommendations seem to be:

1. Become well acquainted with the graph drawing program that you're using. There's a big demand for graphs, so you'll tend to be too busy to explore more than the essentials of the program (and hence under-use it) unless you discipline yourself to explore all its resources.

2. Develop style guidelines: graphs need them as much as does page layout or typography. Start with the standard recommendations (above) and add and adapt as your circumstances require.

3. Build and maintain a 'swipe file': a collection of impressive graphs that you meet with in your reading. This file can be a rich source of ideas over time.

4. Save all your own graphs; they're often re-usable, with alterations. Keep hard copies of all of them, for quick reference.

5. It pays to acquire at least a small, selective bibliography on constructing graphs, if you have to produce them in any quantity. The literature on creating charts and diagrams, though not extensive, is of good quality, with excellent guidelines on how to go about presenting numbers-intensive material.[16] So you can rapidly become competent at creating graphics of this type.

When and How to Use Algorithms and Flowcharts[17]

WHEN PLAIN ENGLISH IS NOT INTELLIGIBLE

People tend to have difficulty with complex instructions or regulations, no matter how simple the language in which they are expressed. Language gadgets like 'unless', 'except for', 'provided that' are hard enough to follow on their own; in strings they make for formidable difficulties in comprehension.

The logic underlying such strings is that of the branching decision tree or algorithm/flow chart. So, to make such instructions or regulations intelligible, a representation of this branching decision tree should accompany the text: see Diagrams 4. 4 and 4.5.

PAYOFFS FROM USE OF THIS TYPE OF INFORMATIONAL GRAPHICS

This graphic format provides several benefits:

1. It sets the information out in a logical, structured fashion, so that the reader can check that the key criteria have all been included.

2. It enables the reader to discontinue irrelevant lines of thought, lessening the total cognitive load involved in working through the instructions or regulations.

3. It goes through the decisions that have to be taken in the most logical way, thus leading the reader to appropriate solutions with the minimum of intellectual effort.

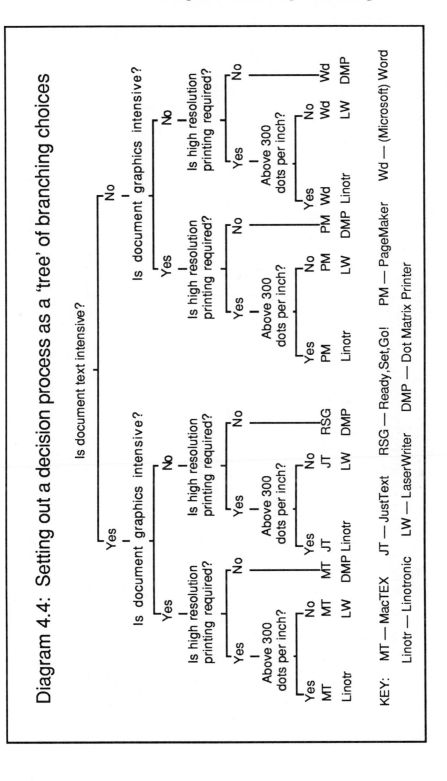

Diagram 4.4: Setting out a decision process as a 'tree' of branching choices

KEY: MT — MacTEX   JT — JustText   RSG — Ready,Set,Go!   PM — PageMaker   Wd — (Microsoft) Word

Linotr — Linotronic   LW — LaserWriter   DMP — Dot Matrix Printer

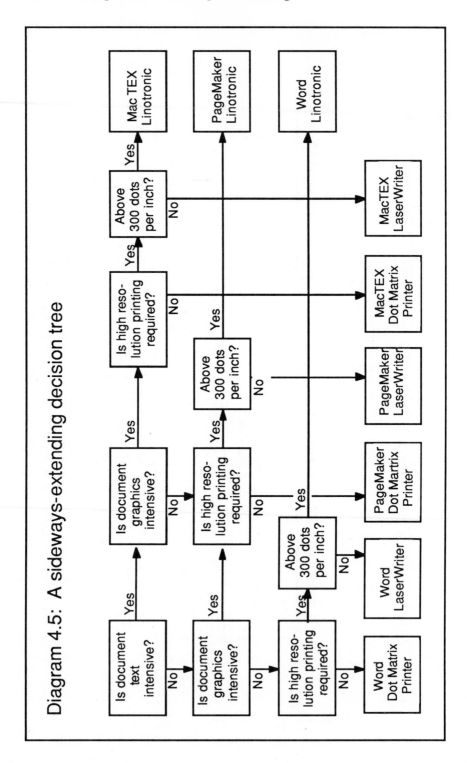

Diagram 4.5: A sideways-extending decision tree

It may be that the downward-running type of decision tree is easier to follow, for most people, than the algorithm with its crossed lines. However, tricks like enclosing the decision end-points with heavier lines make such algorithms easier to follow.

Summing Up

THE TECHNOLOGY

Major changes are currently occurring, very rapidly, in computer graphics. Much more versatile and powerful second-generation drawing programs have recently become available. The resolution capacity of bit-mapped graphics programs has also been much improved. So much higher quality graphics are now possible, and the quality will continue to improve. Also, the library of available computerized art work is increasing, very rapidly, to include object-oriented as well as bitmapped art work.

THE USER PSYCHOLOGY

Desktop publishers are achieving a measure of graphics literacy –a new phenomenon. These changes are cumulative, and will result in many more uses for, and many more users of, computerized graphics. Signs of this new literacy are increasingly in evidence in our survival reading –the reading we must do to keep up-to-date in our fields of expertise. We read specialist magazines or newsletters, often cheaply and quickly produced: they have to be, to reach us fast and frequently.

For easy reading, these are set out in visually informative text layout, and contain numerous infographics. So, too, 'How To' books, which nowadays relate other topics other than technical ones (such as small group communication skills, for instance, or wellness training), now sport many diagrams.

The fact is that certain concepts are more easily expressed with a combination of pictures and words:

1. A social support network, for instance, is better grasped if you have a sociogram to refer to. A sociogram sets out the big picture –the whole, interrelated set of relationships– at a glance, holistically. The text then laboriously and sequentially explains the details. See Diagram 4.6.

2. Likewise, schedules are best explained via a combination of words and diagams. The flow chart gives the big picture, acting as a kind of framework focusing the verbal explanation. The flow chart lets you see, at a glance and holistically, how and where the string of details set out in the text relate to one another.

3. A force field diagram sets out the forces –groups and individuals– ranged pro and con the component parts of an isue, mapping out the alignments and intensities of those forces. Then the narrative plods along, explaining the whys and wherefores in detail.

4. Then there's the 'systems chart', that useful standby when you need to set out the ramifications of a concept. It lets a reader get an overall view of the various subconcepts involved, and of how these relate to one another. Holding this big picture in mind, or referring to it, the reader can follow the complex argument that's needed to explain the concept.

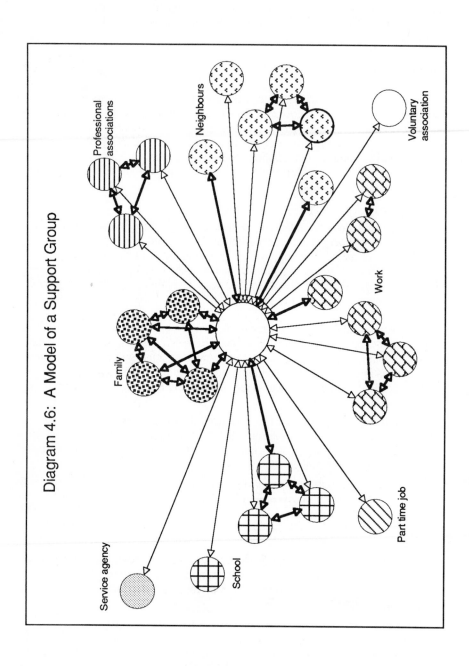

Diagram 4.6: A Model of a Support Group

5 Quality Control over What You Publish:
Content, Format and Copy Editing

Formats Underlying How We Explain and Describe Things
SCRIPTS AND STORY ARCHITECTURE

Two people observing the same event will see a different reality, if the way in which they describe it subsequently is anything to go by. Explanations of how this comes about involve a stimulus : perception : response model. It appears that what I 'see' depends on how I look at things and what I'm looking for. What determines how I do this looking is a 'script' that I've developed.

This script shapes my current understanding of the event that I'm looking at; it's a framework for explaining and describing the event to myself and others. Some of this framework I may have consciously put together; some of it I've unconsciously and unthinkingly taken in.

> Suppose the stimulus I'm looking at is an example of alcoholic behaviour. As I know about the build up of THIQ in some people's brain tissues, I now know that alcoholism really is a disease. But I'm carrying around with me a lot of stereotypes dating from my childhood, and these may unconsciously shape my attitude –and thus my response.

These frameworks of reference are socially constructed: they develop in discussions with the people with whom I habitually talk –people whose judgment I respect.[1] These persons change, as I do, over the years. So the frameworks change, too. Each event that attracts my attention has to be 'made sense of'. Sometimes the framework has to be adapted to fit a particular event into my scheme of understanding.

So I have to make sense of my perceptions in terms both of a mass of these scripts (which are changing over time), and of their background –a network of changing conversational partners (who also are changing over time). I have to keep reconstructing and then re-integrating my various pictures of 'reality' to accommodate continuously incoming, continuously interpreted information. Adapting my scripts is the cognitively economical way of doing all this continuing reconstruction.

IMPLICATIONS FOR EDITORS AND WRITERS

This model of the social construction of reality has important implications for our newsletter editor. If the material she's presenting is to make sense to readers, it must be compatible with the scripts that they're accustomed to.

Material presented in a form that differs radically from the reader's scripts is likely to be perceived as out of touch with reality.

Hence, the wider the audience that you're trying to reach, the more you must format the material in ways –scripts– that are widespread among a great variety of people, and so readily interpretable by them. At least some of these 'ways' have been identified, and their power to inform has been further developed.

THE 'DEEP STRUCTURE' OF STORY FORMS

Writers put this differently. As they see it, underlying any story type is a 'story architecture'. This architecture provides the 'deep structure' of the story: the way of most effectively writing it; the way that strikes a chord in readers' minds, attracting them to it.

There's more to this idea of the deep structure of a story form. We're story-telling creatures.[2] Group participation in reconstructing an event determines how that event is perceived by the group –'what the reality was'.[3] In construct-ing such narratives, we go by 'what makes for a good account'.

There's a logic in good explanations and well-scripted stories. They have to explain things in a way that's inherently probable; they have to be consistent in all their details; they must fit with the personal experience of their listeners –and they must take a form that's worth listening to.

We all know a good explanation/story when we hear one. These accounts have a definite form: an *in*formal logic. It appears that, much of the time, we don't reason by strictly following either inductive or deductive logic (how many syllogisms have you used today –correctly?) Instead, we tend to use a mix of both. Stephen Toulmin's model,which I've adapted slightly, indicates how we do this: Diagram 5.1 illustrates.[4]

How Toulmin's Model Works

1. We reason from data to conclusions (Toulmin's 'claim'), justifying our rea-soning by corroborating evidence (Toulmin's 'warrant').

    For example: 'Pornography (in its sexually sadistic form, not mere eroticism) demeans and endangers women by promoting an atti-tude, in persons habituated to pornography, that regards women as masochistic sex objects.'

2. We'll note exceptions to our our line of reasoning caused by special circum-stances (Toulmin's 'reservation').

    'Unless some other values' –in this case, religious beliefs– 'strong-ly endorsed by a valued reference group cause those exposed to such pornography to reject it.'

3. We'll also indicate the limitations within which our conclusions are likely to hold good (Toulmin's 'qualifier').

    'Depending on the amount of pornography watched and the institu-tionalization, in the viewer's immediate environment, of practices –such as massage parlours and table dancing– which reinforce the message of the pornographic material.'

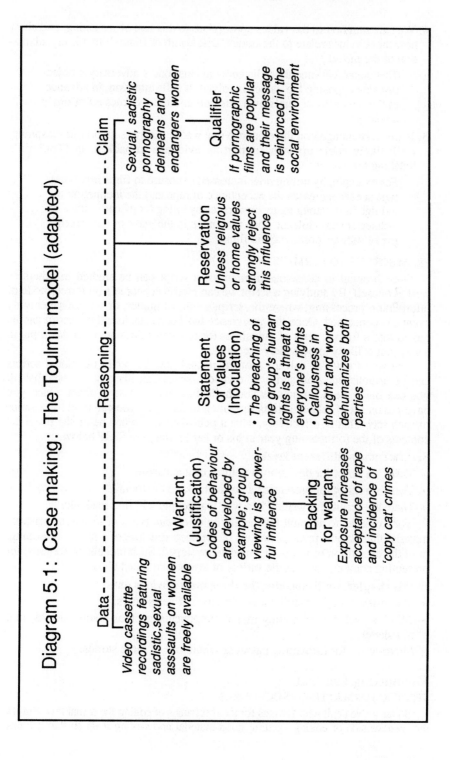

Diagram 5.1: Case making: The Toulmin model (adapted)

Data - - - - - - - - - - Reasoning - - - - - - - - - - - - - - - Claim

Data
Video cassette recordings featuring sadistic, sexual asssaults on women are freely available

Warrant (Justification)
Codes of behaviour are developed by example; group viewing is a powerful influence

Backing for warrant
Exposure increases acceptance of rape and incidence of 'copy cat' crimes

Statement of values (Inoculation)
• The breaching of one group's human rights is a threat to everyone's rights
• Callousness in thought and word dehumanizes both parties

Reservation
Unless religious or home values strongly reject this influence

Claim
Sexual, sadistic pornography demeans and endangers women

Qualifier
If pornographic films are popular and their message is reinforced in the social environment

4. We call attention to the values appropriate to this line of reasoning, and show how these values relate to the issue ('Disclosure of Biases': this is my adaptation of the model.)

> This statement inoculates listeners against one's adversary's objections by exposing the values involved. It calls attention, in advance, to the strengths of one's own position and the weaknesses of one's adversary's.

5. If we're challenged on the evidence that we've used to support our reasoning, we'll likely come up with supporting evidence to back it up (Toulmin's 'backing for warrant').

> For example, by noting how increased exposure to films involving rape scenes increases the acceptance of rape and the inclination to indulge in it among male viewers, or by citing 'copy cat' crimes of sadistic sexual violence done to women in the wake of the screening of sadistic pornographic films.

FROM SCRIPTS TO FORMATTING

Once brought to conscious awareness, a script can be studied in others as well as oneself. By studying a script we can establish people's preferred mode of information processing, where the script's subject matter, or way of perceiving events, is concerned. Once this preference has been established,the script can be turned into a format: a set of guidelines for relaying information on this topic in a way that is likely to be widely accepted.

One script tends to call up another, related one. So *series* of related scripts can be established. And series of related *formats* can likewise be established: you can build these formats as you build formats for a style sheet. Once you have got on set of related scripts formatted in this way, you can plan for a series of such sets. This is, effectively, what a publisher does when he or she plans the contents of the forthcoming year in his or her journal: see SHIP below.

Scripts come at different levels:
- There's a script for designing a volume of a magazine.
- There's a script for presenting a particular kind of story.
- There are scripts for writing in a way that people will find readable.

For example, to account for the ability of certain types of format to generate material that attracts readers, models of the deep structure of a line of reasoning, or of the exposition of a case, have been developed. Such models, or formats, for presenting content, come at the variety of levels mentioned above.

In this chapter, we'll consider the three most obvious ones:
- Macro-level: for formatting a whole series of newsletters.
- Middle-level: for formatting major components, such as feature stories, in a newsletter.
- Micro-level: for formatting passages within one of these stories.

Formatting Content
SPECIFIC FORMATTING PROCEDURES

So far we've dealt with formats for the mechanics of editing the actual text. But it's the *creative* side of editing –getting good material and writing it up so that it holds readers' attention– that finally determines whether a publication attracts and holds readers. There are formats to help in doing this, too. In fact the wider the readership, the more formulaic the product has to be. It's the only way to guarantee that a wide variety of readers, habituated to this kind of formatting, can understand you quickly and easily.

MACRO-LEVEL FORMATS: STORYBOARDING

Possibly the most labour-saving uses of formatting, so far as content is concerned, are involved at this highest level. If a periodical is to attract and hold readers, experience indicates that it must contain certain kinds of information. The acronym SHIP sums them up. There has to be:
- Some form of Service piece (a 'how-to' article).
- A Human interest story (a story about how major developments regarding the periodical's main topic are impacting on the lives of ordinary people).
- An Informational or news piece (an exposé, trend survey or the like).
- A Personality profile (details about the lives of major personalities involved in the topic focused on)[5].

The core of any periodical is five or six such articles. There will also, most likely, be the regular 'housekeeping' departments: sections devoted to the preoccupations of various SIGs (special interest groups) among the membership. As these departments act as outlets through which the SIGs can publish their news, they can generally be relied upon to keep editors supplied with newsworthy items. These departments, together with the SHIP items, make up an issue of the periodical –in this case, the newsletter.

So, with the SHIP categories, and one more –the major pictorial theme for each number of the periodical (often highlighted by one particular picture as a kind of centrefold)– you can make a 'storyboard'. This is what its name implies: a board containing an indication of the stories you need for a year's run of your newsletter.

The status of these stories is indicated in a giant matrix (usually a wallboard, with the matrix formed by vertical & horizontal strips of tape). Along the top are the names of the months. Down the side is the acronym SHIPP (the second P being for the pictorial theme). With such a board, yousee at a glance the months and categories for which you have –and haven't– got material (see Table 5.1).

The regular departments are generally kept supplied with specialized news items, aimed at their particular readerships, by the SIGs. But you'll be well advised to list the departments too. Then you can remind each SIG secretary, in advance, when you need his or her material for the next issue. So you'll want to keep a record of the status of incoming –and outstanding– material on the board. Then you can spot shortfalls at a glance when the deadline for providing material comes up.

MIDDLE-LEVEL FORMATS: STORY ARCHITECTURE

There's another kind of format. It involves story 'architecture', which is equally useful for organizing your writing. Interviews with successful writers, and analyses of successful writing in various genres, have revealed the architecture underlying various types of story. There are now outlines of the principles underlying the writing of each type of story involved in the SHIP acronym, for instance.

Table 5.1: Storyboarding

Monthly issues

Types of article	Jan.	Feb.	Mar.	Apr.	May	Jun.	Jul.	Aug.	Sept.	Oct.	Nov.	Dec.
• Service piece												
• Human interest story												
• Information piece												
• Personality profile												
• Pictorial theme												

KEY:
- Service piece: 'how to' article
- Human interest story: big things happening to little people
- Information piece: trend survey; informational background piece
- Personality profile: little things about big people in the business
- Pictorial theme: motif underlying the photos and/or graphics & artwork

Such outlines make an editor's task much easier when it comes to assessing, or even writing, such pieces. These principles are easy to learn. Before we review them, however, we should first consider an intermediary problem: how to get started on stories of this type. Writing the 'lead' (the opener to these stories) is a difficult task.

So difficult, in fact, that, over the years, a group of micro-level formats has been developed to cope with it. If you know how to use these mini-formats, you'll find the task of writing these SHIP stories –and other journalistic pieces– much easier. So you may chose to jump ahead, to the section on micro-level formats, to read the piece on writing leads before going on to the SHIP stories (which come next).

THE 'HOW-TO PIECE'
(= the 'S' –the Service piece– in SHIP)

These pieces are among the easiest to write. After all, readers are attracted to your newsletter precisely because some of its contents directly address their special problems (such as "How to Get More Use from Your Hard Disk"). So you don't have to win their attention via a sales pitch on the value of the 'how-to' that you're about to divulge. But your lead does have to get to the essence of the problem and quickly explain it.

Example:

"A hard disk is essential for a desktop publisher: the combination of a set of memory-hungry programs and a large volume of text and graphics requires it. Hard disks provide vastly larger amounts of memory, and quicker access to data, than do floppy disks. But hard disks can be incompatible with some of your programs and can function sluggishly if overloaded with data.

Apple introduced a hierarchical filing system (HFS) to cope with the latter problem. But the combination of the new Mac Plus –required to run the new technology– and the HFS on the new hard disk, proved too much for the system-driving software (which also had to accommodate 512K Macs *without* hard disks *and* allow for a new LaserWriter printer).

While the bugs are being worked out of this software, various short-term solutions have been improvised to keep the desktop presses in operation. Here are some of the better solutions: ....".

The above is an analysis of a problem. It consists of a recap lead: a survey of a situation familiar to readers (upgrading of the technology for more memory, speed and ease of use). The twist at the end (a witches' brew of technological fixes made this situation unexpectedly trouble-prone) comes in the general statement of the problem, which focuses attention on What Is To Be Done. Then follows a list of prize solutions, each accompanied by a commentary and appraisal and including quotations from top technical experts.

An informational style of writing is involved: KISS English with homely analogies and straightforward descriptive accounts, accompanied by diagrams and/or illustrations.

THE HUMAN INTEREST STORY
(= the 'H' in SHIP)

This is generally about some kind of disaster: large impersonal forces catching little people unprepared. The disaster may be a hurricane coming unexpectedly and rapidly towards the shore and catching some weekend boaters out at sea. Or it may be structural unemployment devastating a whole community, wrecking the lives of couples in their forties who hadn't seen it coming and whose chances of career switching are slim.

The centre of attention –and the villain of the piece– is the impersonal force. The little people caught up in the situation are there to add human interest and to show the immensity of the forces involved by providing a human scale. Essentially, a multi-track story, with several story lines, has to be managed in print –film manages such things better.

Example:

It's Black Friday: a retirement in force is being carried out at the plant. John Doe, 46, comes home, numb with shock after being laid off, to find that his wife, Jane, a secretary in another company, is also to be laid off. As John and Jane try to plan a new future, its bleakness adds to their shock: neither of their firms is going to survive.

Meanwhile, in a cutaway to the big picture, there's a review of the impact of structural unemployment in their industry, with special reference to one-industry towns like theirs and to middle-aged persons who are laid off.

Then we return to John Doe as he attempts to find alternative employment with obsolescent skills and with more and more fellow workers being laid off. Around him, adding to the economic blight, local property values are plummeting downwards and small businesses are failing. As the situation worsens, John begins to succumb to the usual grim consequences of a hopeless job search: alcoholism, wife beating, deepening depression.

Meanwhile, in another cutaway to the big picture, there's a review of the emergency measures that are being put into effect by the government, itself being drained of tax dollars. The magnitude of the disaster looms appallingly larger, as it dwarfs the government's attempts to retrain and/or relocate huge numbers of laid-off people.

Then back to the man in the street: John is still job hunting, seeking desperately to find a means of economic survival –some days. On his good days, he rallies, holding to a dimly remembered sense of self-worth; but there are many bad days, with their frequent relapses into alcoholism and despair. John and Jane's marriage, like them, is breaking up. Then, beyond hope, Jane, who had done some in-house publishing for her old firm, starts getting odd jobs as a desktop publisher for small businesses, with John helping her by drumming up business.

The problem with this type of story is twofold:

1. How do you manage a multi-track story within a brief narrative frame which effectively only allows of a single storyline?

2. How are you to bring the bewildering mass and complexity of events to an intelligible focus? Remember that you haven't got a lot of space to do it in: you're writing a short article, not a short story.

The solution is:

Select a victim who is in some way typical and present the situation through his or her eyes. The catch in this is that you have to research the whole issue thoroughly before you can tell who is a typical victim.

As the main actor is an impersonal force –a storm, spin-off disasters caused by a new technological fix, or the like– it can't provide a human interest storyline. So the human interest is provided by alternating depictions of the struggles of the main actor's human victims, with cutaways to the big picture: first, factors leading to the disaster, and then, when it occurs, society's struggles to cope with it.

The resulting format is roughly as follows:

- The lead involves a scene-setting event: the storm hits; the lay-offs start –whatever; you choose typical victims and get them caught up in the action. With this type of lead, the story hits the page running, so to speak.

- Then a general statement provides an overview of the disaster: what led up to it, and its ramifying consequences now that it has occurred.

- Then the story goes back to the victims as they struggle to cope, while the disaster engulfing them grows steadily worse. This worsening situation leads them to their darkest hour; they somehow struggle on, hoping beyond hope.

- Then comes a second cutaway to another survey of the big picture, this time achieved by surveying society's attempts to save those in peril from the disaster.

- Next the story returns to the even more desperate victims, to finish on an upbeat note as they somehow escape from their plight.

- A 'What we have learned for the future' note is now struck, to maintain this sense of problems solved/uplift.

THE TREND STUDY
(= the 'I' –the Information piece– in SHIP)

American journalists have made the trend study into something of an art form. American scholars in Journalism have worked out the deep structure, the story architecture, of this art form. The following is a brief account of the format and its rationale.

The main problem, when writing about trends, is the mass, variety and apparent unconnectedness of the data; many subtle changes are occurring in diverse areas. It takes a lot of research to find out what's causing them. Yet you have to grasp this big picture before you can spot the main causative factor –and trend studies must focus on one main causative factor; if you try to explain complicated data in terms of a complex of factors, you merely compound confusion.

The trend study has four component parts.
- There's the lead –normally a bullet lead– and a general statement of the main cause of all the subtle shifts and changes.
- Then there's a description of what's happening,
- an explanation (in psychological, sociological, economic or cultural terms or whatever) of why it's happening,
- and some evaluation of the likely consequences of all these changes.

Known as the DEE model (from the elements of description, explanation and evaluation listed above), this format has the same time sequence –present, past, future– as the personality profile which is discussed next.

In each of the three DEE stages, statistics and quotations occur in a kind of point : counterpoint fashion. The data are accompanied by quotations from the relevant experts. Colourful quotations are sought –contradictory ones, in the stage where the future implications of the trend are being evaluated.

It's estimated that this organization of the format and procedure for writing a trend study can save up to 70% of the time normally taken to research and write one of these pieces.

THE PERSONALITY PROFILE
(= the 'P' in SHIP)

Owed originally to Robert Ruark, this format is brilliantly described by J.T.W. Hubbard, whose work is the basis for the following outline. Diagram 5.2, adapted from Hubbard's, provides an overview of the components of the format and should help you to follow my commentary on it.

> The lead anecdote is easily the most important component in writing a personality profile.

The lead anecdote sets the scene and mood. It's basic to the success of the piece, as it has to grasp the attention of someone who's browsing or skim reading and lure him or her into reading on. The lead anecdote describes an event in the earlier life of the subject of your personality profile, an unusual or startling event that will arouse the curiosity of the reader. This event must exemplify the essence of your subject's personality –as the reader will gradually come to realize.

This lead anecdote is the hardest part of the profile to write. You have to have done a lot of research on your subject before you can identify an incident from his or her life that's perfect for your lead. In fact, the first and last elements in the personality profile are apt to involve as much as a third to a half of all the work involved in the writing the entire piece.

It's best if you've thought out what you're going to use for the last element before you write your lead. Indeed, you may well write all the rest before you write the lead: the main, middle section is much easier to write, being essentially a synopsis of your research.

Having caught you reader's attention, you must persuade him or her to continue reading. You do this by briefly outlining two or three of your subject's accomplishments. These should be chosen so that they all differ one from another, and so that it's hard to see how one person could get involved in such apparently unrelated activities. They lead naturally into an account of what your subject is currently up to –an easy unit to write.

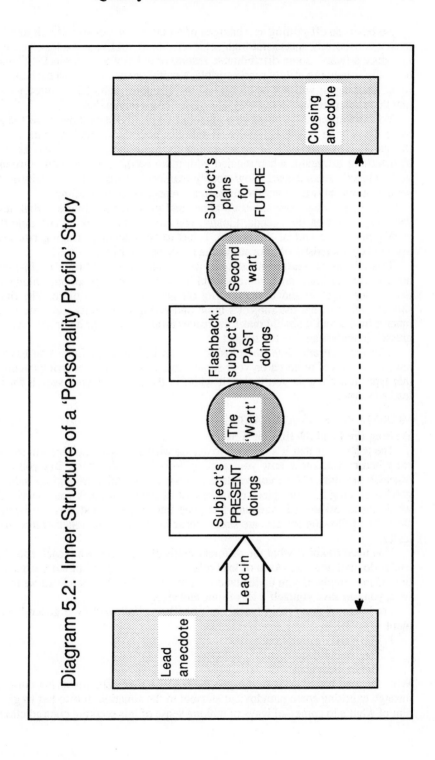

Diagram 5.2: Inner Structure of a 'Personality Profile' Story

No one is so off-putting as a paragon of all the virtues, or so difficult to relate to as a consistently successful high achiever. So, to hold your readers, you now introduce a 'wart': some discreditable feature or habit of your subject's. (This is normally something mildly reprehensible, a moral or social blemish such as vanity or drinking. It will not be a criminal or villainous habit.) Reassured to find that this superman has feet of clay, the reader keeps on reading.

You now insert a flashback to your subject's past, to show how he or she got to be the way he or she is now (wart and all); how the formative years shaped this particular personality. More achievements, most likely. Readers are likely to start turning off again, when regaled with more heroics, so you now introduce your subject's second wart. Now doubly reassured of his or her superiority (in some matters, anyway) over the subject, the reader keeps on reading.

Next you review your subject's hopes and plans for the future –what he or she sees as next on the agenda. Finally, you close with a striking anecdote that clearly marks the end of the profile. It has to be dramatic, bringing out some essential characteristic of your subject in his or her later life.

This closing anecdote isn't easy to write, either It should refer back, somehow, to the lead anecdote; there should be some clear connection, linking the two stories together and thus rounding off and finishing the piece. The finale should further reveal the subject's basic underlying personality, or some major inner growth. And it should make the reader aware of how far he or she has progressed in understanding the subject.

Like the lead anecdote, the closing section isn't easy to find. You have to have done a lot of research on your subject to be able to spot recurring events of this type. It's possible you'll find it while in the throes of your search for the lead anecdote.

MICRO-LEVEL FORMATS, PART 1

Writing the Lead Section for a Story

The problem is that it's difficult to decide what will be a good lead-in to your story before you know how you're going to organize the story. But you can't organize the story before you've decided how you're going to begin. Finding a good beginning for your piece can take half as long as it takes you to write the whole piece. So lots of ingenuity has gone into finding good ways to begin a story. The following formats are simply these bright ideas put together systematically.[6]

You need to know what the different kinds of leads are; what each can –and can't– do, and how each kind of lead relates to different kinds of story organization. Quite simply, if you understand the potential of the lead, and can write one well, you can save yourself a lot of time and effort.

Leads are of three main types, each one being followed by a general statement:

1. The startling assertion.
2. The 'bullet' lead.
3. The indirect lead.

What the lead has to do is to intrigue the reader by arousing his or her curiosity through exposing some paradoxical element in the situation. It also has to give a hint of what's to come –of ways of making sense of this seeming contradiction.

Lead 1: The startling Assertion

Lead no. 1, the startling assertion, may involve an unexpected fact, followed by a general statement about the issues which it raises.

Example:
- Fact: over-25 year-olds are now the biggest group of university students.
- Statement of issue: a smaller proportion of the 18–22 year-old cohort is now choosing to attend university, while a larger proportion of the over-25 year-olds are choosing to come in, or to come back. The implications of our learning society are becoming evident: life-long continuing learning is on the increase; mature, self-directed learners are attending university in unprecedented numbers. But few faculty have the instructional expertise to facilitate the latters' learning appropriately.

The advantage of the startling assertion is that it leads straight into your story. It makes an excellent starter if that story is straightforward. But it's not suited to a complicated story, such as a personality profile or a trend story.

Lead 2: The 'Bullet' Lead

The bullet lead –so-called because it shoots facts at the reader like machine-gun bullets– sets out a series of apparently unconnected facts (usually from 2 to 4.). The reader's curiosity as to how all this hangs together gets him or her to read on and find out. Thus the bullet lead is well-suited for a trend study. After all, the latter involves a pulling-together of a mass of apparently unconnected facts.

Lead no. 3: The Indirect Lead

The indirect lead, approaches the story from an oblique angle. It comes in three varieties: the anecdotal, the scene setting and the 'recap' leads.

- The first of these, as its title suggests, starts with an anecdote; a story about a person, let's say. Initially, this anecdote grabs and holds the reader's attention. Then, as the reader gets into the piece, he or she comes to realize that the anecdote gives fundamental understanding of the personality of the subject of the story.

  This type of lead makes an excellent introduction to a personality profile. The only snag is that you have to be very familiar with the person's life history before you can pick out one incident with this kind of insight.

- Alternatively, the lead may be an story which sets the scene for the piece that's to follow. Not as intriguing as the anecdotal lead, this 'scene-setter' lead is, however, easier to find and to write.

- Lastly, there's the 'recap'. This recapitulates, or goes over, a situation that has developed, generally a well-publicized situation. It's a story that ends with an unexpected twist (your generalized statement). This twist –an unexpected way of looking at the situation– is developed as the theme for the piece that follows. This is a highly effective lead, if you can re-conceptualize the conventional wisdom about an issue that's much talked about.

MICRO-LEVEL FORMATS, PART 2

Readability Formulae: Sentence and Word Length

By readability is meant the ease with which the meaning of a passage can be construed by a reader.[7] This depends on a variety of factors, the most important of which is the combined use of long words and long sentences. So readability formulae have been developed, to monitor the level of clarity of expression. They have come to constitute yet another type of formatting device, at the micro level of composition.[8]

> Of the 1,000 commonest words in English, only 36 are more than two syllables long; and only 4% of the commonest 300 are of more than three syllables.

Readability formulae are based on a measure of average sentence length and the number of words of 3 syllables or more in those sentences. Gunning's 'Fog' index[9] is a well known formula; it works as follows:

1. You pick several passages at random from the text whose readability you wish to assess. Count off 100 words in each passage and continue counting to the end of the final sentence. Divide this number of words by the number of sentences that they contain. This gives you the average sentence length in each passage.

2. Now count all words of three syllables or more. Ignore proper names, compounds made up of simple components (for instance, 'hard-to-get-at', as opposed to 'inaccessible'), and verbs which are three syllables long only

> To get some idea of the implications of this research, consider the following. At 16 words, on the average, per sentence, and 150 syllables per 100 words, you've lost 24% of your potential readers. At 18 words and 160 syllables, you've lost 48% of them. At 22 words and 170 syllables, you've lost 76%. *Reader's Digest* averages 14–17 words per sentence; *Time* averages 17–19.

because of the endings -ed, -es, or -ing. This gives you the number of difficult words in each passage.

Divide this number by the total number of words in the passage, to get the percentage of hard words.

3. Add the figure for the average sentence length to the percentage of hard words; then multiply by 0.4. The result is Gunning's Fog Index. It's expressed in school reading levels; so a '12' means twelve years of school education.

A score of 13 or over indicates writing that's too difficult for most people. *Reader's Digest* scores 10; *Time* and *Newsweek* score 11. The (now no longer existing) *Atlantic Monthly* and *Harper's* scored 12. No popular magazines score 13 or more.

Computer programs are available which can calculate a variety of readability scores for you. A wise editor will aim to write at a level that's slightly below the reading level indicated by the average reader's years in school. People are most comfortable when reading somewhat below the top level at which they can read. Writing slightly below this top level is readily forgiven (when noticed); writing above it is always taken amiss.

Readability Formulae: Paragraph Planning and Structure

Other features too can make for difficult reading. Long paragraphs are notorious for doing so. Actually it's not easy always to construct paragraphs of an ideal length (which seems to be from 5 to 7 lines) while steadily and clearly advancing your argument. Paragraphs are like a flight of stairs. Each should be built around a single idea. Each should move your argument or exposition along a single step. Overall, the progression of the ideas that they represent should be obvious.

All this requires a good deal of planning, at two levels. First, at the conceptual level, you make a dummy of your argument, just as you make a dummy of your layout. The obvious way to do this is by roughing out what you're trying to say via a spoke diagram or mind map –a procedure that takes very little time. Number the arrows of the diagram and convert it into an outline. Then write this outline up, one paragraph per main sub-idea (cluster of arrows) in the diagram.

Now you need to plan the structure of each paragraph. It's best to start with a topic sentence, one that announces the paragraph's theme. You'll need two or three more sentences to explain and illustrate this theme. Short paragraphs of one to two sentences simply aren't up to doing this. They tend to move your argument along jerkily. Most readers dislike them; some readers are irritated by them.

Readability: Choice of Words, Sentence Types and Range of Punctuation

There's more to readability than this KISS (Keep It Sort and Simple) formula, however, as the discussion on algorithms in the last chapter indicated. Besides, slavish adherence to *any* formula makes writing dull. To keep your writing lively, you should:

1. Use strong and vigorous words and use intelligible compounds rather than their multisyllabic alternatives: choose 'to-the-point' rather than 'unconvoluted', for instance.

2. Prefer the verb and noun, respectively the first and second strongest parts of speech, to the adjective and adverb. The latter tend to suggest value-judgments. But, besides this, frequent use of words acting as qualifiers tends to make writing appear finicky. 'Power speech' is more direct.[10] Power speech commands attention, finicky writing doesn't.

3. Prefer active to passive verbs, concrete to abstract nouns and positive to negative expressions (that is, "Do this, or you'll find that.." rather than "Unless you do this, you'll find that..").

4. Write in the natural subject-verb-object order, and keep sentences short; 16 to 18 words is a good average length to aim for. But beware of writing a series of short sentences. They make it appear that you're writing down to your readers, and this will be taken as an insult.

To avoid this, use a variety of long and short sentences and simple and more compound sentence forms. Semi-colons allow you to use compound –coordinate– sentences while keeping readability easy. The occasional complex sentence is inevitable when you're involved in explanations. The complex sentence, after all, was designed for subordination of one idea to another.

Another feature of writing that makes for difficult reading is punctuation. Most people tend to overuse certain punctuation marks and underuse certain others. Overused are:

- Brackets: many readers dislike them when they occur in quantities.

  There are exceptions to this, of course. For instance, where technical writing is involved, clarity has to come first, and may involve frequent bracketed asides, containing definitions or brief illustrations.

- Dashes: when these are overused, the writer gives the impression of being scatterbrained.

- Exclamation marks and question marks: the former tend to be perceived as hysterical, and the latter as histrionic.

Underused are:

- Hyphens: these allow you to make compound words from simple components, as in 'difficult-to-argue-with', instead of 'incontrovertible'.

- Colons: these are perceived as businesslike; their most frequent use is for point form expressions.

- Semi-colons: these effectively make a long sentence into two short ones. This allows use of long as well as short sentences, which makes the writing style more varied without raising the readability score: for more on this point, see below.

  Use of the full range of punctuation marks is advisable: they were each invented for a purpose. They indicate relationships between the thoughts that you are expressing, making it possible for you to write more simply. They're the equivalent of non-verbal language in speech.

Formatting of text:

As we've seen, the layout of your text blocks is critically important. Visually informative text (VIT) goes with readability formatted writing. VIT makes emphases, key passages and asides stand out at a glance.

  Point form sentence fragments are possibly the commonest way in which the VIT format can help to make a text's content immediately intelligible.

In this way, VIT lessens the need for difficult vocabulary and complex sentence structure to get complex ideas across.

Readability: The Human Interest Element and Coorientation

People find what interests them easiest to read. To generate interest, whatever your topic, make people, rather than abstractions, the subjects and objects of your sentences. Provide plenty of illustrations, verbal as well as graphic, of what your abstractions mean. Generalizations without explanatory illustrations are a major reason why readers fail to follow what a writer is trying to say.

Actually, coorientation, as getting on the same wavelength as your reader is termed, is a difficult feat. You're unlikely to manage it on your own. It's advisable to find someone like your target reader. Have him or her read your piece critically before you typeset it. Keep rewriting until this representative of your targeted readership understands the piece as you want your target reader to understand it.

This representative of your targeted readership should be asked to do you an additional service, by reading between the lines of your writing for 'metamessages'. A piece of writing always sends implicit messages. Simple, everyday words, set out in clear sentences, 'say' that you want, first and foremost, to get the point across. Multi-syllabic words, set in complicated sentences, 'say' that you're either trying to show off your knowledge or that you're woolly in your thinking. Your reader should alert you to passages which convey these and other undesirable impressions.

Simplicity combined with the occasional well-turned phrase is what attracts readers. Currently, the way to pique readers' interest is by giving a subtle twist to a common expression, completely altering its meaning. Such feats, like producing simple yet hard-hitting writing, aren't easy to manage. As with a concert pianist, so with a writer; practice pays.

As all of the above commentary indicates, reader-friendly writing involves a lot of effort. Many people don't want to admit it, but the undeniable bottom line is: quickly-dashed-off writing makes for difficult reading.

Developing Your Own In-house Copy Editing Primer
THE NEED FOR CONSISTENCY IN COPY EDITING

As we've seen where typography, page makeup, and business graphics were concerned, there must be consistency behind one's presentation. Inconsistencies indicate sloppiness; they're non-professional, and they're ruinous of trust in the editor's commitment and competence. The reader may not consciously critique the whole piece. But, unconsciously, he or she just won't treat it seriously.

Providing this consistency is what copy editing is all about. Producing text which is consistent in all its details is the hallmark of a competent editor. It's no easy task when you're editing newsletters: they're complicated, and writing tends to come in, in a rush and from a variety of writers, just before your deadline.

To maintain standards in such a situation, you need a copy editing manual or style sheet.[11] Copy editing is largely concerned with (a) punctuation marks, (b) typographical matters and (c) words that can be correctly handled in more than one way. It's the editor's job to see that such items are presented in a uniform way.

"Easy," you're thinking, "–just use a manual on editorial style." Actually, this isn't a very practical solution. There *are* copy editing manuals which set out what a good established style is. But they're not easy to use. You've got to work out what the particular instance confronting you is an instance of, before you can find out from the manual how to handle it.

English is a language that's unusually rich in alternative ways of expressing things. And it has come together over a long time, from a multitude of sources and peoples. So its ways of doing things have historical, rather than logical, reasons behind them.

This means that there are generally several ways of classifying any one item. And that means long searches through the manual's indices before you find the right classification. Besides, no one style manual will cover all instances that can come up. Some of the complexities involved can be seen from even the briefest review of the literature:

Brief Literature Review

Major reference works:

The standard reference is *The Chicago Manual of Style* (University of Chicago Press; the 1982 version was the thirteenth edition). But even this master work, product of a press which has produced thousands of learned books on a myriad topics, isn't adequate. You'll need supplements, such as the *U.S. Government Printing Office Style Manual* (Washington, D.C.: Government Printing Office, 1984). This deals with technical terms, hyphenated compounds and standard abbreviations.

Most large publishers generate their own copy editing manuals. For instance, Prentice-Hall has produced a writer's guide for issue to its prospective writers: the *Prentice-Hall Author's Guide* (Englewood Cliffs, NJ: Prentice-Hall, whatever the year of the current edition is). This gives guidance on such things as writing style, quotation practices and libel, as well as copy-editing-type matters. The Washington Post's 'manual' has been published: R.A. Webb, *The Washington Post Deskbook on Style* (NY: McGraw-Hill, 1978). This book gives advice on writing standards and ethics, legal issues, matters of taste, and so on, as well as copy editing. It's brief, inexpensive, and very readable.

Specifically on copy editing is K. Judd, *Copyediting: A Practical Guide* (Los Altos, CA: Kaufman, 1982), a book which provides a thorough coverage of copy editing. M.E. Skillin & R.M. Gay, *Words into Type* (Englewood Cliffs, NJ: Prentice-Hall, 1974) is a minor classic, which gives guidelines on setting out a book as well as on copy editing.

Back-up books that you'll find useful (for writing as well as for copy editing):

- The classic *Roget's Thesaurus* (Harmondsworth, Middlesex: Penguin; whatever the current reprint is). This comprises collections of words by theme, all exhaustively cross-referenced. It's the forefather of the thesaurus that comes with the spelling checker in your word processing program.
- A.F. Sisson's *Sisson's Word and Expression Locator* (West Nyack, NY: Parker, 1972) is a dictionary in reverse. You use it when you know the thought that you're trying to express, but don't know the word for it. Sisson's book will locate the word for you. It also enables you to locate a famous quotation when you can only remember roughly the gist of what was in it.

  "Overkill," you're thinking, "–I don't need such resources for my little newsletter." You're right.

CREATING YOUR OWN COPY EDITING GUIDELINES

The reality is that you won't have time for such searches in the few hours before the newsletter has to be made up for the printer. Editorial style manuals are too cumbersome to use under such circumstances.

Besides, you don't need such elaborate bibliographical resources. All you need is to achieve consistency. So you can make your own little 'manual'.

Use a set of 5" X 3" file cards with tabbed sections, starting with some of the categories suggested below and adding others if you need them. In general, use a separate card for each contingency, and where possible, arrange cards numerically or alphabetically within their sections. Choose which form of expression you prefer, note your choice on the card, and then do only that in future.

There are only a limited number of items which can be expressed in more than one way. They won't all come up at once or straight away. So you can build your card indices around these items, as follows, *gradually*.

Copy Editing Guidelines in the Form of a Card Index

1. Numbers: 'Seven' or '7'? 'A half' or '1/2'? 'Per cent' or '%'? '7,000' or '7000'? 'One and a half megabytes' or '1.5 megabytes'? 'fifty billion to sixty billion' or '50–60 billion'?

2. Compound words: the question is when to hyphenate. Dictionaries disagree; but there are rules, based on whether the hyphenation makes for added comprehension.

3. Alternative spellings of a word: your spelling checker may help you by providing you with the option of using its American or its British dictionary. But there are still choices: 'formulae' or 'formulas'? 'kidnapper' or 'kidnaper'?

4. Abbreviations and acronyms: 'Calif'. or 'CA'? 'I.B.M.' or 'IBM'?

5. Foreign words: are you going to include their accents? Put them in italics?

6. Proper names and place names: decide on a case by case basis.

7. Miscellaneous. One card should suffice for each of these categories, as there won't be many queries:

   a. *Punctuation*:

   The series comma. In a list of three or more items, are you going to write "database management, spreadsheets and word processing" or "database management, spreadsheets, and word processing"?

   Apostrophes: are you going to use s-apostrophe or s-apostrophe-s –'Jones' or Jones's?

   b. *Emphasizing words*: are you going to use *italics*, small capitals, **bolding**, **bolded italics**, or 'ALL CAP(ital)S'?

   c. *Footnotes and bibliographies*: decide on a standard format for your entries.

   Note: Also record where the computer style sheet resides. Then remember to use these formats in your page makeup style sheet.

8. Principles governing your decisions. As your indices grow, you'll find it convenient to develop rules from the specific choices that you've been making. Keep these in a section of their own.

CREATING YOUR OWN COPY EDITING MANUAL

Your work will bring you in contact with only a limited range of the above copy editing problems. After the burst of activity when you start your card indices up, there will be only a small, steady trickle of new items.

The advantage of building your own card indices is that you'll be able to find things in them quickly and easily.

If you keep a copy of everything on disk, your collection of card indices can easily be printed out as a small manual, should your operation get large or complicated enough to require it. You can also use the work that you do in building your copy editing guidelines to customize your computer software, as follows:

- Add a special dictionary to your spelling checker.
- Add an exceptions dictionary to your hyphenation checker.
- Save the formats you develop, by putting them in your style sheet, glossary, key board enhancer, or wherever you stow such things.

> Work done on copy editing completes and rounds off your other editing activities –as it has completed and rounded off this chapter.

6 Desktop Publishing and Networking:
Cooperative Writing Teams and Group Composition

Editing and Networking
NETWORKING: YET ANOTHER SKILL REQUIRED IN DESKTOP PUBLISHING

A desktop publisher has to be competent, as we've seen, in typography, production of graphics and page make up. As an editor, he or she has to know appropriate formats for writing up materials of different kinds, as well as having copy editing know-how.

The newsletter was chosen to illustrate the complex of skills needed in desktop publishing because it is a common assignment; yet it makes extremely exacting demands of the desktop publisher. It has an extremely varied mix of features; it requires complex layouts; and securing a continuous flow of quality material, while under constant deadlines, is an onerous task.

This last task requires yet another kind of skill, over and above those so far mentioned: skill in networking. So we'll end our review of the skills needed by a desktop publisher by considering the networking involved in publishing a newsletter.

SOCIAL SUPPORT IN ONE'S RECONSTRUCTION OF REALITY

As indicated in chapter 5, 'reality' is socially constructed. If you're thinking of making a major change in your lifestyle –pondering whether to buy a computer, let's say– you'll consult a number of sources of information. Some of these will be people. Some will be printed materials (such as the *Whole Earth Software Catalog*, which annually lists and rates recommended microcomputer hardware, software, books and journals, suppliers, and services).

The more complex or technical the innovation, the more difficult it is to find the kinds of people whom you need to consult. In fact, the only place you're likely to find them is in the pages of a specialized publication concerned with such innovations. So the editor of such a publication has to build an editorial board which can act as such a reference group for readers.

Something is now known about how innovations spread and how social support groups function. So editorial boards can be built to incorporate the kinds of expertise, and to function in the kinds of ways, known to facilitate the type of support that readers need. There are principles involved, so that you can quickly learn what has to be done. These principles are set out in what follows.

WHAT READERS WANT FROM A NEWSLETTER: A CASE STUDY

Imagine that you have to make an important decision: whether to adopt a complex new technology –the computer, let's say– in your work. If you're like most people, you'll seek advice before deciding. Diagram 6.1 provides a general outline of what happens;[1] it may be helpful to refer to it while reading the following discussion.

The Social Construction of Reality in Practice

Your initial mind set is critical. Particularly important are the following: your attitude to risk taking and problem-solving skills; your value system (you'll have to give up many things to become proficient in this technology); your intellectual ability; how much you're 'in the know', and your views on the importance of 'keeping up to date'.

Interacting with this mind set, influencing it and being influenced by it, is your perception of the situation. What's involved here are things like the degree to which your organization and your social set accept innovations; the extent to which the economy requires (or can't afford) them, and the general conditions in your profession/industry.

You may come to feel that you should check this computer business out. This feeling makes you notice computer-related messages among the barrage of media-borne messages that bombard you everyday. As a result of your heightened sensitivity to these messages, you'll likely seek out a book or a specialist journal for in-depth study. Someone in your group will find out what you should read.

Your interest by now aroused, you seek out the person in your reference group who 'knows something about computers'. He gives you some general guidance, then suggests that you go and talk to someone who, ahead of the rest of the people at work, has already started using a computer there. With this innovator coaching you, you try out a personal computer on a task you've been thinking of using it for: spreadsheeting, let's say.

All the time you've been gathering information, you've been considering the advantages and disadvantages of buying your own personal computer. What use will you get out of it? How hard will it be to master? Will it fit your working habits? Can you try before you buy? You talk to the person at work who specializes in getting people up to speed on personal computers; she knows a lot about how these machines can be useful in your working environment.

Let's suppose that you finally decide to buy a machine. After buying it, you fall prey to the usual second thoughts that follow any major decision. Would you have done better to buy a different kind of machine? Maybe the money could have been better spent on the house, and so on (and on...). You find a group to talk these problems over with; typically, this is the user group for the type of machine that you've bought. Not only do they quiet your doubts –they become your new reference group. Imperceptibly, you too become a believer.

Information Brokers We Rely On –and Where We Find Them

We construct our realities socially: we talk to significant others in our lives when taking an important decision. These others provide different kinds of information, for people play special rôles within their groups. See Diagram 6.2.

For instance, when you were initially thinking of making a change in your way of looking at things, you probably sought out someone more in the know

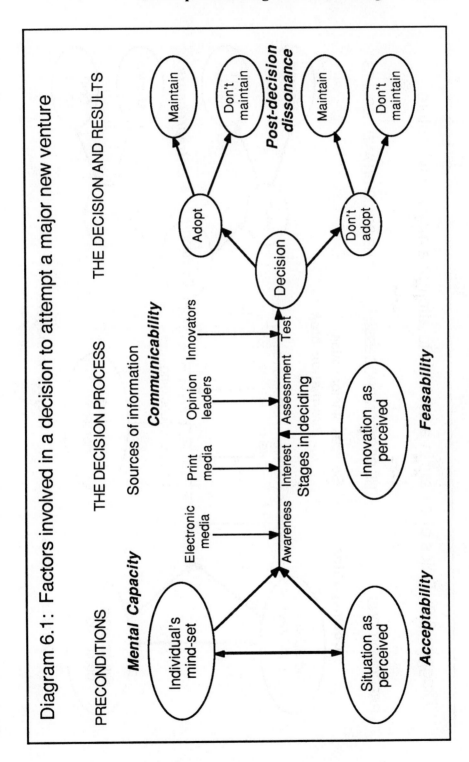

Diagram 6.1: Factors involved in a decision to attempt a major new venture

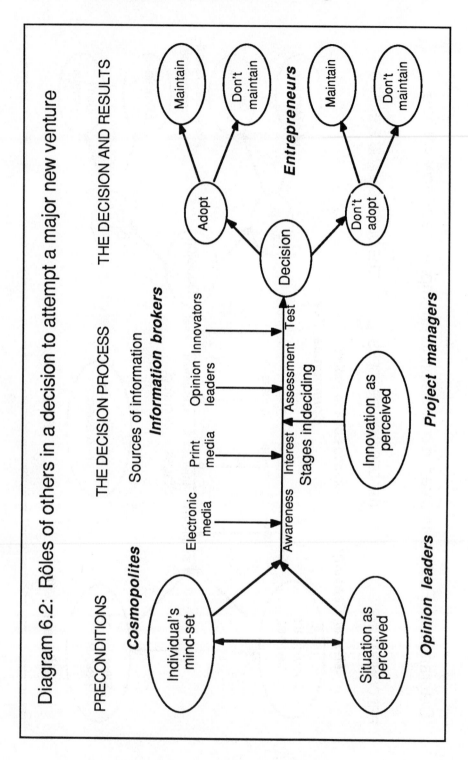

Diagram 6.2: Rôles of others in a decision to attempt a major new venture

than yourself: a 'cosmopolite'. Cosmopolites tend to be somewhat marginal to in-house in-groups. Their set of acquaintances may be scattered across several countries, extending right across 'the trade'. These are people whom the cosmopolites meet at the conferences that they're always going to. So cosmopolites can give you the trends, the big picture.

The local opinion leader, the person who's at the centre of your group's social activities (and much else), is the person who'll be able to tell you how acceptable it will be to your group if you make this change. The person who found out for you 'what the book to read is' would be a 'liaison' –an information broker. Liaisons are connected with, but not part of, many groups; they're generally accepted because of the information they can get and will trade.

That person who was in the know about computers would be a task-oriented group leader, possibly a supervisor –someone well known for being the person to work with when you want to get a job done. For this job, you chose a task-oriented computer freak. He knew enough about the field to identify someone who was using the personal computer innovatively at your level.

This innovator probably wasn't exactly 'in' your group. Innovators are almost never insiders in groups. They're always into something new; and half the time they're on the wrong track. So people mistrust their judgment. Instead, the group relies on its opinion leaders (social or task-oriented) to tell them when an innovator is on to something. Then the group's early adopters get on to it too.[2] The early adopters are followed, after a judicious interval, by the late adopters –and there are generally some diehards, who refuse to follow.

The person whom you spoke to, to check out how useful a personal computer would be in your work situation, would be someone like the micro-manager at the organization's information centre. She's a task-oriented leader who's expert at getting more done for the organization by getting the right people into micro-computing. Not necessarily knowing too many details about how computers work, and not fanatical about any one make of computer, she knows what the different machines are useful for on the job.

Finally, the bigger the decision, the more options are foreclosed by taking it; so the bigger the post-decision misgivings and second thoughts. We normally lay these to rest by talking things over with others who've made this same decision before us. Their considered opinion generally quiets our unease: our perception that we took the decision that was best in the circumstances is reinforced by theirs. Finding kindred spirits is a heart-warming process. We'll find lots of them in the user group associated with our brand of personal computer.

Building A Masthead
THE EDITORIAL BOARD AS REFERENCE GROUP FOR READERS

What has all this got to do with the newsletter editor? A great deal. Few of us can put together a full complement of such highly informed specialists in more than one or two areas. So, for the other areas, we turn to specialized periodicals to find them. A newsletter provides a reference group, or rather, a network of significant others, in print.

For us as readers, newsletters provide the society of minds that we can rely on for reconstructing our reality when this involves important changes to it. For the newsletter editor, the SHIP format provides guidelines as to what kinds of informants readers need for this society of minds. The format guarantees a mix of cosmopolites, liaisons, task-oriented leaders, and opinion leaders, in the know about acceptance of trends. It's a format that has made specialist journals hugely successful. Reread your favourite newsletter or periodical to see how many different kinds of information purveyors appear in it.

TYPES OF INFORMATION PURVEYORS NEEDED

What a newsletter editor has to do is build an editorial board that provides readers with a variety of information purveyors. Needed are:

1. Someone who sees the big picture of what's going on in the field and what's likely to be coming up in it: *a cosmopolite*.
2. Someone who has a feeling for the socio-cultural and cultural implications of what's going on: *an opinion leader*.
3. Someone with real expertise in the technology of the field: *a task-oriented expert*.
4. Someone with experience in managing the field's technology so as to get results: *a task-oriented leader*.
5. Someone in the know about personalities and events in the field, who can find answers to out-of-the-way questions: *a liaison* (the archetypal gossip columnist).
6. A variety of leading-edge practitioners, identified by your liaison, for special purpose assignments: *innovators*.

Also important are the 'departments' within your newsletter that are concerned with in-house events. They keep readers informed about what's going on in the organization and why, by telling them:

• who's done what, and what its significance for the organization is;
• what's going on, and why;
• what the competition/customers/suppliers/regulators are up to;
• what's happening in the various technologies on which the organization relies.

THE ROLE OF THE MANAGING EDITOR

As the newsletter's managing editor, you are a key informant about the affairs of the supergroup –the organization or association with which you and your readers identify. Such an informant has to give readers the bad news as quickly as the good. That's how you build their trust.

They should, ideally, read the bad news in the pages of your newsletter before it appears in the local media. This is only possible if you're running a weekly in-house newsletter (an in-house, *electronic* newsletter is even better) that can be produced quickly –even ahead of schedule in a crisis.

A newsletter gives its readers a sense of belonging. It provides a communication network spanning the whole organization, something that no one person can construct alone:

1. It gives the organization the feeling of being a 'neighbourhood', with its classified ads and notices of sporting events or other off-site activities.
2. It sets events in a stream of past, present and future activities, so that readers can get into the swim of things.
3. Its 'Letters to the Editor' and the replies to these letters give readers a sense that somebody up there cares, and will go out and get information to respond to their concerns.

Securing material for a newsletter is an unending struggle. A team of people with diverse kinds of information (or leads to it) is required. The names of the members of this team constitute your 'masthead'. The variety of designations for such informants –consulting-, contributing-, 'theme-' or visiting-editors, stringers, and so on– reflect the ingenuity needed to build an effective masthead. To do such building, an editor has to be knowledgeable about the topic on which the publication is focused.

Modems make it possible to use contributors, consultants and stringers who live at great distances from the editor, if they and the editor can handle this technology (or can find intermediaries who can do so). In this way computerized telecommunications provide even small newsletters with access to a talent pool that simply wasn't open to them before modems existed.

'Trans-team Building': Building A Board of Directors

BUILDING SUPPORT GROUPS

The model outlined in Diagrams 6.1 and 6.2 shows the diverse skills needed in a team that has to get an organization-wide job done. Identifying people with these skills and making a team out of them is called 'trans-team building' because you have to pull people together from all over the organization to do it.

For your board of directors, you don't need an informational network –your masthead provides that; what you need is an in-house power base to advance and protect your newsletter's interests. If you 'trans-team build' your board of directors, you can tie your newsletter into your organization's power structure.

You choose these people for their communication skills, so they will appreciate the potential of a newsletter and be natural supporters. Choose the right mix, and you can cover all the bases, providing your newsletter with a godfather, an early warning system and connections to the organization's inner circles of power. Diagram 6.3 illustrates what –and who– is involved.

One new term in this diagram –*gatekeeper*– refers to someone whose official position is such that he or she controls the flow of information down into his or her department from above, and up and out of it from below. Normally this person is the head of a unit, section or department in an organization. (The term comes from studies of the influence of newspaper editors.)

TYPES OF NEWSLETTERS: THE DIFFERENCE IT MAKES TO THE EDITOR

How much freedom you'll have to build your own board of directors depends largely on the type of newsletter that you're editing. Normally, the bigger your budget, the smaller your control over who gets on the board. Broadly speaking, there are three levels of newsletter:

Big budget operations:

Representative of this type is the weekly newsletter in newsprint –virtually a newspaper– for a giant organization, such as a university campus of 50,000 persons and a large number of interested outsiders.

In such cases, the newsletter editor has to keep defining and redefining, for both insiders and outsiders, what the organization is, in that he is reporting what its current goals and activities are. The editor is frequently involved, along with appropriate committees, in major policy decisions about public relations matters.

Editors of such big operations are normally chosen because of their background in public relations. This is usually a very senior position. Such editors

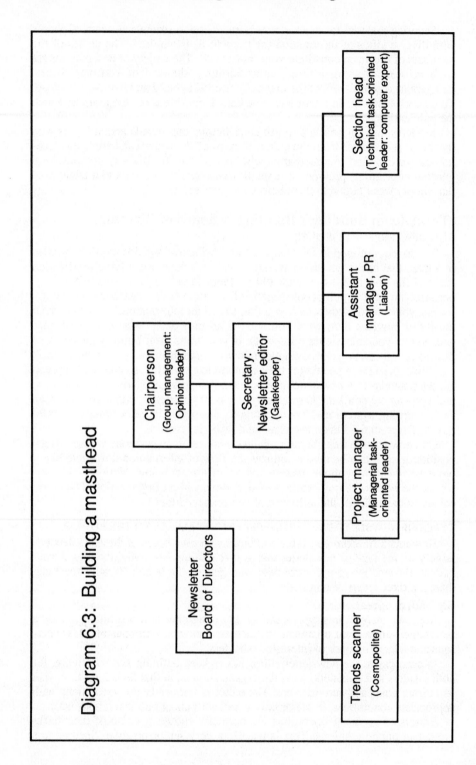

Diagram 6.3: Building a masthead

Newsletter Board of Directors

Chairperson
(Group management: Opinion leader)

Secretary: Newsletter editor
(Gatekeeper)

Trends scanner
(Cosmopolite)

Project manager
(Managerial task-oriented leader)

Assistant manager, PR
(Liaison)

Section head
(Technical task-oriented leader: computer expert)

are not likely to be practising desktop publishers themselves. But they are likely to introduce their staff to desktop publishing, in order to:

1. Save time and money via in-house page make up (sending the made-up copy outside for final printing).
2. Improve their staff's morale and upgrade their skills by helping them acquire computing skills.

Medium-sized operations

Representative of this type are newsletters with a circulation of several thousand. They're usually in-house publications –mini-magazines– for large organizations or well established, national associations. These operations have adequate funding.

In these cases, the editor's primary tasks are to:

1. Provide information about the doings and future prospects of the organization and its competitors.
2. Maintain and develop his or her readers' sense of identification with, and identity within, the organization.

Many of these editorships have been quite recently established. Only recently have organizations come to realize the importance of communicating with their members frequently and freely in print. This realization has grown as the development of the desktop publishing technology has made it ever easier to do so.

Generally, the editors of these newsletters got their jobs because they once, as a sideline, ran a modest newsletter for their division or whatever (on-site news and events, in a multilithed form). Such persons tend to be the ones promoted to run the newer, frequently appearing, large-circulation, professionally printed newsletters. They have acquired desktop publishing skills, mostly, for two reasons:

1. To keep costs down.
2. To meet production schedules that often involve last-minute alterations or additions.

   This type of editor is likely to be a hectically busy desktop publisher.

- Typically, associations which are newcomers to the desktop publishing of newsletters soon expand their range of publications into things like books, curricula, and manuals. So their editors have to expand their editing and publishing skills.
- Typically, too, this editorial position is high in 'visiposure': visibility to important persons, and exposure, via task force membership, to people with in-demand expertise.

   So this kind of editorship can act as a career springboard, if you have networking skills.

Small scale operations

Representative of this type are newsletters which serve to build and then to maintain a special interest group (SIG). They're rarely well-funded, and their editors are usually involved in a search for advertising income to help finance the newsletter.

The primary purpose of such newsletters is the provision of information for members. Editing such a newsletter is usually a disheartening business; where a small-budget operation is concerned, securing advertising often costs more than the ads return in revenue.

The editor is usually chosen because he or she has the desktop publishing hardware and software and the skill to use it. He or she is a valued, overworked and unpaid member of the organization's governing body. The job is generally an avocation, often an avocation that blights the editor's regular career. It takes time, money and energy that would otherwise have gone into career advancement.

The Career Death Wish:

Opting for, or being cajoled into, service as desktop publisher for voluntary or professional associations is apt to lead to exploitation without appreciation or recognition. And, once you're recruited, it's resented if you attempt to quit the long hours of drudgery that result.

Unless such an editorship is likely to lead to a career position in desktop publishing, you would be well advised to think long and hard before becoming involved in it. There's a high risk of being exploited. Few others will volunteer to replace you in such a dead end assignment, yet association members will take it amiss if you defect, even after long service. It's all too easy for a desktop publisher to end up slaving away in a hidey-hole somewhere, his or her services taken for granted and going generally unrecognized.

ELECTRONIC NEWSLETTERS AND DESKTOP PUBLISHING

These are the obvious extensions of the medium and small scale newsletters A variety of electronic publications is involved here:

The electronic journal

Electronic journals are usually prestige publications outlets for academic or writers' associations. They have a board of recognised contributors: writers of some reputation, who have been further 'recognised' by admission to the journal's board of contributors. Only recognised board members can contribute to the journal. Often several writers compose interactively on the board from their distant sites. Association members can watch articles coming together in this way, and 'download' material (copy it to their own micros via modem) for a small fee.

Few other types of associations are wealthy enough to support the editing of an electronic journal: they're really for writers. Besides, relatively few computer users have modems. Those who do have them normally band together into small SIGs (special interest groups). They're usually heavy users of a variety of electronic bulletin boards. These people keep one another informed by using the electronic mail service of their organization's mainframe computer. They can find their way around *any* bulletin board's announcement boards; they don't need an electronic newsletter.

The electronic newsletter

The electronic newsletter is much more common. This is simply information provided weekly, and posted in-house, on an electronic bulletin board running off the organization's mainframe or minicomputer. In these cases, the editor keeps an electronic bulletin board replenished with association or organization news. The board itself is generally maintained and cleaned up (that is, obscenities that are inserted get removed) by a technical expert, the 'sysop' (system operator).

In-house electronic bulletin boards are frequently used: it's easy, and inexpensive for organizational members to access the board at any time, via the mainframe, through their personal computers as well as their office terminals. Running an information service for an in-house electronic bulletin board may be part of the desktop publisher's duties. It's a duty to be sought after, as videotex and telecommunications skills are increasingly prized in large organizations.

The disk-based, computerized newsletter.

A more recent development is the disk-based, computerized newsletter. This is shared with, or sold or traded to, electronic bulletin boards inside or outside the organization. The disk contains articles, 'technical support' ('how-to' advice from experts), ads and public domain software, which users of these boards can download.

This form of newsletter could proliferate. It provides a useful service that gives wide exposure (via telecommunications) to the editor's organization or association, at a fraction of the cost of normal publication. Its potential, and the equivalent of a SHIP for its contents, are as yet largely unexplored. Also largely unexplored are its possibilities as a novel career growth path for a desktop publisher.

Developing Task Forces
THE BREAD AND BUTTER ACTIVITIES OF DESKTOP PUBLISHING

Editing a newsletter is likely to be the most demanding of the common tasks to come a desktop publisher's way. But it's unlikely to be the *commonest* task: predominant among the bread and butter items of desktop publishing are forms. Great cost savings are possible for an organization which prints them in-house. (This applies also to manuals; but these are not frequently-occurring items like forms.)

Designing forms takes a lot of expertise –expertise which the desktop publisher doesn't have. But, if she has networking skills, she can find out who the in-house experts on forms are and get them on to a task force for designing forms. And there are a lot of these mundane, but critically important, bread and butter items for which the desktop publisher can perform this service. Let's review them.

Forms

If forms can be quickly designed in-house, as specifications change, and run off cheaply in small numbers (in the form of photocopies of a LaserWriter print out), savings can be enormous.

Why should this be so? Because the design and printing costs of regular print shops are so high for forms that large print runs are required, to achieve economies of scale. Then, when –as inevitably all too quickly happens– changes have to be made in the form, the organization must do one of two things. It can remainder its large inventory, taking a financial loss. Or it can continue to make do with a now inadequate and inefficient form, till the stock of the old form is used up.

This is an area where in-house desktop publishing really pays off. A wide variety of highly effective, attractively designed, computerized forms, custom letters (to customers, clients, employees, stockholders, suppliers and so on) and memo formats is available:

1. Collections of formats (which can be easily customized).[3]
2. Programs specifically for creating forms.
3. Many, if not most, database management programs allow for easy development of business forms.

    Also, all kinds of specialized database management programs are being developed. For instance, some databases now produce files based on *graphics* images: real estate agencies use them to generate a picture of a property with a wide range of details appended. Bibliographic software has been designed specifically for storing and retrieving bibliographies, and comes with twenty pre-designed forms.

4. There are 'expert system' programs that enable you to construct a form and at the same time construct a program providing step-by-step procedures for filling in the form. These procedures appear on screen as prompts for the clerk, asking for the relevant details needed at every point. An attorney, for instance, can build such a combined form-and-program, to enable a secretary to compose a letter to a client involved in a real estate deal.

To use some of these programs requires some programming capability. Most desktop publishers won't have such a capability, initially anyway. But what the desktop publisher needs most is to be able to:

- find out what software is available and what it can do;
- find out who knows what needs to be done;
- find out who can help program what has to be done;
- combine these people into a task force.

In a large organization or association, it's easy enough to find someone with the (relatively low-level) programming skills needed to operate these programs. It's also easy to identify someone with the specialist job-related knowledge needed to generate the contents, and promptings for relevant details, needed to construct the forms. A combination of these two 'someones' makes up the desktop publisher's 'form producing team', in such a case.

It's these small task forces (known as 'skunk works' in productivity circles) which are a prime source of energy and initiative in effective organizations.[4]

Mailing Lists

Developing mailing lists may be simply a matter of getting the central computer service to provide known client or customer addresses. Alternatively, the desktop publisher may have to start from scratch to put a list together. In such a case, there are agencies which sell mailing lists, which they will configure to your specifications. Extremely well-targeted lists can be built by further developing lists originally purchased from these agencies.

Forms have to be mailed; so do newsletters, for that matter. Programs have been developed to meet this everyday need. These programs turn your mailing list into a database and provide postal area-code sorting, label formatting, and much more. There are programs, too, for mail merging.

These programs produce a 'template' letter containing everything but the addressee's name & address and the 'Dear Mr/Ms X' greeting and any other personalized inserts required. These inserts (name & address etc.) are entered on a separate list. The program merges these two components, inserting the addresses etc., to generate a mass mailing of thousands of individually addressed letters containing personalized messages.

A task force can be put together to develop mailing lists and to despatch mail merge letters. Alternatively, with a little help, the desktop publisher can herself learn how to use the programs involved. Initially she may need a little help in learning such programs. But learning them is a valuable learning experience: it provides an easy introduction to database management –the beginning of programming skills.

Manuals

Publishing, and thereafter upgrading, manuals is the other major area where in-house publishing is a real cost-saver for organizations and associations. The desktop publisher won't actually put the manuals together. The specialists in the production or training or accounting units or whatever will do that. Manuals are typically produced by small, highly interactive task forces. The desktop publisher's rôle is crucial to such a task force. She provides advice on presentation and production, from page makeup to printout of camera-ready copy, and copy editing (critically important for consistency).

Production advice is crucial because the manuals have to be produced to rigid program specifications:

1. It must be possible to input the programs for entering text and graphics into a page makeup program that can accommodate them all.

2. That page makeup program is chosen because it can drive the best quality laser printers and phototypesetting equipment available. (The latter may be available off-site at a computer typesetting agency.)

So the entire operation of producing a manual will have to be pre-planned, before the people who are to write the manuals commence writing. Besides, the desktop publisher is apt to have special knowledge about programs which make the writing up of a manual much easier:

1. These programs have a number of editing capabilities built into them. This is especially helpful for someone whose strength may be in technical expertise rather than in writing skills. For instance, such programs provide the following range of writing aids as you create your text:

   - readability checking   • spelling checking   • grammar check[5]
   - sexist language check   • automatic hyphenation   • cliché checking
   - contents generation   • index generation   • key board macros

2. The programs are also designed so that their output can be fed into powerful word processing programs for final typesetting and text formatting. In turn these programs feed into the desired page makeup programs.

There are many other types of programs that a desktop publisher can beneficially bring to the attention of writers of manuals. Outstanding among these are the following:

1. The 'idea processors': outlining programs which facilitate putting your ideas together when drafting a position paper. You can type ideas in as headings, in any order, then regroup them, move them around (along with the text accompanying each heading or set of headings), or alter relationships, making what was subordinate superior, and so on. Living Videotext's *More*, currently top-of-the-line among such programs, can also generate decision trees, or organizational charts, or flow charts from your outline.

2. The flowchart generators are beloved of engineers, who frequently have to calculate critical paths, or PERT or Gant charts.[6] They're also invaluable for anyone involved in constructing job aids or 'playscript' documents.

   • A job aid is a flow chart set out as a sequential set of instructions for doing one particular task.[7] Bank tellers have booklets full of such job aids. There'll be an aid, for instance, to ensure that they go through all the steps in carrying out an international funds transfer. Job aids are particularly helpful when there's a rapid staff turnover in a particular job or location.

   • Playscript sets out the flow chart of a complex operation as the script of a play. It's meant for people who aren't familiar with PERT, and are daunted by flow charts complex enough to show the critical path of an operation. It's used when several different work groups must interact at different points in a complex procedure, but when their job demarcations break up the overall work flow so badly that none of the persons involved can see the operation as a whole, in an integrated fashion. With playscript's familiar format, such people can see which scene of which act they come in for, what led up to that act, who they must hand the stage over to, at what point and why, and so on.[8]

THE BATCH PROCESSING DILEMMA

The problem that triggers it

When a manual has to be produced, what generally happens is this. Each person involved uses his or her own favourite hardware and software. The result is a series of documents word processed by several different programs and micros, and graphics likewise produced via a variety of programs and machines.

The desktop publisher has to turn this motley collection into a text with properly made up pages of integrated text and graphics. This text will then, almost inevitably, go through a series of extensive, last-minute changes as the manual writers remember things to insert, delete or change. (Manuals go through up to thirteen revisions on average, with some revisions always coming close to the deadline for printing.)

Manuals pose a major challenge to a publisher. They contain a lot of text as well as a lot of graphics. Their text blocks have to be laid out to very exacting specifications: they must be positioned very precisely in relation to their diagrams. And each of the innumerable revisions causes changes producing massive side-effects that cause alterations in the rest of the layout.

Sophisticated batch processing programs have been developed to deal with publications of this nature. Such programs can cope with multi-column, variable column-depth tables; they have 'try tables' that reposition graphics, avoiding splitting them between pages, when an addition or deletion occurs elsewhere in the text.

A batch processing program can change the typography and formatting of an entire document in minutes, simply by changing a few macros in its style sheet. It can set text blocks of any length and width with superb accuracy. It controls the typography with equal precision, providing refinements like feathering, full justification with micro-spacing, and kerning. And it automatically generates tables of contents and indices as you lay the text out.

You just can't do this kind of re-formatting with an interactive,WYSIWYG program like *PageMaker*. Such a program sets text and graphics one page at a time. So a major change to that text requires you to reset it one page at a time.This is likely to take almost as long as it took to lay the text out in the first place –and you'll have to redo your table of contents and indices by hand. Besides, you just don't have precise control over the demarcation of text blocks if you're using an interactive, wysiwyg program that flows text round graphics.

So, if you're going to be publishing a lot of manuals, you'll have to use a batch processing program of some kind. But batch processing programs are difficult to learn, *precisely* because they're not WYSIWYG and interactive:

- You can't see what your formatting looks like as you lay it out (as you can with any WYSIWYG program).
- All you see on screen is plain text interspersed with macros –coded commands.
- Get one of these macros wrong (which is easily done when you've got to input lots of them), and strange things happen to your layout.
- But you won't see what your layout looks like till you print it out.

The benefits and costs of learning batch processing
What you decide about learning batch processing determines what kind of a desktop publisher you're going to become. These programs aren't for occasional users. They're tedious to learn, even on the Mac; and you must use them constantly to maintain and develop your grasp of their complex programming commands

> The desktop publisher as a twentieth century Renaissance Man is a myth.

If you become expert in using one of these programs, you're going to become a specialist in printing. There won't be time for networking. You could be stepping into a career closet, not on to a career springboard, for the following reasons.

As has become apparent, desktop publishing is really a group activity:

- Most people have an aptitude for either typography or graphics –for left-brain hemisphere or for right-brain hemisphere specialized tasks.
- Most publications are put out by a team. This applies to forms, form letters, manuals, newsletters, you name it.
- Networking (the use of LANs etc.) is at the core of maximizing computer effectiveness in organizations.

Besides, desktop publishing activities occur in context. What's required of a desktop publisher depends on the level of desktop publishing activities in your organization. Low-end activities –newsletters, promotional fliers and brochures– don't require expertise with batch processing programs. Middle level activities

–long documents, technical manuals and books– do require it. High-end activities –glossy magazines, with colour separation– are for professional printers, who have always used batch processing programs.

The dilemma

Obviously, you can't afford to restrict yourself to low-end activities only. But few desktop publishers will ever work on the high-end activities, unless they're employed by a major publishing house (and in such cases they'll be recruited from persons with a background in printing). So it's clearly advisable to take the middle ground –to opt for activities at levels 1 and 2, with some time and opportunity to develop networking skills. The question is: "How can one do this?"

Towards a solution

There is a way out of this dilemma. There are now wysiwyg batch processing programs: these allow you to see the results of your programming on screen before printout. This feature makes them much easier to learn than batch processing programs which require you to operate 'blind', so you don't have to pay an exorbitant cost in time and effort to learn them.

But you –and your employer or Board of Directors– will have to explore your options with great care. Expensive hardware and software is involved if you want this kind of programming capability: it's at the leading edge of the technology:

1. Batch processing programs with a wysiwyg pre-screening capability differ enormously in ease of learning and of use. A program like Quark's *XPress* is much easier to learn and use than any of the varieties of *TEX* that are currently available. *XPress* is nearly as powerful as *TEX*, and it's constantly being upgraded.

2. *XPress* is expensive, however. But the version of *TEX* that's resident on many mainframes (that is, that comes 'free') is the non-wysiwyg variety. The wysiwyg varieties of *TEX* (*MacTEX* from FTL Systems and Addison-Wesley's *TEXtures*) are more expensive than *XPress*.

3. You'll probably need a Mac (an SE at least, preferably) to run *XPress* or any of the wysiwyg versions of *TEX* –these are all big, memory-hungry programs.

   This decision is probably the most critical one in a desktop publisher's career. It deserves to be taken with all due care and circumspection, and in close consultation with the work group.

LANs and the Desktop Publisher
WHAT THE LAN PROMISES

LANs (Local Area Networks) are right at the centre of the connectivity issue. They're probably getting more attention from organizational management than any other feature of computer technology, at the moment.

A LAN consists of:
1. The microcomputers or terminals in place in the organization.
2. Cabling, to connect them into a network.
3. An interface connection device (a box or a board) to connect each machine to the network.

4. A network 'file server': a microcomputer equipped with a hard disk, dedicated to managing the files and documents produced by the network.

5. Peripherals –such as printers and modems– shared by network users.

6. Special software for networking, to drive the network as an operating system.

7. Application programs, installed on the hard disk, which may be shared by everyone on the network (that is, for which there is a site license).

Sales of LANs have more than doubled in the past two years. This is because most organizations have a motley collection of different kinds of microcomputers and software, as well as their mainframe or minicomputer. The LAN promises to:

• Tie all these hitherto incompatible machines and programs together.

• Get them talking to one another.

• Link them to the mainframe.

There's an enormous amount of computing power scattered around most large organizations today. This strength is being frittered away because of lack of connectivity: there's too much incompatibility of micros and of programs. But the cost of re-equipping users of the current hodge-podge of micros with a new, uniform set of micros, and of training them in the new software involved, is prohibitive.

Besides, the present micros already run powerful programs, and their users have developed the expertise to exploit these programs to their full potential. If the present micros could be tied to the resources of the mainframe computer and thus to one another, their power would increase exponentially. The LAN promises to achieve this feat.

PROBLEMS WITH THE PROMISE

It's proving difficult to get this promise to materialize. Often hardware and software has been bootlegged in by individuals: engineers, for instance, tend to use Macs no matter what the MIS (Management Information Systems) manager ordains. So, it's difficult to accommodate all the different hardware on the organization's LAN –especially as users won't share their toys. They want their own printer and hard disk, and the prospects of electronic junk mail and LAN system crashes aren't much of an incentive to give them up.

Consequently, it's difficult to decide what type of LAN –there are many varieties– to buy. So the wise organization does three things:

1. It hires a consultant to match the prospective LAN with what the organization needs and can afford (LANs are expensive).

2. Generally, it decides to purchase on condition that it can hire someone competent to install the LAN, since installation can be a complicated business.

3. It appoints a network administrator, since maintaining a LAN involves a constant succession of technical problems. Typical problems are: getting copy protected programs to run on the file server; ensuring that there's 'record locking' (provision that only one person at a time can make changes to the central database), and security against people breaking into the database.

THE DESKTOP PUBLISHER AND THE LAN

Where does the desktop publisher fit into all this? Purchase, installation and maintenance of LANs call for advanced computer knowledge, which few desktop publishers have. The opportunity niche for the desktop publisher comes, as before, via his or her specialist knowledge of desktop-publishing-related hardware and software.

When a LAN is being chosen, the desktop publisher can make sure of not being painted out of the picture; he or she can press for LANs that support the Macintosh. Only a Mac-user is likely to be closely following Apple's persistent and ingenious attempts to make its Macs easy to connect to PCs. So the Mac-user may well have information of which the PC-oriented network administrator may be unaware.

Peripherals and Connectivity in Desktop Publishing

MODEMS

Uses of telecommunications equipment in desktop publishing

Any desktop publisher will be involved in networking. So he or she has to know about modems. The first thing to know is when a modem is needed. Here are the situations in which a modem is a necessity:

1. When the two micros exchanging information don't share a common disk format (you can always send text in ASCII between a Mac and an IBM PC via a modem).

2. When you have to send information often and quickly.

3. When a number of different machines have to access information from a central storage system (an electronic bulletin board or an electronic mail system).

4. When you have to get information from a large database remote from your work site.

5. When you're on the road and must keep in touch with your organization by sending in and receiving reports.

It's possible for the desktop publisher to acquire special, 'street smarts' expertise on this topic:

Modem technology is developing very rapidly, so it's difficult to keep up with it across the board. As most micro-users have PCs, they're likely to keep up only with developments in modem technology for the IBM PC. So the desktop publisher can become a specialist in modems, and communication programs, for connecting the Mac and the PC. As getting IBM PCs to run on the LaserWriter printer is often critically important, this kind of expertise is likely to be in demand.

Current questions related to using modems

Hayes Microcomputer Products dominates the modem industry, currently selling about 80% of all modems. So the Hayes command set has become a basic industry standard for communications programs. Virtually all communications packages for IBM PCs are Hayes compatible. It would be most inadvisable to adopt any modem and/or communications software that isn't compatible with Hayes' products.

Currently, controversy rages over modem speed. Are you best advised to buy a 300 bits per second (bps) modem, or a 1200, 2400 or 9600 bps one? (10 bits make one character, on average.) In practice, the 300 bps modems run too slowly, and tie up the phone lines. So most organizations have moved to the 1200 bps variety. But they're jibbing at purchasing the 2400's, though these cost very little more than the1200's. Result: 90% of modems currently in use are 1200's.

Insider advice is that you buy a 1200 bps modem and its software, which are currently priced very cheaply, and use it while waiting for the next generation of modems. These will be much simpler and more economical, as well as faster and more powerful, and will come as integrated elements within your micro.

Implications for developing desktop publishing as a job

Of all the features of computer technology, the LAN and telecommunications look like being the central concern of management for the next few years. So the desktop publisher would be well advised to adopt the following job skills development policy:

- Gain practical experience of using modems. This is likely to be easily done, as the work will often call for their use.
- Seize every opportunity to become familiar with modems and software that produce compatibility between different types of programs and machines (primarily between the IBM PC and the Mac).
- Grasp any opportunity to work with telecommunications packages and utilities.

This job skills development policy will rapidly lead to the accumulation of the type of computer expertise which is growing in demand and is basic to in-house –and, indeed, inter-organization– communications.

HARD DISKS

Developments in hard disk technology

Hard disk technology is also developing very rapidly at the moment. Prices are dropping as storage is increasing; in response, sales for hard disks are increasing –while sales for personal computers are flattening out. Most IBM PCs are now sold with hard disk drives: the latter are easier for a new user to work with than a multitude of floppies. 20 megabytes (MB) is currently the standard minimal storage capacity for a hard disk, but 30–40 MB will soon be standard (and much larger storage capacity will come with optical disk drives).

The hard disks for the IBM PC and compatibles are amazing in their variety and cheapness; those for the Mac are expensive by contrast. But, now that the Mac has a standardized SCSI (small computer system interface) port, a larger (and cheaper) variety of hard disks is becoming available for it, too. Only the desktop publisher is likely to be conversant with developments in this Mac hard disk market, so rapidly are they occurring.

Backing up hard disks

Oddly, hard disk backup systems don't come as a standard feature of most LANs. Yet every organization has to make provision for such systems, so prone are hard disks to crashing. Crashproofing is already here, in the form of Iomega's almost crashproof Bernoulli Box hard drive system with its removable

5 or 10 MB cartridges. This system, once more expensive and somewhat slower than others, is dropping in price and picking up in speed. It's a very attractive option.

Most of us have to make our own provision against crashing. With a lot of self-discipline, you can back up your day's work on to floppies as you go. Streaming tape does it much more quickly and conveniently. Removable cartridges are equally convenient, and especially attractive when they come encased in Iomega's Bernoulli Box system.

Improvements in hard disk back-up technology are appearing on all sides. There's even software for automatic backup of (only the *new* parts of) one's work. So risking invaluable documents by not purchasing some form of this technology is becoming increasingly penny-wise and pound foolish.

Implications for the desktop publisher

The LAN's network administrator has too much on his or her mind to be likely to keep up with advances in hard disk technology for the Mac. This situation provides a yet another window of opportunity for the desktop publisher: he or she can acquire expertise and knowledge that can be useful in further integrating and improving the security of the network.

For instance, knowing how to exercise a 'rent rather than buy' option for an initial test period can facilitate a wise decision when your organization is deliberating over which hard disk system to adopt. Such knowledge, the computer equivalent of street smarts, comes only from practical experience.

SCANNERS AND PRINTERS

Again, the technology is advancing very rapidly where these peripherals are concerned. If you know what's available, you can save your organization a lot of money. And no-one is as centrally concerned with this particular technology as the desktop publisher is (just as no-one is as knowledgeable about plotters as the engineer/engineering draftsperson).

So printers and scanners constitute the prime area in which a desktop publisher should aim to build up expertise. This is, after all, your turf. So, if you don't become familiar with it, who in your organization will?

Scanners

A scanner is a machine that turns marks on paper –text, graphics or both– into similar marks on a file in a computer disk. It saves retyping a typescript, or redrawing a complicated picture, to disk, thereby achieving gains in convenience and savings in money and time. Scanners, so far mostly used only in the word processing centres of large organizations, have been very expensive. But things are changing:

1. Dedicated word processors have been outdated by microcomputers. So a new market has had to be developed, a market for the micro user. This means that prices have had to drop: individuals don't have at their disposal the money that organizations have. Result: scanners have dropped drastically in price.

2. Scanners have up to now been mostly used for office work, for reading typescript to disk. Now, however, they're increasingly used for desktop pub-

lishing. So their resolution has had to improve. 240 dpi may have been sufficient for office documents, which mostly consisted of text only. But for the graphics which are essential for desktop publishing, a 300 dpi standard has become established. Insiders are now predicting a very reasonably priced scanner that will be able to turn a photograph into a magazine-quality halftone by the end of 1987.[9]

Meanwhile, just as scanned text can be read into the major word processing programs, so the major page makeup programs are developing the capacity to support scanners. The latter are now saving to disk in the TIFF format, discussed in chapter 2, which promises to become an industry standard. Also, write once read many times (WORM) optical disks promise the storage capacity to store graphics and photographs on disk. (Currently one halftone can take up several megabytes of memory.)

The desktop publisher will most likely be following events in the scanner (and digitizer) market more closely than anyone else, being more closely concerned with its products than anyone else, so is best situated to become the organization's resident expert in this area.

Printers

The same holds true of printers. Most members of the organization only need to know how to handle 'Betsy' –the beloved dot matrix or letter quality printer on their desk. So this is the other area where the desktop publisher is best situated to become the organization's resident expert. Such knowledge will likely prove very useful to the organization: insiders predict that printer price wars are pending because:

- The market for the daisy wheel printer has probably vanished. For most office purposes, top quality dot matrix printout is good enough. If it isn't, then LaserWriter printout is now as acceptable as the product of the daisy wheel.
- Dot matrix printers have saturated their markets. To keep selling, even at their currently reduced prices, they've come up with higher resolution (by employing 24 dot, instead of 9 dot, print heads) and tri-colour (ribbons and) printout.
- Laser printers are currently overpriced. To gain market share, developers are increasing resolution or dropping prices. Agfa-Gevaert has a 400 dpi printer, and Varityper has one that produces *600* dpi. This is four times the number of dots per inch that the LaserWriter produces (at four times the cost). 600 dpi is true print quality, the desired goal in Laser printout.

Developments in the technology of printers are likely to bring about particularly dramatic changes in desktop publishing. So all desktop publishers will necessarily be following these events closely.

The Information Centre and the Desktop Publisher
THE DEVELOPMENT AND DECLINE OF THE INFORMATION CENTRE

In the beginning was the mainframe, lorded over by the MIS (Management Information Systems) Manager. The treatment afforded mainframe users in those early days was, in large part, what sparked the microcomputer revolution in the early '70's. People bootlegged personal computers into their work environment to gain independence of the Master of the mainframe.

126   Desktop Publishing and Networking

A brief history of the revolt by the techno-peasants against the domination of the lords of the main-frame.

The puny early micros weren't taken seriously by the MIS Managers. But the micro gradually became a force to be reckoned with, as its numbers began to swell, and its programs became more sophisticated. So organizations set up Information Centres, to provide help for personal computer users and advice for those thinking of getting a personal computer. The micro manager arrived, as director of such a centre.

Most micro managers came in the back door, later in the '70's. Usually they had been initially employed for their expertise in accounting, or scheduling or whatever. But they were also dedicated personal computer users. So they could help out when personal computers began to proliferate in the work place. They understood what personal computer programs could do to give their particular business an advantage, and they knew how to help novices start using these programs to achieve this advantage.

The micro managers weren't technical experts with degrees in Computer Science. But the best ones were good negotiators. They needed to be: they had to negotiate with upper management, the data processing people, the end users, and the vendors of hardware and software. Micros were by now no longer thought of as puny little toys. Rather, they had become status symbols, and people strove to have one on their desks.

By the early '80's the micros and their software had become much more powerful. They had by this time virtually brought about the demise of the dedicated word processor. Management became increasingly concerned to harness its enormous investment in personal computers, so as to maximize their effectiveness. For this, the micros had to be linked together and tied in to the mainframe. Enter the LAN. The MIS Manager now got the chance to integrate personal computers into his mainframe system via the LAN.

Network administrators began to appear, reporting to the MIS Manager. Such administrators need formal training in data processing, extensive mainframe experience and telecommunications experience. They are professionals. They began to replace micro managers, as the MIS Managers strove to regain control over in-house computing.

The Empire strikes back –again and again (currently the weapon is SGML –the standardized general mark-up language).

It's now becoming increasingly difficult, in most organizations, to come into a job managing computers by the back door. Micro managers of long standing survive because of their proven usefulness in some special area. This may be in getting a unit computerized, or in providing in-house training for computer novices, in a range of application programs, or in providing end user support when difficulties with hardware or software occur.

THE DESKTOP PUBLISHER AS A KIND OF INFORMATION CENTRE MANAGER

Essentially, the desktop publisher is being cast in the rôle of a new kind of micro manager, entering by a different back door. Until there are courses or degree majors certifying desktop publishing, this situation is likely to persist. Lack of formal qualifications usually has to be made up for by prodigies of work, as the uncertified person has to keep proving his or her worth.

The desktop publisher has to know the business well enough to identify where savings are obtainable by in-house publishing: fliers, forms, manuals, newsletters, position papers –whatever the combination is. He or she also has to be familiar with a range of applications programs and computer peripherals, and have (or quickly acquire) skills in telecommunications and networking.

Printing, by its nature, puts the printer in a power position; it frequently happens that desperately needed work is submitted late by and for power-wielders. What's required in a desktop publisher is some diplomatic ability and the ability to organize work quickly and then do it efficiently, fast. Without these abilities, exploitation and burn-out is all too likely. Desktop publishing is as demanding a job as it is rewarding.

Currently, what seems to be happening is that desktop publishing is usually found in the traditional publications units –graphics and publishing– of most organizations. There are also, usually, a few individual desktop publishers scattered around in various other departments (producing newsletters and the like). The pattern is little pockets of activity, without overall integration. Absence of a coherent overall plan is good neither for the organization nor for the individuals involved.

A centralized desktop publishing unit, under a kind of information centre manager who's familiar with the technology, seems likely to be an effective solution. Desktop publishing requires many programs to work together. So it's at the centre of the movement towards greater connectivity discussed in chapter 2 Consequently, it makes sense for a desktop publisher to become conversant with the economic politics of the production and distribution system that drives computing. The next chapter reviews what's involved.

Social Support Reconsidered

TECHNOSTRESS[10]

Perfectionism and Workaholism

Computing contributes massively to tendencies towards perfectionism –a frame or mind that inhibits one's initiative and saps one's morale.[11]: you have to follow follow the computer's instructions set perfectly. Desktop publishing compounds the compulsiveness of perfectionism. You've got to get many programs and peripherals to work perfectly together. And printing is a totally unforgiving business. There must be NO errors –this when you're putting out long, complex documents, to a tight time schedule, via a multi-stage process.

Desktop publishing adds workaholism to perfectionism: a common –and disastrous– combination.

> Workaholics, the Stakanovites of capitalist cultures, are often thought of as heroes. The people close to them, however, think of them as dry alcoholics. The workaholic has all the self-centredness of the alcoholic and is as unreliable in relationships in private life. It's the same behaviour; only the crutch is different: work instead of alcoholism. Many workaholics are teetotal 'hero children' who have made their escape from an alcoholic parent and home via over achievement through work. Such persons are terribly at risk if they get involved in desktop publishing.

There's unremitting demand for the services that a desktop publisher can render. There are always newsletters, forms, flyers and advertisements to get out for some Great Cause –and usually at short notice ("You can easily make the change –you've got everything on the word processor).

The mystique of computing is reserved first for programmers and hackers, and then fornumber-crunching researchers. Desktop publishing is seen as akin to typewriting. It is accorded all the respect and status accorded to secretarial work. So work is relentlessly and inconsiderately pushed on the in-house publisher. Revisions are required from him or her that wouldn't be considered if an outside printer had to be paid for doing them. 'Proper' printers, notorious for their abruptness when pressed to turn out work at short notice, still have a status, and are accorded a respect, that isn't generally given to a desktop publisher.

The human costs of the desktop publishing revolution:
It's easily possible for a desktop publisher to be reduced to the hectically harried lifestyle known as techno stress. Its characteristics are:

1. A speeded-up sense of time. Work time and computer-using time, that is; it's usually combined withchronic lateness for meals and forgetfulness of social engagements.
2. Perfectionism and workaholism, as noted above.
3. Mental strain, from long hours of solitary and concentrated work before a computer screen, resulting in mental fatigue.
4. A negative self-concept. With so much to do and so many things that can go wrong and so many readers to point each one of them out, it's hard for the desktop publisher to see the wood (the major achievements) for the trees (the many trivial and inevitable errors). Perfectionists don't have much sense of proportion.
5. As the desktop publisher becomes more and more wedded to his or her microcomputer system, isolated by over-involvement in long hours of solitary work, his or her social relationships become strained. Often, they wither.

THE CLAN OF THE COMPUTER BEAR
From building contacts to maintaining a social support network
Building a netowrk of persons on a '(persons I) need to know' basis is treating people as instruments to be used for one's own career purposes. But it's our loved ones who make life liveable and give it human meaning. These are the poeple we care for as people, not for what they can do for us –though, in a crunch, they WILL do things for us (as we will for them) as no one else will.

Diagram 4.6 sets out a model social support network. It's much larger and looser, much less contrived and organized than are the work support groups considered so far in this chapter.You may care to compare it to your own social support group. Important characteristics are[12]:

1. Heterogeneity: it's made up of different kinds of people, from different kinds of ethnic and socio-economic backgrounds.
2. It's big: about 25 persons.
3. There's a lot of give and take: relationships are reciprocal.
4. There are 'weak links' (people you're friendly with but only see occasionally) as well as 'multiplex' relationships (people you see on all sorts of occasions).
5. Low density: the network has all kinds of sub-groups who barely know one another –gives you chance to experiment with new rôles.

7 Developments in Computing:

Their Relevance for Desktop Publishing

A Short History of the Micro

FROM FIRST TO THIRD GENERATION

The third generation micro is now with us. Judging by the history of its first two generations, we can expect it to have a life of about five years. (The *next* generation's chips are already here, according to industry gossip, in prototype.[1]) That's how long it takes to develop software that fully exploits new hardware. By the time the software is in place, both the need and the technology for a more powerful micro will also be here.

The first generation

The first generation micros date to the middle '70's: Apple's first microcomputer appeared in 1977, with 48K of RAM (up from the 16K that the Tektronix 4051 had possessed in 1973). These were 8-bit machines, made by Apple, Commodore,Tandy Radio Shack and so on. There were no industry standards, though the CPM drive operating system could be made to run on various of these machines. There was little transferability of text files or connectivity in general.

These macros could do word processing; some (the Apple IIs) could do some rudimentary graphics; they could all run (rather rudimentary) games. Then came the invention of the spreadsheet –a new concept of what a computer could do: change one thing in one place, and everything everywhere else changed automatically. This program, *Visicalc*, running on the Apple, gave micros a practical use in business. So the micro came to be regarded as a serious business machine. Sales soared, creating a big enough base of established users to make it worthwhile for third party developers to upgrade the hardware and software.

Apple adopted an 'open architecture' concept, which means that:

1. The hardware vendor makes schematics of the central processing unit's mother board, and a good deal of the ROM (Read Only Memory) BIOS (Basic Input-Output Source code) available to developers under 'non-disclosure agreements'.

2. The central processing unit (CPU) can be opened; inside is a 'mother board' (also termed a logic board) with slots into which 'cards' (small plastic boards containing microprocessor chips –themselves tiny computers) can be inserted.

3. 'Ports' (apertures) in the rear of the CPU allow for printers and modems and the like to be attached to the mother board or the cards.

This led hardware developers to design peripheral devices for the Apple II line, providing it with more RAM (Random Access Memory), better printers and modems, and a variety of enhancement cards. As the micro's capabilities were, as result, much enhanced, software developers began writing programs for it.

The Apple II was easy to assemble and repair –and to reconfigure, given the abundance of peripherals available for it. It came to have a library of 4,000 programs written for it. User groups of Apple II hobbyists grew up around it. It was the Volkswagen of micros.

> But open architecture had made cloning possible. Cheap versions of the Apple II, of the II+, and even of some of the later models proliferated. Sales slumped: Apple's developmental costs had financed others, to Apple's own cost.

The second generation

The second generation micros came with IBM'S 16-bit personal computer (speedily dubbed the PC) in 1981. The PC's Intel 8088 microprocessor chip had a 1 MB address space, a gigantic increase from the 64K of the 8-bit micros. The PC's DOS (Drive Operating System) made 640K of that space available for applications programs. IBM's strength in mainframe development made it a market leader from the outset. The new micro was a runaway best seller. So the PC set a standard with its 16-bit chip, PC DOS and open architecture.

Developers abandoned the 8-bit micros for this new, more powerful machine. An impressive range of cheap peripherals was quickly produced by developers working on the 'bleeding edge' of the technology (so called because few survived in the cut-price competition that resulted). IBM-compatible micros and outright clones proliferated, too. Many were cheaper and more powerful than the PC itself. An enormous established user base developed. Figures vary, but there must by now be more than 8,000,000 PCs and PC compatibles out there.

Applications programs of much greater power and sophistication were developed for these more capacious 16-bit machines, which had larger RAMs, and lots more memory (in their amazingly cheap hard disks), than the 8-bit machines had had. The age of the big programs arrived. Lotus Development Corporation's *Lotus 1,2,3* (a spreadsheet with the power to do graphs) and Ashton-Tate's *dBase III* (a database [that is, a records] manager) themselves have enormous bases of established users. Golden oldies, such as the word processing program *WordStar*, were also ported, in enhanced versions, to the new micros.

> The software available for the Mac and PC is obviously likely to vary from country to country. I'm referring to the most popular programs in North America (and, later in the chapter, to programs that are currently 'state of the art'). These programs may not be equally well known in Britain and on the Continent. Please take my specifics as examples of the trends I'm talking about in such a case.

These programs could run on all of the 16-bit machines, whose users came to number in the millions. An enormous library of business programs –over 14,000 by now– grew up around the PC. But IBM –which did not generally lead in technological or programming innovativeness– lost market share to the clones and compatibles. There was no market leader: it was a clone-driven feeding frenzy.

Meanwhile Apple had come up with a 16-bit machine of its own –and a new concept: closed architecture.

> The machine was the Lisa. The Lisa's case could not be opened without voiding the warranty. Enough specifications were made available to enable developers to produce peripherals and write software to the closely defined standards laid down by Apple. But Apple kept close control over its proprietary ROM chip, the basis of its revolutionary 'desktop' user interface.
>
> Apple's new machines were designed to be user-friendly. The 'desktop' was a transparently clear, well documented work space, not a cursor-driven, empty screen requiring programming skills to get it operating. It was easy to learn and to use. It was also graphics (rather than character) based. The first WYSIWYG micro had appeared. All programs and all peripherals for this micro had to work with Apple's desktop user interface, so they could all flow into one another. Total integration.

This time, with closed architecture, there were to be no clones.

This policy required Apple to keep developing its technology, so as to stay ahead of possible imitators. Apple moved to the Macintosh, a smaller and cheaper machine incorporating the developmental work poured into the Lisa. The first Mac –the 'skinny Mac'– had only 128 K (thousand megabytes of memory in the RAM). It was a toy. So Apple developed the 'fat Mac' with 512K of memory. This left a trail of technological orphans, as the Lisa and the skinny Mac ceased to be supported by Apple.

This was no way to treat developers or the user base. And the 'black box' machine wasn't compatible with the PC. So, in a vicious circle, growth of established user base was slow, and developers were also slow to commit their futures to this funny-looking little machine. Programs, in consequence, were few, and slow to arrive. Peripherals were likewise scarce, and lacking economies of scale, expensive.

Re-inventing the (use of) the computer

Then came the invention of desktop publishing –as with the invention of the spreadsheet, this was yet another new concept of what a computer could do. Aldus' page makeup program, *PageMaker*, combined with Apple's LaserWriter and Adobe's page description language, *PostScript*, to exploit the potential of the Mac (which Apple forthwith developed into the Mac Plus, with a megabyte of memory).

The PC and its clones and compatibles couldn't compete. The payoffs from desktop publishing were enormous, and the Mac had this lucrative market niche all to itself. Business began to adopt the Mac. The number of users grew –rapidly: the millionth Mac was produced in March, 1987. By that time, the Mac was the best selling micro around, and Apple's market share and stock were rising as IBM's were dropping. Developers were by now flocking to the Mac: programs began to pour in, some of them, such as Microsoft's spreadsheet, *Excel*, the best of their kind. So did peripherals.

Apple was meanwhile racing to develop the first of the next generation of micros. The technology was ready; Apple had purchased a Cray supercomputer to assist in research and development –and had a new concept: semi-open architecture.

The third generation

So it was that the third generation micro arrived in 1987 –minus software, of course– in the form of Apple's Mac II (accompanied, naturally, by yet *another* updated Mac: the Mac SE [System Expanded]).

Now, clearly, the first machine of its generation tells little about what subsequent machines will be like. But it does tell *something*: the PC, after all, shaped most of its generation. Important new features of the machine will rapidly become minimum standards. So let's briefly review the first machine of this new generation, to get an idea of the advances that the new generation represents.

The Mac II's CPU is driven by a 32-bit, Motorola 68020 chip. It has a 68881 floating point math co-processor chip, with a 68851 memory management chip as an option. It comes with a standard one MB of RAM, expandable to 8 MB. This micro runs at 16 MHz.

> **To prevent cloning, there is a proprietary ROM chip, containing a new user interface, under continuous development.**

The Mac II has an internal drive for an 800K floppy disk. Plans for a 1.6 MB floppy are at an advanced stage; and the micro's power supply is enough to accommodate them. There's provision for a second internal disk drive, either another floppy or a hard disk. A –*very* fast– 40 MB hard disk is standard.

There are six 32-bit expansion slots. One slot is for an MS DOS card with an Intel 80286 chip: the Mac II is intended to be able to run any PC program. A Nubus system bus, compatible with Intel's Multibus II, will allow of fast development of add-on cards by third-party developers. The SCSI (Small Computer System Interface) port will do the same for peripherals.

> A 'bus' is a pathway, or connecting channel, for control signals to the motherboard's slots for peripherals. The Nubus bus is 32 bits wide (rather than 8 or 16), and is 'microprocessor independent': it can handle signals from any chip. It has a 'multimaster design'; any of the cards using the bus can assume mastery of it at need.

There are two serial ports, for a printer and a modem. There's a stereo sound port for four-voice stereo and amplifiers. There are two Apple Desktop Bus ports for a keyboard, mouse, graphics tablet, and joystick. (These peripherals can be chain linked.) The slots are meant for cards such as a network connector or a video display card.

A variety of monitors is available: a 12" (monochrome) or 13" (colour) screen, with 640 X 480 pixels, or one of the large (19") screens with over a million pixels. The video card has an optional add-on chip with another 256K of RAM. It can refresh its graphics screen *very* quickly, and provides 256 shades of grey, or a choice of 264 colours from a palette of 16 million. This colour display system is independent of application software (that is, it can run anything).

This system will be capable of running under *Unix*, and will be inter-faced to an Ethernet LAN. It will run other languages, too: C, Fortran-77, Assembler, with MPW Pascal as an option.

BACKGROUND TRENDS

The impact of a 'communications tool' technology:

Essentially, a microcomputer is an extension of its user. It's the first user-definable tool. You can alter its hardware and software at will, making what is virtually a new machine out of it.

You can adapt, and continuously re-adapt, a micro to fit your needs. It's a multi-functional machine, which rapidly becomes a virtual co-worker.

Consequently it has come to eliminate a series of machines dedicated to a *single* function. First to go was the dedicated word processor: the micro does word processing and spread-sheeting, data base management and numerous other things. Next to go was the dedicated typesetter.

Desktop publishing is now the driving force behind the development of microcomputers.

Soon the ability to do desktop publishing will be simply another basic feature in such computers. The Mac is currently in the lead in the race to produce a micro with this ability. High-end desktop publishing requires a workstation; the Mac II is a cheap workstation.

So it looks as if the next to go will be the dedicated work station, the mini-computer on which engineers produce computer-assisted, three-dimensional drafting –30% of their time. The other 70% of their time they're number crunching, managing data bases and word processing. They can do all of these things now with one machine –which is much cheaper.

The signs are already on the wall. Companies servicing minicomputer users are beginning to port their software to the micros. The long-term trend has been for the gap between the micro and the mini to close. The next-but-one machine to be phased out by the micro looks like being the mini.

The next-but-one task scheduled for the micro is multitasking: the running of several programs simultaneously –the forte of the mini. The third generation micros have the capacity to do this. They have capacious RAMs (1.5 *gigabytes* at the time of writing –July, 1987– on the Mac II), and their largest hard disks (of well over 100 MB) are about to be dwarfed by new, magneto-optical, hard disk technology. All that's required is the software.

The prime rôle for the micro is turning out to be that of serving as a tool for enhancing the creativity and judgment of skilled workers: applications that provide heuristics, set out decision alternatives and projections, and *speedily* organize –or jump about within– information, in various configurations (see the discussion on *Guide*, below).

Re-inventing the Computer: Different Views of What Computing should Entail

THE CONFLICT OF PHILOSOPHIES

The issue: What *kind* of continuing learning?

Underlying most of what's going on in microcomputing today is a conflict of philosophies, epitomized by two machines: the PC and the Mac.

- The PC will take you through the 'boot camp' of MS DOS, giving you some knowledge of programming: it'll make you a 'power' computer user, and induct you into the priesthood of computer programmers.
- The Mac provides an easy learning environment, in the belief that what's important is what you want to achieve by using a computer, rather than you 'should' learn to accommodate to the algorithms of some proprietary software.

This conflict of philosophies has to do with how one learns and why one learns –and with getting clear about means and ends. Essentially, then, we're going to explore some issues basic to experiential learning and to self-expression through work. Adoption of a new communications technology (which is what computers are) has serious long-term consequences for the adopter.[2] Learning an application program is like putting on an electronic skull cap which enables the thoughts of many other gifted persons to interpenetrate and subtly change one's own thoughts.

We're going to attempt to get a sense of the different directions in which this technology may take us, so as to choose between them with discrimination, rather than merely go unthinkingly along with one option or the other.

> In the two and a half years since its introduction, the Mac has changed the way people go about microcomputing. The IBM PC and its compatibles and clones now have interfaces that are similar to the Mac's, both in appearance and in ease of use: they sport icons, windows, pull-down menus, dialog boxes and desk accessories, and are mouse-driven. The Mac's 3.5", 'hard shell', 'floppy' disk is becoming widely used. The top programs for the IBM PC are being ported across to the Mac: *Dbase III Plus* (which already has a Mac-like interface) and *WordPerfect*.

The two microcomputer work environments have edged closer together by the IBM PC's edging closer to the Mac. This is because of what insiders refer to as the 'Mac advantage'. Let's see what this amounts to.

THE 'MAC ADVANTAGE'

The user interface

The Mac was specifically designed, using what's known about how people learn, to be easy to learn and to use. It has a highly visual, point-and-click, easy-to-learn user interface –its famous 'desktop environment'. You're not confronted by a blank screen and blinking cursor when you turn the machine on; so you don't have to learn strings of commands before you can make anything happen.

You can be using the machine in minutes. It's far easier to learn (as comparing training costs shows, more than five times easier) than is the PC. Let's see what this user-friendly 'desktop' consists of:

1. A menu –a series of words strung out in line across the top of the screen. These words are the titles of pull-down menus: each word expands into a series of related component items as you place the mouse-driven pointer on it and 'pull' it downwards. Click the mouse on any item, and a dialogue box (sometimes a series of dialogue boxes) appears, guiding you through the various decisions involved in carrying through the activity involved.

   Once you become familiar with the menu's lead words and their component items, you can substitute 'power commands' for them. You hold down the command key and simultaneously strike another key to execute the 'power command' you wish to use. For example, command-X, in many programs, cuts selected text and graphics from the screen and disk.

2. The mouse allows you to activate a menu item (some of which are 'icons' –little pictorial symbols, making recognition of their functions easier) simply by pointing at it and clicking on it . There are many 'point and click' movements that function as power commands –in the scrolling areas of the screen, for instance.

3. The Mac has 'smart' software: it keeps a visible and continuously updated record of what's in which drive; where your application programs and your data files are; which disk and file you're saving to, and even how much memory is available and needed.

4. You can open up a number of files one after another and have them all on screen simultaneously, each one overlying and concealing its predecessor. Or you can alter their on-screen size, so that they all appear together in 'windows' on the screen, and transfer data between them. These 'windowed' text files represent the file folders that you have on the top of your desk.

This visual interface with its transparently meaningful displays enormously lessens the cognitive load when you're learning to use the micro. And, when you know its menus by heart –as you very soon do– you can use 'power commands', involving a couple of key strokes, to bypass the menus for speed and convenience. These power commands also appear in most of the programs that run on the Mac. So, once you've learned one program, you've learned a good part of.the next one you have to learn. Typically, Mac-users learn more programs than do PC-users.

The Mac's graphics capabilities

The Mac was specifically designed as a graphics-based machine. Essentially, it draws pictures –graphics or screen fonts, rather than characters or numbers, on the screen:

1. The Mac has a standard graphic file format. Any graphic produced by a program that runs on the Mac can be cut or copied to its 'clipboard', and then 'pasted' into any other graphics document –and most text files.

   There is no such standard for the IBM PC. Until quite recently, each graphics program was unique and couldn't be read by any other. Attempts have recently been made to provide more compatibility among graphics programs for the IBM PC (see chapter 4).

However, the PC was originally designed only to print letters and numbers on its screen. So, to get it to draw diagrams and pictures, you have to buy a graphics 'card' (another chip, to drive the micro). And in a clone-driven market, there is no standard for these cards.

Consequently, a uniform graphics file format has yet to be agreed on. So, economies of scale not being possible with several products competing for the one market, the cost of each of the various graphics cards is very considerable.

2. All kinds of operations can be carried out on a Mac graphic, whether that graphic is bit-mapped or object-oriented. These operations are designated by small icons: pictures symbolizing the operations that they represent. Apparently, we grasp the point of a well-thought-out graphic over twenty times faster than we'd grasp the same point if it were set out in text.

This feature has been exploited with great success in telecommunications programs for the Mac (especially in Hayes' *Smartcom II*). The multitude of operations involved in transactions between modems are represented by icons, making for much easier understanding of what is involved in the various steps of getting on line with an information utility or the like. The processes involved become 'transparent': you can visualize what's going on and why.

Drawing can be by mouse-driven, point and click movements, or by establishing precise coordinates on a gridded screen (again, by using the mouse).

A recent invention (*Personal Writer* from Anatex Inc.) takes advantage of the Mac's graphics capabilities to allow you to write –longhand– to disk. You simply write with a stylus on a graphics tablet attached to the Mac. The software learns to recognise your writing and transfers it –and any corrections– to the screen (and to disk) in a typeface (scaled to the size of your writing). A 100,000 word dictionary corrects your spelling. The resulting text file can be accepted by pretty well any software that runs on the Mac.

Heralded as "the next computer revolution", this software adds a new meaning to user friendliness, where computers are concerned.

Typographic Facilities

The Mac has built-in typographic facilities:

1. Its system folder can store a large number of typefaces, each in a range of font sizes.
2. From the desktop 'bar menu' (the line of words along the top of the screen), you can also bold, italicize, shadow or underline (or set any combination of these on) any font.
3. You can change the typefaces or font sizes contained in your system folder at will.
4. Each of your fonts is represented on screen by a screen font.

This means that the Mac's screen, with its relatively high screen resolution (relative to the IBM PC, that is), is easy to read, despite its small area. This is important. Text visible on a computer screen is harder to read than the same text visible on paper (it takes 20–30% longer to read, and there's less chance that you'll spot typographical errors), unless:

1. Both upper and lower case characters are displayed. ('Allcaps' are hard to read; there's inadequate variation in letter size and shape.)
2. The letters are in high contrast. (The Mac's black on white characters are easier to read than the IBM PC's green on black ones.)
3. The text is presented in a dynamic way. It should scroll; there should be horizontal and vertical spacing, and attention should be focused by blinking characters. (These features require a fast operating central processing unit.)

    There's no colour monitor for Macs other than the Mac II as yet. This is no great handicap, except for games. Certainly word processing isn't something that's assisted by having a coloured screen. You can print in colour on the ImageWriter printer.[3] But you can't reproduce your printout en masse, except by going through an expensive process.[4] So there seems little point in colour printouts. Colour is still a feature of high-end printing, currently.

The IBM PC wasn't designed to handle graphics or fonts: its screen resolution is lower than the Mac's; it's slower;[5] it doesn't have a range of fonts, and it can't display different fonts on screen. Admittedly, its graphics and fonts-using capabilities can be improved by adding a Hercules graphics card (which permits colour displays) and by employing T/Maker Graphics' *Clickart Personal Publisher* application program. But this only slows a PC down still more. Consequently, graphics is an area where the Mac is clearly superior to the IBM PC. (More on the consequences of this below.)

Program Integration and Compatibility
For Mac users, program integration and compatibility is high:

1. All programs written for the Mac must employ the standard Mac interface.

So there's a coherent, standard menu-structure extending across these programs. This means that, generally, you'll already be familiar with about 40% of any new program that you come to learn.

2. More: there's a software 'kinship' that further increases the compatibility between programs for the Mac.

Mac software is dominated by Microsoft products: 53.5% of software sales come from their programs. Add Apple's own programs –closely integrated with those of Microsoft– and Aldus' *PageMaker*, which is largely compatible with both Microsoft's and Apple's software, and you have 81.3% of the Mac's software coming from one large extended family.

This high compatability makes for much easier learning of programs. Easy learning means that you'll go deeper into any programs that you learn and that you'll be more inclined to learn new programs. The reverse tends to result from the difficult learning associated with what has come to be known as the "MS DOS boot camp". Mac users, typically, use a lot of programs, whereas IBM PC users tend to learn fewer. (Indeed, some of them refer to the PC as "my *Lotus* machine".)

Any work environment in which a lot of employees have to acquire familiarity, individually or as a group, with a wide range of programs requires management to take this ease-of-learning factor into account when deciding whether to buy a Mac or an IBM PC. Not surprisingly, business attitudes towards the Mac –especially in small businesses and among professionals– are becoming more favourable.

3. *All Mac programs use the same 'cut/copy to the clipboard/scrapbook and paste from it' routine.*

This uniform feature makes data easy to transfer between programs, especially as there's a standard graphic file format. So it's easy to put complex graphics into a text file. Accessibility is the mother of familiarity: proportionately, many more Mac users than users of IBM PCs employ graphics programs –and the Mac users use a wider range of graphics programs.

4. *A range of desk accessories (which you can add to, or subtract from, very easily) is part of the Mac's desktop.*

So this collection is available to all programs running on the Mac. Third party developers have added many more such programs to those that came originally with the Mac.

5. *The Mac's latest system, with Multifinder, enables you to switch very rapidly between programs.*

Indeed, you can print in the background while word processing or the like. For Macs without the RAM for Multifinder, there's a utility program called *Switcher*. *Switcher* has come into its own on the Mac Plus and the SE, especially when these have a hard disk. It sets up a cluster of programs in the RAM, allowing you to switch between them at electronic speeds –and, of course, to paste material from one application to another via their common RAM.

Development of the Mac's Artwork Library

Common standards encourage the development and accumulation of software. This is particularly noticeable where graphics for the Mac are involved:

The Mac's basic graphics application program, *MacPaint* , has just undergone major development: see the discussion in chapter 4, especially the commentary on *SuperPaint* and *Illustrator*.

Clip art libraries are being turned into 'click art' libraries for the Mac. Object-oriented (as well as the easier-to-construct bit-mapped) graphics are now appearing in larger numbers. This is partly because of the standard file format, partly because so many newspapers are using the Mac, largely because of its graphics capabilities, for page make up.

To visually catalogue the growing library of click art, graphics management programs have long since been developed for the Mac. A number of programs have recently been developed that considerably enhance the Mac's 'Scrapbook' desk accessory program –that is, that actually improve on the Mac's own desktop.

Other consequences of the Mac's easy-to-use graphics are:

1. There's considerable use of graphics in the database programs that run on the Mac and can benefit from referring to pictures: personnel records, inventories, real estate transactions and suchlike.

2. There's a greater range of planning tools and outliners for the Mac than for the IBM PC, because of the facility with which the Mac's programs can utilize graphics –essential for setting out flow charts, outlines, decision trees, and decision support systems.

> The diversity and range of outlining programs –called idea processors– for the Mac is outstanding. For brainstorming and preparation of project outlines these programs are so useful that they rapidly become essential for everyday planning and writing.

3. It's much easier to develop that greatest of all integrators, the page make up program, for the Mac than it is for the IBM PC. This is why the 'Big Three' page make up programs were developed for the Mac, not the PC.
4. There's now a wide range of programs (over 1400) available for the Mac. These in no way compare in number with the 14,000 available for the IBM PC. But the best programs for the Mac do compare well with those for the PC in quality. *Excel* (a spreadsheet), *The Fourth Dimension* (database management), *Word* (word processing), *PageMaker* (page makeup), *Microphone* (communications), *MacDraft* (drawing) and *MacProject* (flow charting) seem to be as good as anything that runs on the PC. And the PC is chasing after the Mac to develop programs like *Illustrator* and the various 3D drawing programs that first ran on the Mac.

> As a result, a Mac does all that a PC can do and more: it enables an organization to conduct all the usual business operations and do its own in-house publishing.

How things currently stand in the marketplace

The amount of software for the Mac in no way compares with that available for the IBM PC. But, as a result of the factors and developments outlined above, the amount of software for desktop publishing on the Mac is greater. And, in quality, ease of use and cost, the Mac's software tends to have a superior performance-to-cost ratio.

This is the basis on which the Mac's dominance in the desktop publishing niche rests. It's why 70% of all desktop publishing is done via the Mac and LaserWriter, and why Apple is now the biggest seller of printers (Laser-Writers) in North America.

Re-inventing the Computer: Different Views on Marketing Strategies

THE OPEN ARCHITECTURE ENVIRONMENT

Advantages

1. Third party developers rapidly expand hardware and software resources.
2. The market spurs on constantly leap-frogging growth in these resources.
3. The user can expand his or her system as his or her needs grow.

Disadvantages:

1. No industry standards; incompatible hardware and software; files are not transportable between applications.

Diagram 7.1: A Desktop Publishing System:

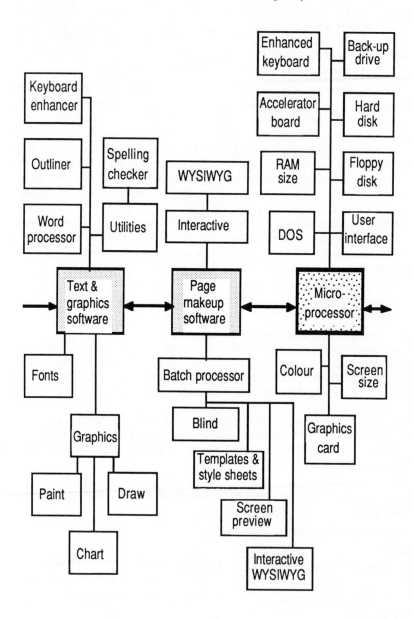

Choice Points

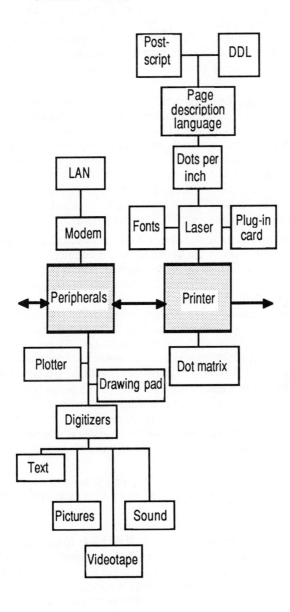

2. Solutions compound these difficulties. Thus MDS's new 10" X 8" screen for the PC, which gives it 100 dots per inch (to the Mac's 72) is incompatible with certain of the cards designed for producing graphics on the PC, runs into problems with the 'barrier' in the RAM after 640K, and, if virtual memory is used on the new more powerful chips, requires DOS 5.0 –a fourth variety of DOS.

3. No-one is responsible for the overall system of microcomputer and peripherals. There can be no support for end-users: it's a retail mass-market. Besides, the dealers can't know more than a fraction of the products that they're handling. No concerted, focused growth plan is possible in a clone-driven market.

4. The beginning end-user is paralyzed by over-choice when putting a micro together (let alone a system).

> To do desktop publishing on a PC, for instance, you'd have to add an EGA (expanded graphics adapter) board, a 'windowing environment' and a mouse. This would require boosting your RAM to 640 K, and adding at least a 10 MB hard disk drive. And after all this, you still wouldn't have much choice of fonts –and you'd be much better off with the 80286 chip that's in the PC AT.

> On top of all this, the command-driven PC and its non-compatible programs make for a difficult learning curve. Learned helplessness or reactance (obdurate resistance to learning) result.

Consequences when you're assembling a desktop publishing system:
The consequences of all of the above are that a beginner desktop publisher requires someone with expertise to tell the beginner how to put his or her system together. Diagram 7.1 (above) indicates how much more complicated it is to set up a system on a PC than on a Mac.[6]

1. All software that runs on the Mac is compatible, and you can load all of it into the Mac's page makeup software. The Mac is a graphics-based, interactive, WYSIWYG micro; so you can ignore the central box. All peripherals that run on the Mac are compatible; so you you can ignore the 'peripherals' box. The Mac outputs to the LaserWriter; so no problems with the last box either.

2. Box one: the PC doesn't have a variety of fonts to screen or print, and it can't handle graphics unless you enhance it. Also lots of graphics programs that *can* be made to run on it are mutually incompatible. Box two: there's a range of page makeup programs that run on the (enhanced) PC. You'll have to chose the one you need. Each page makeup program will only support certain graphics programs.

> The 'micro' square is crucial. You're going to have to have to add an accelerator board, a graphics card and a hard disk, and increase the RAM size –carefully (only certain combinations of these peripherals will work together).

> Peripherals: there's a wide choice; you'll be easily to put a compatible combination of these stage four peripherals together (except for sound). Printer: if you want to use the LaserWriter, you'll have to do so via a Mac or via software that supports the LaserWriter. Unless you've allowed for this, you'll have to go back to squares one and two and start over....

This complexity leads to 'turnkey' solutions: someone chooses a whole system –his– for you; sets it up; teaches you how to run it, and then turns it over to you in running order. Such 'solutions' tend to be costly: you get oversold.

Meanwhile, the PC has become the standard tool for composing and editing (rather than publishing) text: its word processing and text-editing programs surpass those available (so far) for the Mac.

CLOSED ARCHITECTURE: THE 'SINGLE, COHERENT DESIGN CENTRE' APPROACH

Advantages:

1. Uniform, user-friendly interface:
   a. Easy to learn (the Mac interface has an 8:1 advantage, in ease of learning, over the PC's DOS).
   b. A WYSIWYG (What You See Is What You Get) screen.
   c. Program compatibility reinforces learning.
2. Standard graphics file format –and PictureBase (a database management system for graphics) as an additional pressure towards standardization:
   a. Graphics are transferable from one program to another.
   b. Libraries of clip art pour in for computerization as click art.
   c. Novice users can buy, and easily install, fonts from an extensive and expanding collection of typefaces –from many languages (including Arabic, Greek etc.).
3. Portable software files:
   a. Microsoft's programs (which are among many of the best selling programs for the Mac) form a 'family' which is especially portable to the key Apple programs (designed in close consultation with Microsoft).
   b. Even a relative beginner can leverage his investment in program expertise: each new program learned reinforces previous learning while adding to it.
4. Planned growth is possible: this is virtually a one-company market niche.
5. Planned support programs are affordable in a one-company market:
   a. For users: user groups; specialist magazines and electronic bulletin board services.
   b. Dealers: vendor support (as with *PageMaker*).
   c. Desktop publishers: editing services.

Disadvantages:

Desktop publishing involves a market of opportunity. The idea of porting a high-end publishing program to the Mac-LaserWriter combination was Paul Brainerd's. Apple's planning and technology was positioned to take advantage of such a development. But the move into desktop publishing involved taking advantage of a suddenly available niche market; it wasn't planned from the outset. So there are some problems.

1. Not all programs are in fact fully transportable. The SCSI ports on the Mac Plus have made some adaptation of pre-existing software necessary. But this is a minor problem compared with the incompatibilities which plague the PC environment.
2. The dealers know less than even relatively beginning users, as the latter are quick to use a wide range of programs (including utility programs).

3. Neither the vendors nor the dealers are able to deal with bugs in the overall system –that is, where bugs involve, or occur in, interaction among a supposedly integrated complex of hardware and software. In practice, users in distress consult other, experienced users, or –if they can't help– laser setting shops (who have *lots* of experience in getting hardware and software to work together).

4. The Mac isn't compatible with (IBM's) mainframes or with the PC. These are problems that can be handled by software, however: Tri-Data's *Netway 1000A* makes the Mac emulate a 3274 mainframe's controller; Centram's *TOPS* links Macs and PCs on a LAN, and Apple's *MacLink Plus* couples the Mac and PC. Likewise, the lethargic communications exchanges caused by the slow serial port on the Mac Plus have been coped with by the communication cards now available for the SE and Mac II.

Consequences for the would-be desktop publisher:

The resulting easy-to-install, plug and play desktop publishing system is saleable through dealers, thus realizing a decrease in price for the end-user. This marketing strategy produced the first publishing system to be sold through retail outlets. It resulted in a lucrative niche market dominated by one machine: the Mac Plus and the Mac SE have become the standard page makeup terminals for 70% of desktop publishing.

> Networking to mainframes and beyond, LANs and modems have posed perennial problems for all micro users. (If PC compatibles are *too* compatible, lawsuits over patents result.) As these things go, the Mac is a relatively easy computer to connect to a network or a LAN.

The Influence of the Established User Base
THE ATTITUDE OF PC USERS
The costs of success:

What a computer maker can do depends, to a large extent, on what its base of established users expect of it, and what they'll put up with.

In this respect, IBM is somewhat a victim of its own success. The company's great contribution was to bring a 16-bit standard to the micro market. All PC-users, including owners of IBM compatibles, expect IBM to provide continuity of service to the business community (whose favourite saying is: "Nobody ever got fired for buying IBM")

IBM has sold its products, to a large extent, because of its service ethic and because (the PC Junior excepted) it doesn't leave its customers with technological orphans on their hands. There's a huge base of established IBM PC users (estimated at 4.2 million worldwide), made even larger by all the compatibles and clones (maybe another 3 million machines).

When an organization owns thousands of PCs, the prospect of upgrading them is daunting. The largest single cost associated with computers occurs in training people to use them. The retraining associated with major program upgrades is long and costly. Besides, 90% of users don't use the full resources of the programs they've already got.

In fact, most micros are PCs with 8088 chips, running outdated software. This is, however, still perfectly functional and effective (whereas new software and new hardware are rarely free of bugs). Transferring the contents of tens of thousands of 5.25" floppy disks on to 3.5" disks is not an enterprise to be lightly undertaken, either.

Consequently, most corporate owners of PCs don't wish to have to dispose of them –and their associated software– to update to a new generation of PCs. Yet, less than 10% of IBM PCs are ATs (the 80286 chip-based machines needed for desktop publishing), and less than 1% of PC-type micros are new, third generation PS/2 models.

So development by incremental steps seems the only policy feasible for IBM. Its clientele won't appreciate a quick move to the PS/2 that leaves them stranded with technological orphans –or a collection of incompatible micros. Huge sums of money are involved in this (inevitable) model change.

THE ATTITUDE OF MAC USERS

The Mac and the early adopters

Apple's position is rather different from IBM's:

1. In the first place, there's a smaller base of established users.

   But numbers are growing rapidly, since the appearance of the Mac SE 9system expanded) and the Mac II. The 2,000,000th Mac should be sold in October of 1988.

2. More importantly, Mac-users (mostly yuppies –Young, Upwardly-mobile, Professional Intellectuals) seem to have a rather different attitude from that of the (largely corporate) IBM PC users. A relatively large number of them seem to have the characteristics of early adopters of technological innovations:

   - Mac users tend to be affluent; and they're ready to pay to get work done by whatever technology does it most effectively and easily.

   - In big organizations, Mac users tend to be top echelon: presidential and vice-presidential levels –up there. The Mac's influence is from the top down.

   - The Mac appeals to professionals in small business. They haven't time to become computer buffs: they just want to cope more effectively with their work. And they only own a few machines. So an upgrade is a major inconvenience, but not a disaster.

   - Apple has established a niche in academe for the Mac. This means that students go out into the work world with the mind set of a Mac user, so far as computing is concerned. They simply won't put up with what they see as unnecessary complexities in operating a micro: to them learning DOS is like having to learn Latin in order to read the bible. They won't switch to the PC. (Few users will learn a second machine, come to that.)

Experience shows that, in spite of their outcry, Mac users will switch to a new Mac technology if it's introduced. They've not had difficult learning experiences to daunt them. The Mac is an expensive micro, so its purchasers tend to be relatively well-to-do.Consequently, the prospect of a switch is irritating, but not disastrous. It's simply perceived as a financial cost, which will soon be offset by increased effectiveness and productivity. Given these characteristics in their user base, Apple is able to leapfrog the competition, even when it has to cease to support one of its Mac models, leaving it as a technological orphan.

A Guess at the Future
PRESSURE FOR CONNECTIVITY
Making it easy for the PC and the Mac to communicate with one another:
This pressure is coming from two main sources:

1. The need to link the organization's micros to one another and to its main-frame (via a LAN), and beyond (via a network). Such linkage means, as already indicated, that a variety of hardware and software must be induced to work together.
2. The need to achieve the savings made possible by in-house desktop publishing. For this purpose, too, a variety of hardware and software must be induced to work together.

Hardware manufacturers and software developers are striving to achieve greater connectivity. Evidence for this (discussed in more detail in chapter 4) is:

1. Increasing support, among manufacturers and developers alike, for standards –for graphics (cards and programs), printers, and scanners.
2. The ever-more frequent appearance of software facilitating transfer of files between different kinds of disks, different kinds of peripherals, and different kinds of micros.
3. Major applications programs ported from the PC to the Mac, or vice versa, along with programming to make transfer of files between the two varieties of any of these programs simple and easy.

Also, there have been signals from the world's two largest makers of micros –IBM and Apple– that they are taking steps to encourage ease of communication between their machines.

> IBM is developing a library of software aimed at integrating 'multi-vendor environments' –desktop publishing systems and LANs which typically involve a variety of micros and peripherals made by third-party developers. This policy reverses its hitherto somewhat exclusionary attitude towards non-IBM hardware.

> Apple has provided slots for cards to run PC programs in its latest micros. The Mac II is capable of running a card with an Intel 80326 chip on it; the Mac SE is capable of running a card with an Intel 8088 chip. All Macs now have SCSI ports, and the Mac II has a Nubus bus that can accept *any* microprocessor chip.

THE 'OPEN ARCHITECTURE' ISSUE
A new concept: *semi*-open architecture:
After Apple's experience with the Apple II line, and IBM's with the PC, it's clear that cloning poses serious problems for both manufacturers. Yet open architecture is necessary for connectivity and to encourage third party developers.

Apple's solution seems to have been found in the concept of a semi-open architecture. This solution appeared with the Mac Plus and has been taken further in the Mac SE and Mac II:

1. Semi-open architecture, with slots, a standard bus and SCSI ports.
2. A proprietary ROM chip; very limited disclosure of data on the system, the expansion board's logic diagrams, and the BIOS code.

IBM's third generation micro, the PS/2, with its 80235 chip and new OS/2 operating system, seems to be taking a somewhat different route:

'Open' architecture for IBM will apparently involve the following:

1. Physically open architecture that developers can write programs for, containing an expansion bus that they can develop boards for.
2. A *proprietary* bus –the MCA (Micro Channel Architecture) bus. Compatability with this bus will not be possible without infringement on IBM's patent rights.
3. Non-compatible buses won't be able to support the boards that run on the MCA bus.
4. IBM's new operating system, OS/2, won't run on anything but the MCA bus. Conversely, any system that's not completely compatible with the MCA bus won't be able to run IBM software.

> In short, no cloning.

Of course, it's possible to 'reverse engineer' any micro. Uncovering the custom chips to analyze their circuits, and unassembling (breaking down the assembler code of) the BIOS code will reveal the undocumented data. But any cloning will unfailingly result in law suits. Both Apple and IBM have indicated that they will *strongly* defend their proprietary rights by legal means. Their subsequent actions show that they mean to do so.

WHITHER THE THIRD GENERATION?

So the environment of the third generation of micros will be as different from that of the second generation micro (essentially a CPU standardized on the IBM PC) as that generation differed from the (chaotic absence of standards in the) first generation environment. This micro will be a product of a 'constellation' (to be discussed in chapter 8), centred upon one of two major 'intelligence centres' –Apple and IBM.

The Impact of This Technology on Writers and Writing
THE TYPEWRITER MENTALITY PASSES AWAY

Text processing

> Serious writers are switching from typewriter to the micro, as the latter makes them much more productive, and also gives them more power when dealing with publishers.

It's easier to process text on a micro than on a typewriter: less effort pays off more. Typescript is correctable only in small ways, whereas word processed text is easy to correct on a *massive* scale.[7] A heavily corrected typescript is a mess. It's difficult to read, and pencilled-in ideas for changes, additions or deletions get overlooked in its confusion. Corrections and alterations to word processed text involve no mess, so there's none of the confusion common when working with a messily over-written text.

Word processing **doesn't** save time –you do six or seven revisions where you'd have done (at best) one when using a typewriter– but it does produce a superior product.

Typescript is inert; word processed text interacts with you. All kinds of serendipitous combinations occur in text left adjoining after block deletions or removals. You can play 'what if' games with word processed text without losing anything: changes can be undone –and you always have your copy of the original, anyway.

Desk accessories allow a writer to develop an outline, and then insert it into his or her text. So writers do a lot of outlining, and the resulting text is better planned. Revising word processed text is much easier and speedier: there are sentence dis-assembly programs, and global 'search and replace' programs, for text editing. Re-formatting such text is enormously easier. So word processed text is generally better organized than typescript text.

There are programs for automatic indexing and footnoting, and for automatic hyphenation and justification. Other programs check spelling (and provide a thesaurus to generate ideas for other ways of expressing oneself). Yet other programs check punctuation and even (some) grammatical forms. So editing and copy editing is better done.

Product quality is also improved: there's a wide variety of fonts available, and all kinds of graphics, from business graphics (charts and graphs) to line art, and there are style sheets which facilitate page formatting. And the results can be printed out on a laser printer, which confers 'the authority of print' on them.

Using a word processor changes a writer. No one who's used a word processing program ever leaves it to go back to typewriting.

WRITERS RECOVER (SOME) CONTROL OVER THE PUBLISHING PROCESS
New skills give the writer greater control over the finished product
When editors require the writer to acquire and use page makeup technology, they effectively equip him or her with the combined skills of an editor, a publisher, and a team of printers. Such a writer becomes dispensable, especially as his or her ability to produce camera-ready copy is an economic asset, often sorely needed.

Writers also know that the their work can easily be changed in form – form a talk to a general article, for instance– and may be published by different media, such as the electronic journal, for a niche market. Given these terms for publishing and marketing, the power imbalance between writers and publishers is shifting, with the writer making some gains.

Design teams and co-operative writing in general
Publishing a manual in-house is now a highly interactive process involving several authors, illustrative artists, and the page makeup person. The latter is also the editor-publisher, and the desktop publisher –who facilitates and coordinates the team which must be involved in the layout at every stage.

A wide range of skills is required of such an editor.; but the process is likely to be highly productive, innovative, and cost effective.

A New Communications Environment
ATTITUDES TO WRITING AND PUBLISHING ARE CHANGING

1. Text is increasingly becoming seen as an interactive process rather than as a product: it is something that one 'massages', and there are new theories of audience, involving reader co-construction of meaning.
2. There's a changed visual sense: there's much more frequent use of graphics; the producer/director (as an alternative to the author) is seen as a possible model for a writer –in the writing of simulations, cases and suchlike.

3. Composition is, likewise, increasingly interactive: a writer may be jointly composing a work on an electronic network, or may 'download' (import via a modem) material from a database or an electronic utility.
4. Attitudes to literary property are changing as interactive production becomes commoner and as copyright becomes harder to enforce, what with xerox, VCRs, audio-recorders, optical character readers, frame grabbers, copy programs –or computer clones themselves, for that matter. Concepts like public domain software are symptomatic of this change.
5. It's the end of an era, for typographers. Visually informative text is replacing the monolithic text block (product of the hard-to-use batch pagination program). There are niche markets for short runs of specialized books, personal imprint editors, and 'intrapreneurs' (a newspaper chain's graphics artists who sell their work as click art, for example).
6. Common to many of the above developments is a new emphasis on metacognition. To work with this new technology, a writer has to be much more aware than in the past of his or her own thinking process, whether it's a matter of consulting an (invisible) database, or of customizing a computer system, or designing visually informative text, or 'invoking' a reader, or of selecting planning frames in scenario building. New capacities of mind are being discerned. The 'triune' and the 'society of mind' models (the latter an offshoot of work on artificial intelligence), have made us more conscious of the new mind sets and thinking and learning styles involved.[8]

CHANGES IN READERSHIPS

Changed readerships –owed, in no small part, to concentration in newspaper publishing– have developed, with readers oriented towards the types of publications (newsletters and specialized magazines) that are easy to produce via desktop publishing.

Impacting on the other electronic media, the micro has led heavy users of information to favour an interactive, user-initiated approach to communication. Meanwhile a burgeoning self-help/support group movement is gaining strength; regard for the postal services is diminishing, and modems and electronic information services are coming into favour. The result is a 'do it yourself' attitude towards getting out news that is important to the special interest group.

Narrowcasting is taking over from broadcasting among producers of text. Consider the following changing patterns of media use among heavy print-users:

The movement from broadcasting to narrowcasting	
1976	1986
Books and newspapers	Specialist magazines, newsletters, manuals
Typewriting	Word processing
Postal services	Electronic mail electronic information utilities
TV, film & radio	Xeroxing, VCRs, audio-cassettes click art & copy programs

NEW CENTRES AND FORMS OF PUBLICATION

New centres of publication

All major organizations are now involved in publishing. Besides the in-house publications unit, there are networked support-groups and self-help groups producing newsletters and brochures for their clientele (Employee Stock Options Programs, Employee Assistance Programs and the like) A wide range of communications is in use, with far more publishing initiated by the workers themselves.

The author is becoming empowered over against the publisher: economic transfer, once the writer has paid his or her dues for the technology, gives that writer leverage with editors. Such writers are now accompanied by virtual co-workers: their customized and extremely powerful computer systems. This accompaniment can make a writer an irreplaceable member of a publications production team.

The book on a disk

1. The advent of the book on a disk will likely be an intermediary stage en route to CD ROM. Plain text with embedded macros takes far less space on disk than does the variety of fonts and formatting currently provided by a program such as Microsoft *Word* . Besides, a make up language can be coded for security, so as to be unreadable to anyone without a key.

2. A revised edition, also on a disk, could involve as little as an install program and a limited number of changes, for a minor editing. A new disk would be all that a major revision would entail.

3. The in-house publicist could quickly instruct would-be readers about the steps involved in locating specific passages and the commands required to access them. He or she could also quickly produce whatever camera-ready copy was desired, as well as see to getting it printed.

4. Certain texts, such as manuals and job aids, require frequent revision, often by persons scattered through a large organization. In such cases, the in-house publicists in the branch offices or wherever could input the changes made by their branches' technical experts, along with the necessary macros. Indeed, even outsiders, if they had desktop publishing skills, could input such changes.

   As changes came in, the desktop publisher, functioning as the central publishing authority, could collate them. Then, with guidance from the technical experts of his or her branch, he or she could incorporate all changes meriting incorporation, to establish the next edition. So there would be no need for filters, or expensive, high-end editing systems: text in ASCII is readily manipulable.

8 The Desktop Publishing Revolution:

The Logistics of the Microcomputer Production and Distribution Process

The Dream

THE TECHNOLOGY AND ITS REVOLUTIONARY POTENTIAL

'Desktop publishing' means that documents can be produced cheaply and easily which have 'the authority of print'. The costly pre-print stages of document preparation can be done on a micro. Then only the –relatively inexpensive– running off on a printing press remains to be done.

Until recently, the current advertising has it, only millionaires could afford a printing press. Now, anyone who has the price of a cheap car can afford one, in the form of a micro and a handful of word processing, drawing and page make-up programs.

Mastering this technology need not be difficult. Apple's Macintosh, for instance, was expressly designed to be easy to install and use. It is "for the rest of us", rather than for the computer wizards, with its mouse, menus, icons and windows. The Mac, in fact, is the first cheap WYSIWYG workstation –the equivalent of a minicomputer.

If you can print cheaply, you don't have to sell dear. You don't need an expensive distribution system to sell your products and cover your costs. You can make a profit on small sales in a 'niche market' – a market segment interested in your topic which you can reach by direct mail. So cheap publishing makes it possible for small publishers to thrive, with all that this implies for western society and,.indeed, countries throughout the world.

THE ONLY MULTILINGUAL MICRO

The Mac treats any letter or character that it puts on its screen as a picture. So it can put on screen, and print, a wide variety of typefaces (Arabic, Cyrillic, Hebrew, and Hindi, for instance) and even pictographic scripts like Chinese. This is an outstanding feature of the Mac, which the developers of this micro have vigorously encouraged. It has spurred a renaissance in the design and invention of typefaces and in the production of alphabets in non-Roman typefaces. A truly remarkable (and continuously expanding) collection of typefaces is available for this, the only multilingual micro.

The Mac was explicitly designed not to be an 'English-only' machine. Its user interface is dominated by non-linguistic features: it's mouse-driven and employs icons –little pictures. Its menus and dialogue boxes come in a variety of languages. You can choose an interface in the language of your choice, at least where the main international languages are concerned. A third of all Macs sold go to purchasers outside of the U.S.A.

Once you have a text file on disk, you can make a copy of it in a matter of seconds. Then you can send it, on disk, to someone else, or send it by telephone using a modem. Hence its revolutionary potential: potentially, anyone, in any country around the world, can′publish anything and/or transmit it, quickly and unobservably, to anyone he or she wishes to send it to.

This means, potentially, freedom of the press for everyone. Anyone who so wishes can publish his or her views, with the authority of print and with sophisticated graphics and page layouts. Publications that look as though they have been professionally produced need no longer be the perquisite of the élite and the wealthy. This was the dream of those who developed this technology –a noble, Californian dream.

Awakening from the Dream
THE COMPUTER "FOR THE REST OF US"

It's true that you can buy a powerful micro cheaply now: a clone of an IBM PC 8088 sells for under $500. If any micro is a machine "for the rest of us", the PC clone, some contend, is that micro.

The PC employs a 'command-driven interface': you're faced with a blank screen with only a blinking dot when the machine starts up. You have to program it, to get anything to happen. And the programs that run on the PC differ from one another, so have to be individually mastered,′ often with little or no transfer of learning. Not a prospect to relish, especially as the programs themselves aren't always easy to learn. PC-users tend to learn few programs.

Learning to use several programs entails learning quite a bit of programming. Computer programming requires advanced math skills. Both programming and advanced math go together with, and are normally acquired through, a lengthy process of formal education. So any computer that requires a lot of computing skills to run is a computer for an élite group of users, *not* for "the rest of us".

Besides, the PC is a relatively antiquated machine, and you can't do page makeup on it unless you add cards and peripherals (which will cost more than the PC itself did). Diagrams 2.1 and 7.1 should help in understanding what's involved. Desktop publishing involves a 'long linked' technology: lots of pieces of hardware and software have to work together to make it all happen.

Furthermore, to produce a WYSIWYG screen, a micro has to be a graphics-based computer. If it wasn't designed for this (and the PC wasn't), you have to add on all kinds of peripheral devices to make it capable of doing it. These devices require a lot of power, memory and storage space. You'll need a megabyte of memory in the micro's RAM (most IBM PCs and clones have trouble passing the 640,000 byte mark) and a hard disk, preferably with 20 MB of storage space. Such power and equipment is expensive.

Furthermore, the cheapness of the PC clones is owed to the fact that their peripherals were produced by third party developers. Prices dropped as these developers competed with one another for sales. This cheapness has its disadvantages. Many of the peripherals won't work together. Very often you can't take a text file produced by one program and get it to run when introduced into another program.

So getting this long linked technology to work if you're using the PC or its clones isn't cheap or easy. A beginner will need help in setting up a system to do desktop publishing on one of these micros. He or she will find it a costly process, and one that involves learning some quite difficult programs.

The PC isn't the machine for the rest of us to do desktop publishing on.

THE COMPUTER FOR DESKTOP PUBLISHING

This is why 70% of desktop publishing is done on the Macintosh and its (relatively) cheap laser printer, which produces what looks like regular print. There are good reasons for choosing this combination:

The Mac has never been cloned. So Apple, its developer, has been able to require those who wished to develop peripherals and software for the Mac to develop them to Apple's specifications. As result, any piece of hardware for the Mac will work with all of the other peripherals, and so will any software program. As is not the case with the IBM PC and clones, all programs written for the Mac have to employ the selfsame graphics file (Apple's). So all their files are compatible with one another. This means that all the Mac's peripherals are compatible with one another, and you can transfer text files from one program to another.

It also means that, once you've learned one program –which is unlikely to require any programming skills, you'll find that you know 40% of the next program when you come to learn that. So it's easy to learn a new program on the Mac; and each one learned reinforces previous learning. Mac users typically learn a lot of programs.

PRICING THE DREAM OUT OF THE REACH OF THE REST OF US

But this user-friendliness comes at a price:

1. Peripherals for the Mac aren't nearly as cheap as are those for the IBM PC and clones. Until recently there were millions of PCs and clones and very few Macs. So developers competed to produce peripherals for the PC, with the result that prices of its peripherals dropped. Few Macs meant few developers for the Mac. So peripherals were not competitively produced, and therefore were costly. (With over a million Macs now sold, this situation is changing.)

2. Besides, keeping ahead of the clone-makers requires continuous development of the Mac. So does keeping up with demands for ever more sophisticated page makeup capabilities. Together these pressures have produced a *series* of Macs, each of ever greater power, capabilities and expensiveness.

This has all occurred in about three years.

The result is that the Mac isn't a particularly cheap micro. Added to your initial outlay are the costs of having repeatedly to purchase new versions of the Mac, as earlier ones, no longer 'supported' by Apple, become 'technological orphans'. (Only the micros from the Mac Plus on are able to run all of the current software.)

You have to keep buying the new models, to be able to use the new, state-of-the-art software. But having to sell outdated equipment at fire sale prices to buy the new micros adds considerably to the costs of desktop publishing.

Furthermore, buying time on someone else's laser printer isn't really a viable way of getting your printing done, for the following reasons:

1. The Mac has a tiny screen. It's difficult to proofread on such a screen. You get better results by printing out your text and proofreading that.

2. The Mac has a perfectly good dot matrix printer, which does a superb job –for a dot matrix printer– inexpensively and fast. But you need at least a laser printer to get a *print* quality product. However, the laser printer and the Linotronic print two lines less per page than the dot matrix printer does. So all the page breaks change, ruining your page makeup designs.

3. Even at the prices you pay for LaserWriter printing, you can't afford to test-print frequently. Think of the cost of three test runs of a 50 page document (not an uncommon requirement when complex layouts are involved).

> *So, if you're doing a lot of printing, and the documents must look professional, you must have your own laser printer.*

A Mac system for desktop publishing is no longer cheap if you have to buy a LaserWriter printer. For the latter, too, has appeared in a new, more powerful version. Additional parts are used to upgrade the earlier model. So the price of the original model hasn't dropped very much. (People are upgrading them, not selling them.) And the Linotronic is a regular phototypesetter, selling at upwards of $US 30,000.

The Reality
THE ACTUAL USERS OF THE NEW TECHNOLOGY

In practice, the Mac is a micro for big organizations or for professionals. (Essentially, you've got to be able to deduct your personal computer and its expenses from income tax if you're to afford it.) The Mac is becoming the micro of the well-educated, for the following reasons.

1. The Mac's hardware and software have been upgraded to cope with more sophisticated tasks. Both are becoming more complicated. A great increase in capability results. But it comes at the price of a user's having to know how the latest Mac system (the *fifth*) works, and how to get an ever increasing number of programs to work together.

2. Likewise, advanced page makeup programs require you to know a good deal about typesetting. In practice, it's not much use having a printer's team on your desktop if you don't know what they're capable of and how to direct them.

To use the Mac, you have to know a good deal about the printer's craft –you've got to acquire a lot of specialist, printer's knowledge. And you'll need an ever increasing amount of computing smarts. Most of us can only afford the time to acquire this combination of expertise if it's our job to do so. This is precisely the case with many Mac-users: they're employed as in-house publishers.

Such users are normally part of a team. It's rare for someone to have skills in typesetting *and* to be a good graphics artist. Generally, too, the 'lead user' (the expert in the technology on whom others in the office rely for advice) who keeps the local area network, is another team member.

Any but the simplest forms of desktop publishing are generally done by such a group, using several Macs hooked up to a LAN and a LaserWriter. Only big organizations can afford such technology.

THE REAL BENEFICIARIES OF DESKTOP PUBLISHING TECHNOLOGY

Desktop publishing has created a fast-growing, multi-billion-dollar market where none existed prior to 1985. The major beneficiaries of desktop publishing have been, in fact, not the individuals employing it, but their employers, the big organizations. Organizations have saved a lot of money by printing forms, manuals and newsletters in-house. Many large organizations have effectively become their own publishers.

Profit-taking from desktop publishing seems, in fact,to have been the motive behind many large organizations' involvement in this technology:

- What drove the development of WYSIWYG page makeup software seems to have been the desire of newspapers to cut the costs associated with their printing unions.
- Computer graphics programs were developed by the military-industrial complex for the writing of instructional manuals. These programs were then 'ported' to the micros, for spin off profits.
- Likewise the big publishers ported their page makeup software (in the form of batch programs) and collections of computer graphics to the micros, as these, becoming increasingly powerful, were able to use them.
- What's been driving the development of hardware and software for desktop publishing has been the desire of large organizations to do *all* their own printing, at least to the camera-ready stage, in-house.
- The losers in all of this seem to have been the small, unionized print shops.

In North America we are now in a situation where three times as many people read newsletters –many of them the public relations output of big companies– as read daily newspapers. This exposes the fallacy in the contention that owning a press gives you freedom of the press. A *distribution system* is required to get printed matter out to the public and read; and such systems are expensive.

The big organizations, who have the resources to set up some form of distribution system, have made the largest gains in freedom of the press. Most such organizations seem by now to have become publishing houses, putting out sophisticated newsletters and pamphlets to explain what they are contributing to society.

USE OF THE TECHNOLOGY BY PRIVATE INDIVIDUALS

Private persons are only a fraction of the Mac-using population. Most of them are using their micros for business or professional purposes:

- Word processing is the commonest use of the micro by private persons. It increases a writer's productivity by 40%; so anyone who writes a lot for his or her living can ill afford not to use the technology.
- The next commonest use is record keeping via database management; then comes spreadsheeting for keeping accounts.

There's not much sign of a revolution here. And this is in North America, where the desktop publishing technology is (relatively) cheap and available, and its use is unconstrained.

There's little sign that the Mac, or any other micro, has been 're-invented' (that is, that it has had uses invented for it that were not contemplated by those who initially designed and financed it). There has been no efflorescence of new writers, small publishing houses, new forms of writing, or underground presses. Rather the emphasis has been on developing better database, spreadsheet, and word processing programs.

Major innovations have had to do with CD ROM. They involve achievements such as putting the Library of Congress catalog system on one of these multi-gigabyte disks, putting the US zip-code on a (slim) disk, and setting up such a disk with text and diagrams to help Ford's mechanics with their work. Inventory control and operations management figured largely among the things that mainframe technology was devised for. There seems little sign of change in the uses to which the micro technology is being put.

How Real Was The Dream Anyway?
USE OF THE TECHNOLOGY IN THE THIRD WORLD

What of the Third World? As we've seen, even in the United States, where the price of what is, effectively, the most useable desktop publishing system is (relatively) low, most users are middle class and using the technology for their organizations or for careerist purposes. It's hard to imagine that things can be much otherwise in Third World countries, for the following reasons:

> Even when speaking of the U.S., it's misleading to say that you can buy your own printing press for the price of a cheap car. Realistically, a desktop publishing system is likely to cost well over $10,000. This is *not* the price of a cheap car.

> Besides, a car is the second largest expenditure, after their home, that the average U.S. family makes. A car is a *necessity*, given the parlous state of the public transportation systems, and the dangers of nighttime travel, in big U.S. cities. Most would-be purchasers of desktop publishing systems in the U.S. have to choose between a car or a publishing system –and, compared to the car, the latter is a *luxury*.

> This is clear from reviewing the socio-economic characteristics of the families that have a computer (which is much cheaper than a desktop publishing system) in the home.

> The 13.7% of households owning computers are affluent and well educated –and they got their computers for the children, thus perpetuating their families' advantage in computer literacy. Their median income is twice the national average, and the percentage of college graduates among them is above average. And even these homes tend only to have Commodores or Apple IIs.

In reality, both money and education are required for desktop publishing. Money is required because the technology is expensive, and education is required because editing skills require considerable literary training or experience. This technology is more accessible to some than to others.

Still, if past trends are anything to go by, as time goes on, the technology will become cheaper and simpler, and accessible to ever larger numbers of people. Some desktop publishing capabilities will likely be built into word processing programs. It will be possible for anyone to do the simpler forms of desktop publishing –newsletters and the like.

The fact that there have been only 700,000 purchases of Macs (not of the –far more expensive– publishing *systems*) in the U.S. is in accord with the argument that nothing revolutionary is occurring. When those who purchase computers for the home are relatively well-to-do, even in the U.S., how can things be much different in Third World countries? There the price of the technology is higher than in the U.S., and most people's incomes are lower.

Moreover, all countries aren't like the U.S., where freedom of expression and of the press is concerned. Use of publishing technology –or even of photocopying machines and typewriters– does not go unregulated and unremarked in many Third World countries. Only officials in authority, or wealthy persons, are likely to have access to these microcomputer-driven publishing systems. Possession and use of such systems will be widely –and closely– scrutinized. Social revolutionaries are unlikely to be able to use them unremarked.

What chance would you have, for instance, of writing a Kurdish book to disk, and then circulating it widely, if you were a Kurd in Iraq (where the Kurdish language is not for use in publications)? And how would you reach the largely illiterate Kurds in the largely paperless environment of the villages?

The contention that the Mac will conquer illiteracy in the Third World seems also somewhat dubious. The price of the Mac is likely to be a formidable obstacle to such an outcome, apart from the powerful societal and international pressures against Third World mass literacy.[1]

> The same holds true for the contention that the Mac will subvert censorship behind the iron curtain. Simply acquiring a Mac behind the iron curtain would be a major achievement. Besides, totalitarian governments don't normally tolerate any publications critical of their régimes.

Where disparities of power and wealth are even more marked than in the U.S., and freedom of the press less in evidence, the effect of desktop publishing technology is likely to be the exact reverse of revolutionary. It will, in practice, increase and consolidate the communication outreach of big business and big government and further entrench the middle class.

A REVOLUTION IN BOOK PUBLISHING IN THE WEST?

Market structure

To appreciate the potential of desktop publishing in this regard, you have to take the market structure of book publishing into account.[2] The market conditions which largely determine what goes on in book publishing cause considerable uncertainty. For all their efforts, book publishers haven't managed to control all sectors of this market. This lack of control leads to a highly competitive market structure, in some sectors. So here, if anywhere, a revolution in publishing might be expected.

Disproportionate influence of the big publishers

There are some areas in publishing where size confers few advantages: small publishers may produce a better return on investment than big ones with trade books and specialized books, for instance. Printing costs are by now low enough that, depending on what you mean by 'publishing', almost anyone can publish pretty well anything. And they do. The numbers of small publishers, like the numbers of new book titles and of new authors published, are all at record highs –along with book sales (which rose 400% between 1960 and 1980).

These statistics don't necessarily mean that all books which deserve to be published are getting published, however. Consider the following facts, (taken, in each case, from the latest years for which I've been able to find statistics):

1. In 1978, when you count as a publisher anyone who had published one (or more) new title(s) that year, there were 10,803 publishers. However, when you count only persons who had published five or more new titles the year before and three or more in 1978 (by no means big publishers), the number of publishers falls to 1,213.

2. In 1972, There were 1,205 publishers, when you count as a publisher any operation with one employee or more. But the top 27 publishers (comprising firms with 1,000 employees or more) accounted for 45.43% of all book sales. And the top 115 publishers (comprising all firms with 100 or more employees) accounted for 79.82% of all sales.

The rôle of the small publisher

The big publishers operate under 'profit or perish' rules (unlike the 'gentlemen publishers' –owner operators). They owe their financial success to restricting their publications, by and large, either to successful authors (often discovered by the smaller operators) or to authors writing on themes dictated by the big publishers themselves.

So small publishers are critically important. They take a chance on writers the big firms won't consider –and a writer's main problem is getting his or her first book published. If it succeeds, one of the big firms will take the next book. So, as the big firms grow bigger, "new and diverse publishing alternatives to the established industry" are essential in order to allow more new writers to get into print.[3]

Hence the importance of desktop publishing, which greatly increases the viability and vitality of small publishing operations –the 'push cart presses' which are beginning to spring up in areas other than the Northeast seaboard of the United States.

Text books and paperbacks

There are other areas, too, where desktop publishing is going to create new opportunities for the rest of us. These are the areas within the market where the big publishers have managed to establish control over the market for books.[4]

- *Textbooks are one such area.* This market's growth has plateaued out, so competition for market share is fierce. Here size, with its high-end publishing facilities and nationwide sales force, is an advantage to a publisher. Publishers with a small size, less visually spectacular print run, and without a sales force, just can't compete.
- *Paperbacks are another area.* Big publishers are often divisions of conglomerates which have interests, and outlets, in other communications media, vertically integrated with distributors. 'Blockbuster books', promoted by massive advertising campaigns, with multi-media tie-ins, can produce 'surefire' titles –and a restricted range of authors and subjects.

These factors, combined with the rise of the book distribution chains, have led to greater concentration of control in the areas of textbook and paperback publishing and retailing.

However, textbooks are an area where desktop publishing *can* make a difference:

- If textbooks were locally produced, issues of regional interest, and national issues other than those deemed important by big city writers, for that matter, could well be presented in them.
- At the regional or local level, desktop publishing could produce a cheaper product, with more frequent editions to update contents, as well as illustrative material relevant to local conditions and issues. (Learning proceeds best when the subject matter is meaningfully related to the learner's lifespace.)
- Besides, the textbook writing operation could develop a cadre of local writers and critics. The end result would be a fillip to the maintenance and invigoration of regional (and smaller national) cultures.

New technology, old mentality

But, if such local centres are to become active, desktop publishers must organize themselves and make their potential readers conscious of what they have to offer. There's little indication that this is happening. Currently, desktop publishers are a latent group, atomized and without a larger vision of their potential rôle. Desktop publishing is active only in the service of large organizations, professionals' businesses, and careerist interests; no larger social purpose has yet been articulated for it.

Desktop publishing technology is new and undergoing rapid development. Its users are, for the most part, newcomers to their area of expertise. Usually, they don't fully appreciate the importance of their role, or the opportunities and costs that lie before them. How should they? They're in a chaotic situation: the technology is evolving, and new uses for it are continuously being found. But such uses are all within the range of uses established by traditional publishing. The new technology is, for the most part, trapped within the thought ways of the old technology.

One break with such traditional ways of thought is self-publication of electronic journals. An on-line electronic magazine involves no start-up costs. Its publisher can upload material on to a network such as The Source, or Compuserve, or any university mainframe (the latter are all linked by gateways) using a program (*Microfilm Reader*) which its developers (Buck, Wheat & Associates) provide free. Network members can download it as an on-screen magazine, graphics as well as text. Using a publications kit (which the developers sell), they can print out what they've downloaded, paying a shareware fee.

Alternatively, the publisher could send the journal out on a disk, at regular intervals, to modemless readers who are interested in it. There are successful precedents for such a procedure. For instance, *UpTime*, the monthly series of programs and reviews on disk, has sold over half a million copies to date in this way.

> Initiatives of this kind are surprisingly infrequent,
> however. Old ways die hard.

WHICH GROUPS ARE GETTING THE MOST OUT OF THIS TECHNOLOGY?

Personal publishing has most to contribute to the low end and the middle of the publishing business:[5]

1. The high end of the business, publishing large print runs of expensive publications such as books, magazines and newspapers, has its own expensive, high volume publication systems. Here the LaserWriter is used mostly as a cheap means of producing page proofs or graphics (which are printed in very large sizes on the LaserWriter and then reduced by a process camera to achieve high resolution). The Mac is used as a text inputting device, feeding into a central processor.

2. Medium-sized printing operations, like small quarterly magazines or weekly newspapers, unable to afford high-end publishing systems, can do typesetting, graphics, page makeup and proofing on the Mac and LaserWriter. Organizations can produce their own forms and manuals. Besides this, the micros enable them to manage their accounts, keep their inventories, and do mass mailings. They thus give in-house control of the work flow along with enormous cash savings. Currently, such businesses are the ones that are benefiting most from desktop publishing technology.

3. Potentially, however, the biggest impact will be on the low end of the market. There are many small 'mom and pop' newsletters (over 10,000 are published monthly in the U.S., for instance). These can move from the typewriter and xerox machine to print –and manage mass mailings to subscription lists and accounts all on the one machine.

Small typesetting houses are already setting type for small printers, small businesses and persons wishing to publish their own books. Corner copy shops can become 'instant printing' operations, producing menus, flyers and notices for local small businesses as well as running off documents for persons buying time on their LaserWriters. Career counseling agencies can produce more 'professional' looking résumés.

Printing is now cheaply and readily available for the masses. But it hasn't produced an underground press, as multilithing and xeroxing did. Its users haven't reappropriated the technology, by using it for purposes and/or in ways not intended by the military-industrial complex which generated it.

ACADEME TO THE RESCUE?

Academics are not, as yet, proving particularly enterprising in devising uses for this new technology. For instance, it doesn't seem to have dawned upon our universities –or school districts, for that matter– that desktop publishing could provide a solution to the rising costs of (and often to the irrelevance of much of the subject matter in) textbooks.

Faculty could develop their own textbooks, maybe over a period of years, showing concern for local needs and at a fraction of the cost of big-league textbooks. This would enable local faculty to publish, circumventing the vagaries of the marketing process, and keep texts up to date.

This could mean, for instance, Canadian textbooks, produced by and for Canadians, something that the foreign conglomerates with large publishing houses, selling primarily into a huge U.S. market, are not overly concerned about. (How important you consider this to be depends on your views on intellectual colonialism.) A new type of university press could well come into existence, training students –Arts and Social Science students– in an in-demand, practical and professional skill. Such a press would likely use book-oriented students with linguistic and literary skills as interns, rather than maths-oriented computer science students.

Such small-scale 'presses' would make more effective use –group use– of a technology that is rapidly becoming too expensive for the ordinary individual. You need a Macintosh Plus with its megabyte of ram, hard disk, scanner and LaserWriter printer to effectively use the cutting edge of this 'cheap' desktop publishing technology. But a LaserWriter and a scanner can serve a *group* of writers just as easily as they can serve *one* writer –and they're much more cost effective when used by a group of writers. A hard disk can also serve a group of writers almost as easily as it can serve one, if those writers are connected on a local area network.

The Dream As Nightmare
BACKGROUND TO THE DREAM
The consequences of computerization for the workforce
No technology is neutral, because people –usually powerful people– use it for their own ends. So it pays to know how this technology is being used and what the consequences are. The main consequences of the automated office, robotics and telematics have been, and will most likely continue to be, as follows:[6]

1. Jobless economic growth involving structural unemployment (particularly for women) and indirect job losses.
2. De-skilling, job ghettos and a skills gap between the 'smart' and the 'dumb' jobs spawned by these new technologies.
3. A new information world order producing passive consumers of the technologies' information, goods and services.
4. Trans-border data flows and foreign ownership, causing lost business, job erosion, invasion of privacy and loss of small nations' cultural sovereignty.

Desktop publishing within such a workforce
Where does computer assisted publishing fit into this gloomy picture? Desktop publishing has emerged as a career growth path for those without advanced programming and statistical skills. In a work environment, it involves multi-functional skills (and may soon involve use of workstations), and accessing the distributed logic system of the mainframe.

It also provides the editor with an information broker's rôle, and many of the skills of a micro manager: the editor is usually involved with a local area network, telecommunications (receiving or sending data via modem), and getting different machines and programs to exchange data. Besides, in the field of electronic publishing, editors who have done computer assisted page makeup are frequently selected to do page creation for the videotex systems –which will grow in use in the years ahead.

Re-inventing the technology
Second wave computerization –that spawned by the microchip in 1971– normally goes through three phases:

- First there's automation of individual functions.
- Second comes integration of these automated functions into clusters, in some form of automated management of information system.
- Third comes making innovative use of the technology put in place by the first two phases, so as to create new kinds of activities and employment.

This third phase has been noticeably slower in coming about than the other two. It involves re-inventing the technology –re-conceptualizing what the technology might be used for and what it essentially "is", and directing its 'logic' (that of inventory control, parts management, coordinating of data flows and surveillance of operations) into new directions.

Desktop publishers have been no more creative in this regard than other users of the technology.

Take the case, mentioned in an earlier chapter, of learned journals. Few in Canada subscribe to them –perhaps 10% of a professional group's membership: on average, about 800 subscribers. Costs of publishing these journals are escalating rapidly; governmental subventions are declining, and subscription lists are static.

Meanwhile most university mainframes are on line with one another. So an electronic journal would be accessible to (and downloadable at) every university, and thereafter accessible in hard copy to any subscriber.

Electronic journals would seem to be the obvious, if not a very creative, solution to this cost-price squeeze. As we saw in the last chapter, the 'book on a disk' is an economic way to publish. However, there appears to be very little support for such a solution to their dilemma among learned journal editors.

Commentators on trends in computing hold that innovative use of computers to create new features in already existing jobs is likely to be the most frequent way of adding value to computerized work. The new market niches carved out by small entrepreneurs –in copy/print shops and in typesetting, mentioned above– are mildly creative applications of the technology.

Computer assisted publishing seems to be awaiting some radical redefinitions of what publishing 'is' or could be. Developers of artificial intelligence programs, by way of contrast, do seem to have managed such re-invention. Their 'neural networking' programs, simulate the brain's non-linear processes and promise to enable computer systems to 'learn'

PASSIVE CONSUMPTION OF THE 'FREE FLOW' OF COMMUNICATIONS

Desktop publishing offers a chance of a more open information society, a society in which ordinary people use this technology as a tool to help them communicate with one another. In practice, however, there's every indication that we could be reduced to becoming mere passive consumers of technically superb communications sold to us by the 'information-industrial complex'.[7]

This complex, the informatics industry (third largest industry in the world), is largely controlled by a few corporations located in major cities in the industrialized West. It largely controls the 'free flow' of information (and entertainment and so on) around the world. Specifically, the information utilities of this complex provide the huge databases upon which we are coming to rely –The Source and Compuserve and so on. So the data in terms of which we think, and relying on which we do our research, are selected and structured by these databases.

They thus provide our frame of reference and the informational context within which we do our thinking. In a sense they are making up our minds for us. Meanwhile the purveyors of content and the carriers (for instance, CBS and AT&T) are teaming up to exploit the potential of computer assisted publishing and telematics. These corporations are both carriers of electronic messages and, to a large extent, controllers of what is carried.

But there doesn't have to be a replay of what happened with TV:

- Computing is interactive; and personal computing has a tradition of re-directing the technology –hardware, software and firmware– in the user's interests.
- Desktop publishing gives ordinary people input into the print culture, possibly the richest carrier of ideas in our society.
- We're linked by user groups and networks, and there are hackers to redefine what the technology is all about and can be made to do.[8] "A lot of little brains can beat a few big brains", say the Japanese –and look at *their* record.

The desktop publisher can educate his or her fellow workers to see themselves as co-writers of at least some scripts (those that particularly concern them), rather than as mere spectators of the play –the passive consumers upon whom high end publishing relies.

The aim is to get people to think of computers as a means of expressing themselves. Contributing to 'round robin' writing –interactive group writing of a story– or even using electronic mail will get them started. Then they will come to see using computers as just another way of getting writing done.

This is important, because familiarity with computers now increasingly determines one's ability to get 'smart' (rather than 'dumb') jobs. So it determines one's life chances. And such familiarity is currently largely restricted to the middle class, in industrial society.

The 'Constellation': Organizational Format of the Future?
MICROCOMPUTERS FROM THEIR MANUFACTURERS' VIEWPOINT
Maintaining the lead
Now that the 32-bit micro is here, the race is on to develop an operating system that can do multi-tasking –that is, run several programs at the same time. IBM and Apple seem to have decided upon different strategies for doing this.

IBM seems to be trying to develop a multi-tasking operating system, the OS/2 program, for its PS/2 (Personal System generation 2), in one great leap forward. IBM is aware that this development is going to take time, so is anticipating a long lead time and allowing major developers an equally long developmental time frame for adjusting their software to multi-tasking. In consequence, there's likely to be a dearth of such software for many months to come.

The problem with this strategy is that other companies may produce other operating systems in the interim. Then the micros using the Intel 86386 chip could end up with several different operating systems. Such lack of a standard would produce chaos.

Microsoft is also working on an OS/2 (a second-generation Operating System). Microsoft wants its OS to be device-independent, to run on any micro powered by an Intel 86386 chip (this would include a board with such a chip slotted into a Mac). It's clearly in the users' interest to have such a standard –as it was in the case of DOS, the drive operating system that enabled all PCs, whether IBMs, IBM-compatibles or clones, to run the same software. DOS wasn't (IBM's) PC DOS; it was MS (Microsoft's) DOS. It would be better for all users if OS/2 were the same.

Apple seems to be trying to develop its operating system gradually towards multi-tasking. Developers will be able to keep up to the series of small changes in Apple's system as it inches forward towards this goal. Meanwhile, there will be no dearth in software, as there must be with the Great Leap Forward strategy.

The problem with Apple's strategy is that its system is already showing signs of age:

- Third party developers are coming out with improved versions of various parts of that system, responding to users' complaints about them. There are alternatives to Apple's 'finder' and 'desk accessory and font remover', for instance; and there are what are virtually new versions of the 'scrapbook'.
- Some developers are employing dialogue boxes that remind one of IBM-style programs.
- Apple's *Quickdraw* routines are aging and developers are programming in *PostScript* to get around them.

The merit of Apple's system has been that it acted as a standard.

All developers have had to design to Apple's specifications. By now, however, there are signs that Apple is losing control of, and direction over, the direction in which Mac technology is being developed. (Apple is fighting back with programs like *HyperCard*, which reconceptualize system functions.)

Reliance on powerful third party developers

There is also the problem –from Apple's point of view– of reliance on powerful third-party developers. Apple is very dependent on Microsoft's software. Microsoft is far and away the largest independent supplier of software for the Mac, and has developed of the most powerful spreadsheet and word processor that currently run on the Mac. Microsoft's primary ties are to IBM; and Microsoft's porting of the windowing environment to the PC has cut into Apple's lead. This situation of dependence will only worsen when *dBase III* and *WordPerfect* are ported to the Mac.

CHANGE IN ORGANIZATIONAL DESIGN AND PHILOSOPHY AS A STRATEGY

Apple seems to have chosen to cope with these dilemmas by moving to a 'constellation' type of organizational format.[9] A constellation consists of an 'intelligence centre', plus a framework coordinating 'modules' –affiliates and members of the constellation: see Diagram 8.1.

Functions which aren't of crucial importance are transferred from the centre to the modules –other companies. Repetitive or standardized industrial-type activities are likewise spun off. This leaves the centre with the jobs that are on the leading edge of the technology, while allowing it to piggy-back on other companies' technological capabilities.

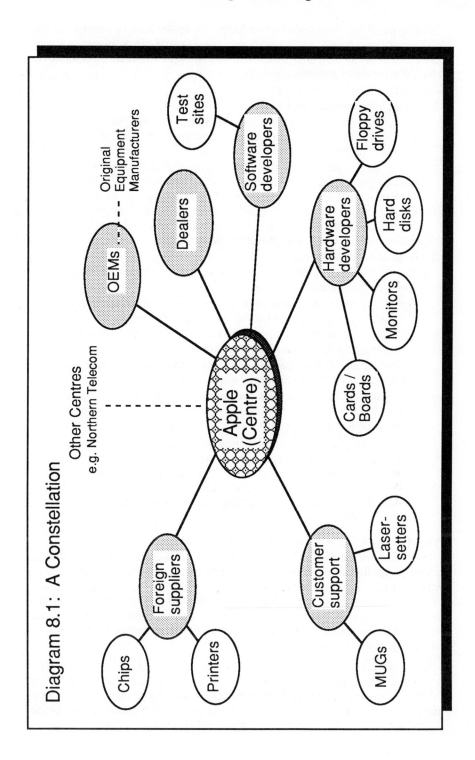

Diagram 8.1: A Constellation

This type of organizational format keeps the centre lean by cutting back on bureaucratic overgrowth (and payroll); decreases capital expenditures; makes for greater flexibility in allocating resources, and strengthens the membership overall by the securing of strategic alliances.

The central core concentrates on:

1. Research and development:
   - Apple has purchased a Cray supercomputer for this purpose, and provides leadership in research and development to all the other members of the constellation.
   - New developments on the part of constellation members are encouraged by Apple's generating third party enterprises (by licensing out its technology or providing support to start-up efforts); by allocation of venture capital; by 'non-disclosure' agreements (which admit promising third parties to inside information on future developments, or patents, in Apple's technology).

2. Maintenance of standards:
   - Seeing to it that all developmental work is in conformity with system specifications for instance:

     Apple has retained control over its operating system (the system; the finder; the utilities) and Switcher. It has also retained its programming languages, its version of Unix, and the telecommunications programs *Appleshare* and *MacTerminal*.
   - Coordination of third parties' activities when several related programs are under development simultaneously.
   - Provision of support services and resources: supporting its dealers and its MUGs (Mac User Groups); and making allocations from its venture capital fund to promising new developers.

     > The ethos of the constellation is that of 'bottom-up' management: everyone involved, in the modules as well as in the centre, is encouraged to come up with innovative ideas –and solicit them from 'lead users' at beta test sites or pushing the technology to its limits in their work.

PAYOFFS FROM THIS ORGANIZATIONAL FORMAT

In a constellation, the staff of the Centre have fewer decisions to make than do staff at similar levels of seniority in more traditional organizations. But the decisions are all big ones, because the staff of the Centre focus on critical issues, at the cutting edge of the technology. Their rôle is to provide the entire constellation with leadership, and to initiate new developments constantly Speedy, flexible and creative response to a wide range of developments is what, above all else, is required of them.

The Centre gets out of capital-intensive activities, and decreases outgoings on manpower and payroll (there have been layoffs and financial 'streamlining' at Apple). Cut-backs and transferring operations out, along with licensing out of patents, frees up money for supporting developers with projects of high potential, and for investment in joint ventures with other good prospects.

Projects which are at the bleeding edge of the technology are spun off to the modules –to new companies entering the constellation. This spreads the risks attendant on innovative ventures. When a spun-off project succeeds, its developers can be encouraged to go public with their stock, increasing the financing and alliances available to the constellation. Dropping back to a minority stockholding position, when such projects succeed and go public, frees the Centre's capital for re-allocation.

A constellation is big enough to be monitored for its social and environmental impact on its host society. So the Centre must watch its policies carefully. For instance, Apple is the only major producer of computers to have refused to sell into South Africa while the apartheid policy is in effect. Moreover, the Centre can avoid activities which could be socially or politically controversial, allowing modules to risk involvement therein.

> The policy of the centre is to undertake, or sponsor, socially approved missionary activities (Apple has positions for "evangelists"), such as providing computers for the schools (to develop a future generation of users), and supporting its MUGs.

Another advantage of a constellation is that no *one* developer, whether of software or of hardware, can dominate the market into which the constellation is selling. Nor does the Centre have to rely on any one company as a major supplier. The Centre's rôle is to concentrate on basic research and development, and oversee and integrate the many related developmental endeavours among the modules. This makes it an intelligence Centre; so it builds an informational base which makes its leadership unassailable.

Leadership also entails the development of game plans. Highly successful ventures can be supported when their developers port them to other types of computers.

An example
After copious infusions of venture capital by Apple, the presentation graphics program *PowerPoint* (which provides computer-designed overheads for convention speeches and the like –potentially a billion-dollar market) became a bestseller. It was then ported to the PC.

These crossovers enable the constellation to invade other markets, encroaching on the market share of leading developers who *aren't* constellation members.

IMPACT OF THE CONSTELLATION ON THE COMPUTER INDUSTRY

Software wars and software prices

It's clearly going to be increasingly difficult for a small company to make it on its own in an industry dominated by constellations. It won't have the capital, the inside information, or the technical support. The bigger companies will gobble the smaller ones up –and themselves be at risk from big companies leagued in a giant constellation.

Mergers and alliances are going to proliferate. Companies need a certain critical mass of programmers, persons to provide over-the-phone technical support, and sales and distribution staff, if they're to provide quality service for major clients. Corporate buyers make a huge investment in software and an even larger one in training their staffs on that software. They won't do this without assurance of on-going support and product development.

A software house which secures a number of major corporate clients has a large captive market for upgrades and add-on products. But it will only retain this market by readily providing customer service and innovative product upgrades that reflect technological breakthroughs. Other software houses will push forward to provide service, if it fails to do so.

Software prices will rise. It's only competition between small, innovative companies, which don't have the overhead of the giants, that keeps prices down. Such small companies won't be able to mount the advertising campaigns that go with securing corporate customers. To make their way, they'll have to become affiliates of the bigger ones.

Insider trading in ideas and other conflicts of interest

The Centre *can't* itself develop software, if it wants third parties to do so:

1. The Centre is necessarily privy to the plans of third parties developing software for its micros: it provides them with technical support. If it is simultaneously developing software that competes with theirs, it can exploit their ideas to its own advantage.

2. It takes several years to develop the next model of a micro. Likewise, it also takes several years to develop the software for it. For the two to appear simultaneously, the software developers must have inside information at each developmental stage of the new model. If any one software house has the inside track, it doesn't make sense for others to undertake to develop programs for the new model.

Apple learned its lesson when it bundled (sold as part of a package deal) *MacWrite* and *MacPaint* with the first Macs. As a result, there were no developers of graphics or word processing software –apart from Microsoft, which had enjoyed an insider position with Apple during development of the Mac.

At the time, Apple had no option. It had to have software available for the Mac, or the machine would have been useless. When introducing the Mac II and SE, however, Apple *did* have options: there are 2,000 programs currently available for the Mac. So, when major developers objected to Apple's plans to put out a data base management program of its own, Apple spun its software development activities off to two modules.

One is a new subsidiary, called Claris, which is headed by Apple's former vice-president for sales and marketing in the U.S. This subsidiary is to become an independent entity within a year, with Apple holding a minority ownership. This module starts as the world's fourth largest software development house (after Microsoft, Lotus and Ashton-Tate).

Owning the best-selling programs *MacPaint*, *MacDraw*, and *MacTerminal*, and all the Apple II application programs,. it immediately proceeded to upgrade them. After many years of neglect, these programs, which have a huge established user base, are now back in contention as front-rank programs subject to constant up-grading. With such support, they're born again market contenders.

This subsidiary, backed by the resources of Apple's constellation, is likely to end Microsoft's reign as the largest independent supplier of software for the Mac. Then Apple will no longer be dependent on a company which has close connections with IBM. Apple wants its developers to be urgently writing their most exciting programs for the Mac, and porting from the Mac to the PC, not vice versa.

The other subsidiary is another new company, called Acius. This is headed by Apple's former top 'evangelist'. It has taken over development and marketing of the database program to which the big software houses objected. Now known as *Fourth Dimension*, this is the most powerful database running on a micro.

In keeping with Apple's tradition of evangelism, Acius has established a certified developers' program, to assist advanced users –targeted as the first buyers of *Fourth Dimension*– .in creating applications programs based upon it for others to use. There is also to be a support program for user groups and dealers, to educate them in the intricacies of the *Fourth Dimension*.

The case for independent software houses operating in an open market

It's in the public interest to have powerful software houses, such as Microsoft, operating independently of the major vendors of micros. Industry-wide standards in software, particularly in the all-important drive operating system software, will come only from such houses.

A free market in ideas concerning this technology –the matrix which fosters such independents– is also in the public interest. The constellation is likely to inhibit the ferment of ideas that goes with an open market place, which has been the environment from which most of the creative initiatives in microcomputing have come. Japan has so far been more noted for superb exploitation of such ideas than for their abundant generation.

THE CONSEQUENCES, FOR THE REST OF US, SHOULD THIS ORGANIZATIONAL FORMAT BECOME WIDESPREAD

The impact of the constellation on the worker

The constellation is the organizational form which underlies the Japanese economic miracle. It goes with a social welfare system and a work ethic which are distinctly different from the ones we are used to:

1. In Japan, if you are fortunate enough to get hired into one of the centre's units within a constellation, you will live out your working life there. Your organization will provide company help with housing and medical care till you retire at 55, with a bonus for your long years of service.

2. You'll need that bonus. There are no state pensions or unemployment insurance.

3. If you've been employed in one of the centre's units, you'll very likely be hired into one of the modular companies of the constellation. There, as vice-president, your inside knowledge of, and contacts within, the Centre can be of inestimable value to the module out on the periphery.

4. But you've lost your company-provided support for housing and medical services.

You'll need the equivalent of $1,000,000 to retire on. You may have been making $64,000 a year, and you'll have been saving hard –VERY hard. But the cost of living is so high in Japan that you probably won't have saved as much as you'll need.

You'll have to live with a member of your family when you can no longer work.

> These savings enable Japan Inc.,under the strategic guidance of MITI (the Ministry of Trade and Industry), to conduct a systematic investment program world-wide.[10]

The above scenario holds only for the favoured few who make it to the Centre. Most don't. And life in the modules is a much tougher business. It's better than life *outside* the constellation, however. These are the labour conditions that produce the driven work force that has created the Japanese economic miracle.[11]

The impact of the constellation on society

The constellation is fearsomely effective as an engine of economic growth. Western societies may have to adopt it to cope with international competition. This form of organization is anyway likely to spread from the leading edge companies in our economy, if previous experience is anything to go by.

The constellation is merely the latest organizational form in a series which started with the traditional hierarchical organization, developed into the matrix, and progressed into 'System 7 S'. The latter is another Japanese organizational form –leadership in developing such forms seemingly having passed to Japan– which seems to be the predecessor of the constellation.[12]

If the constellation becomes the organizational norm in the West, our living conditions are going to change drastically:

The gains so laboriously made by the labour movement over the years will be lost. Pensions will go. Unions will become the production conscious Japanese variety. In-house promotion will be attenuated (ex-Centre members will get all the prize positions in the modules). A stable work environment will be a rarity: the Centre passes on most of the high risk endeavours to the modules, exploiting those at the bleeding edge of the technology. It's economic transfer again, on a gigantic scale.

We'll be working in 'greedy groups' –groups which will require huge amounts of our time and energies.[13] Competition will be endemic: we'll be members of competing groups/teams within our organizations, the groups themselves situated within fiercely competing organizations. Large alliances of companies will be vieing with one another for survival.

Welcome to the desktop publishing revolution.[14]

Footnotes

Chapter 1

[1] See T.F. Carney & B. Zajac, *Communications and Society: A Social History of Communications* (Winnipeg, Manitoba: Natural Resource Institute, University of Manitoba, 1975, chapters 2–6), for a survey of the communications practices associated with each of these major developments in communications-related technology.

[2] See T.F. Carney & B. Zajac, *Communications and Society: A Social History of Communications* (Winnipeg, Manitoba: Natural Resource Institute, University of Manitoba, 1975, chapters 2–6), for a survey of the communications practices associated with each of these major developments in communications-related technology.

[3] S.T. Kerr, "Transition from Page to Screen", pp. 321–44 in S. Lambert & S. Ropiequet (eds), *CD ROM: The New Papyrus*, Redmond, VA: Microsoft Press, 1986.

[4] On the qualifications brief, see R. Lathrop, *Who's Hiring Who.* Berkeley, CA: Ten Speed Press, 1977, chapter 5.

[5] S.A. Bernhardt, "Seeing the Text", *College Composition and Communication*, 37 (1), 1986, 66-79. Table 2 largely follows Bernhardt's table on p. 76.

[6] See E.A. Lind & W.M. O'Barr, "The Social Significance of Speech in the Courtroom", chapter 4 (especially pp. 71-4) in H. Giles & R.N St Clair (eds), *Language and Social Psychology*, Baltimore, MD: University Park Press, 1979.

[7] See R.N. Bolles, *What Color Is Your Parachute?* Berkeley, CA: Ten Speed Press, current edition, for the job hunting script, and M. Treece, *Communication for Business and the Professions*, Boston, MA: Allyn & Bacon, 1978, chapter 6, for the subscripts.

[8] For the research findings that substantiate this contention, see D.H. Jonassen (ed.), *The Technology of Text*, Englewood Cliffs, N.J.: Educational Technology Publications, 1982.

[9] L. Hayes & J. Flower, "Identifying the Organization of Writing Processes", chapter 1, and J. Flower & L. Hayes, "Composing: Making Plans and Juggling Constraints", chapter 2, in L.W. Gregg & E.R. Steinberg (eds), *Cognitive Processes in Writing*, Hillsdale, N.J.: Erlbaum, 1980.

[10] See N.D. Perkins, *The Mind's Best Work*, Cambridge, MA: Harvard University Press, 1981, chapters 6 -7.

[11] Initially termed a 'mind map', it's now known (in the US) as a 'spoke diagram' and being routinely taught in (some) schools. Its originator was Tony Buzan; see his *Use Your Head*, British Broadcasting Company, 1980 reprint (or later).

[12] L.V. Sadler, W.T. Green & E.W. Sadler, "Diagrammatic Writing Using Word Processing: "Larger Vision" Software", *Research in Word Processing Newsletter*, 4 (1), 1986, 2–7.

[13] On the importance of social support, see T.L. Albrecht & M.B. Adelman, "Social Support and Life Stress", *Human Communication Research*, 11 (1), 1984, 3–32.

[14] A. Tough, *The Adult's Learning Projects*, Toronto, Ontario: Ontario Institute for Studies in Education, ed.2 1979, 100–101.

[15] On the importance of the development of a special in-group language, see R. Herman, "Intervening in Groups: A Repertoire and Language of Group Skills for Self-Directed Learning in Decision-Making Groups", *Small Group Behavior* 14 (4), 1983, 445-464. Herman states (p. 448) that "A common language for dialogue is at the heart of collaboration" –it bonds people into teams. The classic exposition of this thesis is that of P.L. Berger & T. Luckmann, *The Social Construction of Reality*, Garden City, NY: Anchor Books, 1967.

[16] J. Naisbitt, *Megatrends: Ten New Directions Transforming Our Lives*, New York, Warner Books: 1982, chapter 8. On computer networking, see A. Glossbrenner, *The Complete Handbook of Personal Computer Communications*, New York, St. Martin's Press: 1985 ed.

[17] N. Lavroff, "Making Waves on Silicon Beach", *MacWorld*, April 1986, 119-120.

[18] S. Darian, "Using Algorithms, Prose and Graphics for Presenting Technical and Business Information", *ABCA Bulletin* 46 (4), 1983, 26-29, and P. Wright & F. Reid, "Written Information: Some Alternatives to Prose", *Journal of Applied Psychology*, 57,1973, 160-166.

[19] For an illustration of this mode of communication in action, see L. Schatzman & A. Strauss, "Social Class and Modes of Communication", chapter 42 in A.G. Smith (ed.), *Communication and Culture*, New York: Holt, Rinehart & Winston, 1966.

[20] On the use of such schematics in writing, see D.N. Perkins, *The Mind's Best Work*, Cambridge, MA: Harvard University Press, 1981, chapters 6-7. On the omnipresence of such scripts in our everyday thinking, see R.C. Schank & R.F. Abelson, *Scripts, plans, goals and understanding*, New York: Wiley, 1977.

[21] This phenomenon is most clearly apparent in social science textbooks. But it's pervasive; it can be seen elsewhere, even in 'trade' books: see the bestseller *Born to Win: Transactional Analysis with Gestalt Experiments*, by M. James & D. Jongeward (Reading, MA: Addison-Wesley, 1973 reprint).

[22] See D.A. Kolb, *Experiential Learning*, Englewood Cliffs, NJ: Prentice Hall, 1984, chapter 6.

[23] See S. Turkle, *The Second Self: Computers and the Human Spirit*, New York: Simon & Schuster, 1984, Parts II and III.

[24] G.R. Miller & M. Burgoon, "Persuasion Research: Review and Commentary", pp. 29–47 in B. Rubin (ed.), *Communication Yearbook 2*, International

Communication Association (New Brunswick, N.J.: Transaction Books), 1978.

25 D.A. Schön, *The Reflective Practitioner: How Professionals Think in Action*, New York: Basic Books, 1983; see chapters 1 to 3 ("Design as a Reflective Conversation with the Situation").

26 See the symposium "Homo Narrans: Story-Telling in Mass Culture and Everyday Life", *Journal of Communication* 35 (4), 1985, 173-171.

27 This is "symbolic convergence theory": see E.G. Borman, "Symbolic Communication Theory: A Communication Formulation", *Journal of Communication* 35 (4), 1985, 128-138.

28 See L.N. Landa, *Algorithmization in Learning and Instruction*, Englewood Cliffs, N.J.: Educational Technology Publications, 1974, for the general concept of raising the overall level of expertise in society in this way, by making the expertise of top experts available to all who are interested in acquiring it.

29 Discussion follows T. Nace, "Lighting the Path to the Future", *MacWorld*, Feb. 1986, 100–106. Currently, the authoritative treatise on this topic is S. Lambert & S. Ropiequet (eds), *CD ROM: The New Papyrus*.

30 A byte is composed of 8 bits. A bit is the smallest unit of computerized information: it just indictes 'on' or 'off', 1 or 0. The combination of bits and their pattern determines the meaning of the byte. See commentary on the ASCII code: chapter 2, note 7.

31 L. Thayer (ed.), *Organization* ↔ *Communication: Emerging Perspectives I*: see M. Heyer, "The Creative Challenge of CD ROM", pp. 55–57.

32 W.H. Gates, Foreword, pp. xii–xiii in L. Thayer (ed.), *Organization* ↔ *Communication: Emerging Perspectives I*.

33 G.D. Ofiesh, "The Seamless Carpet of Knowledge and Learning", pp. 299–319 in S. Lambert & S. Ropiequet (eds), *CD ROM*.

34 M. Minsky, *The Society of Mind*, New York: Simon & Schuster, 1986, Prologue.

Chapter 2

1 Hubbard, J.T.W. *Magazine Editing*, Englewood Cliffs, N.J.: Prentice-Hall, 1982, 4.

2 For the (diffusion of innovations) model, see Rogers, E.M. & Shoemaker, F.F. *Communication of Innovations*. N.Y.: Free Press, 1971, chapter 1.

3 Discussion follows D.B. Davis, "Business Turns to In-house Publishing", *High Technology* 1986, 6 (4), 18–26.

4 See R.M. D'Aprix's chapter, "Communicators in Contemporary Organizations" in Reuss, C. & Silvis, D. (eds), *Inside Organizational Communications*, N.Y.: Longman, 1981.

5 On the critical importance of this type of communication to the success of these stock option programs, see C. Rosen & others, "When Employees Share the Profits", *Psychology Today* 1986, 20 (1), 36.

[6]   Discussion follows S.F. Roth, "Book Publishers Join the Computing Age", *Personal Publishing* 1 (1), 1985, 34–6.

[7]   ASCII stands for American Standard Code for Information Interchange. It's a 7-bit code. As each bit can occur in one of two states, there are 128 variants –differing 7-bit combinations– to a 7-bit code. This is enough for a complete set of numerals and letters of the alphabet (upper and lower case), plus punctuation marks. An 8-bit code admits of 256 variants, so allows many other symbols to be coded in. But the 8-bit or 'high' codes aren't standardized, so can't be read by regular programs.

[8]   The interpretivists are urging upon organizations the need for an "ideal speech situation" ("a situation of true consensus achieved through free and rational discourse"): see L. Smircich, "Implications for Management Theory", p. 237 in Putnam, L. L. & Pacanowsky, M.E., *Communications and Organizations: An Interpretive Approach*, Sage, 1983.

Chapter 3

[1]   See D.R. Moen, *Newspaper Layout and Design* , Ames, Iowa: Iowa State University Press, 1984, 150, for an unusually clear statement of this situation.

[2]   See R.M. D'Aprix, "Communicators in Contemporary Organizations", chapter 2 in C. Reuss & D.E. Silvis (eds), *Inside Organizational Communication*, New York: Longman, 1981.

[3]   C. Rosen, K.J. Klein & K.M. Young, "When Employees Share the Profits", *Psychology Today* 20 (1), 1986, 36.

[4]   Such as *Document Modeler* : see the review by S. Roth, "Document Modeler", *Personal Publishing* 2 (5), 1986, 32–2.

[5]   See the journal *Personal Publishing* for a good instance of this phenomenon in the specialist literature, and W.E. Korbus' chapter (9) in Reuss & Silvis, *Inside Organizational Communications* , for another instance from a 'Reader' (a collection of 'readings' –chapters– by different authors).

[7]   See A. Hurlburt, *The Grid*, N.Y.: Van Nostrand Reinhold, 1978.

[8]   Discussion is much influenced by Moen's chapter 3 in *Newspaper Layout and Design*, "Laying Out Pages".

[9]   This formatting convention is used with great effectiveness in R.K. Yin, *Case Study Research: Design and Methods*, Beverly Hills, CA: Sage, 1984.

[10] The December 1986 issue of *Personal Publishing* (vol. 1, 2) provides a symposium in print on typefaces and setting text generally. The June 1987 issue (vol. 3, 5) provides another such symposium. Comparison of the two indicates how rapidly the field of desktop publishing is developing in these, its early years.

[11] See B.A. Morgan's insightful commentary in Research in *Word Processing Newsletter* 5 (5), 1987, 2.

Chapter 4

[1] See Betty Edwards' deservedly well known and wonderfully liberating book *Drawing on the Right Side of the Brain*. Los Angeles, CA: Tarcher, 1979, Preface and chapters 1–2.

[2] See M. Green, "Zen and the Art of Personal Publishing", Personal Publishing 3 (3), 1987, 28–31; or, even better, his book *Zen and the Art of the Macintosh*, Philadelphia: Running Press, 1986. The book's subtitle sums up its message well: *Discoveries on the Path to Computer Enlightenment*. The book's graphics show something of the promise of the new technology to go beyond outmoded presentational forms.

[3] This is the theme of the January 1987 number of Personal Publishing (vol. 3, 1); see in particular the article by J. Karney, "Absence of Standards", pages 24–26.

[4] The programs referred to are the ones I know about: the leading programs in North America. These may not be equally well known in Britain and on the Continent. Please take my specifics for generics in this case: I'm referring to the types of program that are in heaviest use: those for word processing, spread sheeting, database management and page makeup.

[5] See S. Roth, "The State of the Art", *Personal Publishing* 3 (3), 1987, 24–26. Actually, this whole number, which is dedicated to the theme "How to Use New Art Tools" relates to the discussion that follows in the text.

[6] See D.R. D'Acquisto, "SuperPaint", *Personal Publishing* 3 (3), 1987, 48–54.

[7] See C.J. Weigand, "The Third Dimension", *Personal Publishing* 3 (3), 1987, 34–44..

[8] M. Saenz, "PostScript in Color", *Personal Publishing* 3 (4), 1987, 30–34.

[9] See T. Ulick, "Page of Another Color", *Personal Publishing* 3 (6), 1987, 54–59.

[10] See Karen Keer, "Copier Publishing: The real revolution in personal publishing", and D. D'Acquisto, "The Copier Toolbox", *Personal Publishing* 3 (6), 1987, 38–46 and 50–53 respectively (see especially page 53).

[11] Discussion follows T. Ulick, "Clip Art to the Rescue: Building an art library of electronic art", and especially S. Roth, "Pasting Pictures: The problem with graphic standards for the IBM", pages 21 and 25 & 28 respectively in *Personal Publishing* 2 (6), 1986.

[12] Discussion follows T. Ulick & S. Roth, "Digital Halftones: Size is what counts when it comes to dots", pp. 20–21 in *Personal Publishing* 2 (4), 1986. This issue is dedicated to developments in digitizers and scanners and provides an excellent review of the topics discussed in the text.

[13] Discussion follows H. Mee, "Hard Copy Clip Art", and J. Karney, "Graphic Survival Kit": *Personal Publishing* 2 (6), 1986, 32–5 & 36–7 respectively.

[14] Korbus' chapter in Reuss & Silvis, *Inside Organizational Communication* gives a good outline on graphics (and design) principles. The January 1986 issue of *Personal Publishing* (vol. 2, 1) gives a symposium on computer graphics.

[15] Discussion follows T. Ulick, "Graphs into Graphics: Converting Numbers to Art", and S. Lambert, "Graphing Techniques": *Personal Publishing* 2 (3), 1986, 18–21, and 22–25 respectively, and B.Ostendorf, "Desktop Design", *Personal Publishing* 3 (3), 1987, 90–97.

[16] See especially N. Holmes (*Time* magazine's deputy art director), *Designer's Guide to Creating Charts and Diagrams*, Watson-Guptill, 1984 (very readable; covers both basic and advanced issues); J.V. White, *Using Charts and Graphs*, R.R. Bowker, 1984 (good, cheap paperback; covers the basics, readably); E.R. Tufte, *The Visual Display of Quantitative Information*, Cheshire, Conn.: Graphics Press; 1983 (the classic).

[17] Discussion follows S. Darian, "Using Algorithms, Prose and Graphics for Presenting Technical and Business Information", *The ABCA* (American Business Communication Association) *Bulletin* 46 (4),1983, 26–28.

Chapter 5

[1] Still a classic exposition of this viewpoint is P.L. Berger & T. Luckmann, *The Social Construction of Reality*, Garden City, NY: Anchor Books, Doubleday, 1967. See also R.M. Perloff & T.C. Brock, "..."And Thinking Makes It So": Cognitive Responses to Persuasion", chapter 3, and R.W. Chestnut, "Persuasive Effects in Marketing: Consumer Information Processing Research", chapter 10, in M.E. Roloff & G.R. Miller (eds), *Persuasion: New Directions in Theory and Research*, Beverly Hills, CA: Sage, 1980.

[2] See the symposium "Homo Narrans", *Journal of Communication* 35 (4), 1985, 73–171, especially W.R. Fisher's opening piece, "The Narrative Paradigm: In the Beginning", pages 74–89.

[3] Well shown by E.G. Borman's work on symbolic convergence: see "Symbolic Convergence Theory: A Communication Formulation", in the above symposium, pages 128–38.

[4] S. Toulmin, *The Uses of Argument*, Cambridge, England: Cambridge University Press, 1958. My discussion follows N. Buerkell-Rothfuss, *Communication: Competencies and Contexts*, New York: Random House, 1985, 308–311.

[5] Discussion of SHIP and its story 'architecture' follows J.T.W. Hubbard, *Magazine Editing*, chapters 3, 6 & 7.

[6] Discussion follows Hubbard's chapter 5: "Three Ways to Start A Story".

[7] Thus readability involves the clearness of meaning in a text, whereas legibility involves clearness of the lettering.

[8] See R. Gunning, *The Technique of Clear Writing*, N.Y.: McGraw-Hill, 1968, 31–45.

[9] Gunning, pages 38–43.

[10] See E.A. Lind & W.M. O'Barr, "The Social Significance of Speech in the Courtroom", chapter 4, especially pages 71–74, in H. Giles & R. St Clair (eds), *Language and Social Psychology*, Baltimore, MD: University Park Press, 1979.

[11] Discussion largely follows Marcia Yudkin's excellent piece, "Editorial Style", *Personal Publishing* 3 (3), 1987, 68–70, to which I am also indebted for many items in the bibliography given in the text.

Chapter 6

[1] Discussion follows E.M. Rogers & F.F. Shoemaker, *Communication of Innovations: A Cross-cultural Approach* , N.Y.: Free Press, 1971 (ed. 2); see chapter 3, "The Innovation-Decision Process".

[2] This is why they and the opinion leaders have a better track record than the innovators for successful innovations.

[3] The examples quoted are for the Macintosh, which is currently the personal computer for desktop publishing. There are many more programs for the IBM PC than for the Mac in this area. So, if programs are available for the Mac, they're normally available for the IBM PC too –except for the graphics-based ones.

[4] T.J. Peters & R.H. Waterman Jr, *In Search of Excellence*, NY: Warner Books ed., 1984, pages 211–212 (actually, all of chapter 7 –"Autonomy and Entrepreneurship"– relates to the discussion in the text).

[5] Actually, grammar and punctuation, but limited to a restricted number of types of error.

[6] The 'critical path' is that series of activities within a whole complex of activities which takes longest to complete. Consequently, it determines the overall time to completion; so it is 'critical'. PERT means Program Evaluation and Review Technique. It involves reviewing a program in CPM-like terms. A Gant chart, called after its inventor, is a matrix with activities (down, left) and time periods (across, top). Each activity is depicted by line stretching through the cells when it's occurring. This layout shows at a glance how many activities are going on at any time period.

[7] See P.C. Nasman & K. Machung, "Job Aids: Improving performance without formal training", Training/HRD 16 (12), 1972, 68–70, and D.H. Bullock, Guiding Job Performance with Job Aids", Training and Development Journal 36 (9), 1982, 36–42.

[8] See J. Dawe & W.J. Lord Jr, *Functional Business Communication* , Englewood Cliffs, N.J.: Prentice-Hall, 1974 ed., 384–90.

[9] The current thrust of the technology is to develop grey-scale processing as a feature of the scanner.

[10] Discussion follows C. Brod, *Technostress: The Human Cost of the Computer Revolution*, Reading, Mass.: Addison-Wesley, 1984, passim.

[11] Discussion follows D.R. Burns, "The Perfectionist's Script for Self-defeat", *Psychology Today* 14 (6), 1980, 34–52.

[12] T.L. Albrecht, M.B. Adelman & associates, *Communicating Social Support*, CA, Newbury Park: Sage, 1987, chapter 2.

Chapter 7

[1] This is Intel's 68030 chip: the first use in a micro of a chip with the 'Harvard style' parallel architecture, so far used only in supercomputers The 68030 provides 8 MIPs (Millions of Instructions Per Second), and is nearly twice as powerful as the –currently state-of-the-art– 68020 chip.

[2] E.M. Rogers, *Communication Technology: The New Media in Society*, NY: Free Press, 1986, chapter 4, "Adoption and Implementation of Communication Technologies".

[3] See C. Johnson, "Coming Out in Color", *MacWorld*, July 1986, 112–118, and J. Knott & D. Prochnow, "The Macintosh Brought to You in Living Color", *Macazine* 3 (4), 1986, 87–91.

[4] You can produce coloured overheads cheaply, by using transparent coloured overlays on plastic transparencies: see R. Schwartz & M. Callery, "Picture Perfect", *MacUser* 1(10), 1986, 60–63 & 139.

[5] Of the 4.2 million installed IBM PCs, only 400,000 are IBM PC ATs with the 80286 chip that's needed for the next generation of software (the IBM PC has the less powerful , slower 8086 chip). The Mac runs on the 68000 chip, which is faster than the 80286.

[6] I owe the idea of illustrating the comparison in this way to T. Ulick (presumably; the article doesn't have a by-line), "System Savvy" (on putting a system together), and D.R. D'Acquisto, "Macintosh Publishing: Assembling A System", *Personal Publishing* 2 (11), 1986, pages 24–25 and 32–36 respectively.

[7] I owe many ideas in the following passages to P. Pearson's article "Turning on to Word Processing", in *The Bulletin of the Association for Business Communication* 50 (2), 1987, 19–23.

[8] On the 'triune' theory of mind (as opposed to left- and right-brain theories of hemispheric lateralization), see R.J. Sternberg, *Beyond I.Q.: A Triarchic Theory of Intelligence*, Cambridge University Press, 1985; on the 'society of mind' model, see M. Minsky, *The Society of Mind*, NY: Simon & Schuster, 1986.

Chapter 8

[1] On societal pressures, see P. Friere's classic, *Pedagogy of the Oppressed*, NY: Herder & Herder, 1971. On international pressures, see J.D. Cockcroft, A.G. Frank & D.L. Johnson, *Dependence and Underdevelopment: Latin America's Political Economy*, NY: Garden City, 1972.

[2] Discussion follows P.M. Hirsch, "U.S. Cultural Productions: The Impact of Ownership", *Journal of Communication* 35 (3), 1985, 110–21.

[3] See M.J. Robinson & R. Olszewski, "Books in the Marketplace of Ideas", *Journal of Communication* 30 (2), 1980, 81–88 (the quotation comes from page 88), and W.W. Powell, "Competition versus Concentration in the Book Trade", *Journal of Communication* 30 (2), 1980, 89–97. These articles should be read to qualify the findings of the article by Hirsch just cited.

Footnotes

4   They can finance the advertising blitz behind a 'blockbuster', plan ahead for multimedia tie-ins, and use their back lists (of steadily selling books) and best sellers to get the distributors to foist their paperbacks on to bookrack-sales outlets. And they're big enough to be able to bargain with the bookstore chains.

5   Discussion largely follows R. LePage, "Desktop Publishing I –The Industry", *MacIn-Touch* May 1986, 1–10.

6   Discussion follows H. Menzies, *Computers on the Job*, Toronto: Lorimer, 1982, and H.J. Otway & M. Peltu (eds), *New Office Technology: Human and Organizational Aspects*, (no place of publishing given) Ablex, 1983.

7   For the term and a commentary, see C.J. Hamelink, "Informatics: Third World Call for New Order", *Journal of Communication* 29 (3), 1979, 144–48.

8   Skim reading of the *Whole Earth Software Catalog for 1986* (S. Brand editor in chief; Garden City, N.Y.: Quantum Press/Doubleday, 1985) will reveal the wealth of imagination and ingenuity that has gone into such redefining to date –and this creativity just keeps coming.

9   See A. Toffler, *The Adaptive Corporation*, NY: Bantam Books ed., 1985, Part 6, "Shaping A Super-Industrial Corporation", chapters 10–11. For industry analysis along the lines of that in the text, see D. Bunnell's editorial, "Campbell's Software" and J. Borrell's commentary, "What's in a Face?" in *MacWorld*, August 1987, pages 17–22 and 41–44 respectively.

10   See "Japanese Multinationals: Covering the world with investment", *Business Week*, June 16, 1980, 92–102.

11   See E. van Helvoort, *The Japanese Working Man: What Choice? What Reward?* Vancouver, B.C.: University of British Columbia Press, 1979.

12   On hierarchical formats, see J.D. Thompson, *Organizations in Action*, NY: McGraw-Hill, 1967, Part One; on the 'matrix', see S.M. Davis & P.R. Lawrence, *Matrix*, Reading, MA: Addison-Wesley, 1977, chapter 1; on 'System 7 S', see R.T. Pascale & A.G. Athos, *The Art of Japanese Management*, NY: Warner Books ed., 1981, chapter 3, and Peters & Waterman, *In Search of Excellence*, chapter 1.

13   T. Kidder, *The Soul of A New Machine*, NY: Avon Books ed., 1982. Look at the last two sentences in the Prologue.

14   An earlier version of the thesis expressed in this chapter is to appear in *Politics and Administration in Changing Societies*, a *Festschrift* to Professor Fred Riggs edited by R.K. Arora I am grateful to Professor Arora for giving me permission to use that work as basis for this chapter.